Communications
in Computer and Information Science 1094

Commenced Publication in 2007
Founding and Former Series Editors:
Phoebe Chen, Alfredo Cuzzocrea, Xiaoyong Du, Orhun Kara, Ting Liu,
Krishna M. Sivalingam, Dominik Ślęzak, Takashi Washio, Xiaokang Yang,
and Junsong Yuan

More information about this series at http://www.springer.com/series/7899

Gary Tan · Axel Lehmann ·
Yong Meng Teo · Wentong Cai (Eds.)

Methods and Applications for Modeling and Simulation of Complex Systems

19th Asia Simulation Conference, AsiaSim 2019
Singapore, October 30 – November 1, 2019
Proceedings

Springer

Editors
Gary Tan
National University of Singapore
Singapore, Singapore

Axel Lehmann
Universität der Bundeswehr München
Neubiberg, Germany

Yong Meng Teo
National University of Singapore
Singapore, Singapore

Wentong Cai
Nanyang Technological University
Singapore, Singapore

ISSN 1865-0929   ISSN 1865-0937   (electronic)
Communications in Computer and Information Science
ISBN 978-981-15-1077-9   ISBN 978-981-15-1078-6   (eBook)
https://doi.org/10.1007/978-981-15-1078-6

This Springer imprint is published by the registered company Springer Nature Singapore Pte Ltd.
The registered company address is: 152 Beach Road, #21-01/04 Gateway East, Singapore 189721, Singapore

Preface

The AsiaSim conference is an annual international conference that started in 1999, and has primarily been organized by the three Asian simulation societies: Chinese Association for System Simulation (CASS), Japanese Society for Simulation Technology (JSST), and Korea Society for Simulation (KSS). In 2011, the Federation of Asia Simulation Societies (ASIASIM) was set up to promote the advancement of modeling and simulation in industry, research, and development in Asia and beyond. In 2013, the AsiaSim series finally left the 'Golden Triangle' of China, Japan, and Korea and was held in Singapore for the first time. Then in 2017, it was Malaysia's turn to host the conference.

On behalf of the Organizing Committee of AsiaSim 2019, we are proud to present the 19th edition of the AsiaSim conference series (held in Singapore for the second time).

Asiasim 2019 is organized by the Society of Simulation and Gaming of Singapore, the National University of Singapore, and Nanyang Technological University. The Society of Simulation and Gaming of Singapore is a non-profit professional organization set up to contribute to the development of simulation and gaming in Singapore and the region. It is a focused community for researchers, practitioners, and developers who are keen to further their professional knowledge through learning and working together and promoting the experiential activities to the public.

We received submissions from China, Japan, South Korea, Indonesia, India, Italy, Pakistan, Philippines, Germany, Malaysia, Columbia, and of course Singapore. After an intensive review process by a carefully assembled international Program Committee, where each paper was reviewed by no less than 3 reviewers, we finally accepted 19 full papers and 5 short papers. The following three papers were shortlisted for the best paper award:

- "Digital Twin Technology for Aquaponics: Towards Optimizing Food Production with Dynamic Data Driven Application Systems" by Ayyaz Ahmed, Shahid Zulfiqar, Adam Ghandar, Yang Chen, Masatoshi Hanai, Georgios Theodoropoulos.
- "On Evaluating Rust as a Programming Language for the Future of Massive Agent-based Simulations" by Alessia Antelmi, Gennaro Cordasco, Matteo D'Auria, Daniele De Vinco, Alberto Negro, and Carmine Spagnuolo.
- "Conv-LSTM: Pedestrian Trajectory Prediction in Crowded Scenarios" by Kai Chen, Xiao Song, and Hang Yu.

The accepted papers are consolidated in this volume of the *Communications in Computer and Information Science* series, and are divided into many relevant topics, including Agent Based Simulation, Simulation Methods and Tools, Visualization, Modeling Methodology, and Simulation Applications in Science and Engineering.

The diversity of topics presented at this conference made for a healthy exchange of research ideas and technical exchanges.

We would like to take this opportunity to thank the ASIASIM Federation for allowing us to host AsiaSim 2019 for the second time in Singapore, and we hope that you found the conference enriching and memorable.

We also thank the members of the Program Committee for their valuable effort in the review of the submitted papers. Finally, we would also like to thank our technical co-sponsors and sponsors. Your contributions and support helped to make AsiaSim 2019 a reality and a success.

October 2019

Gary Tan
Axel Lehmann
Yong Meng Teo
Wentong Cai

AsiaSim 2019 Organisation

Conference Chairs

Gary Tan   National University of Singapore, Singapore
Axel Lehmann   Universität der Bundeswehr München, Germany

Program Chairs

Yong Meng Teo   National University of Singapore, Singapore
Wentong Cai   Nanyang Technological University, Singapore

International Program Committee

Anastasia Anagnostou	Brunel University, UK
Philipp Andelfinger	Nanyang Technological University, Singapore
Agostino Bruzzone	University of Genoa, Italy
Gabriele D'angelo	University of Bologna, Italy
Terence Hung	Rolls Royce, Singapore
Dong Jin	Illinois Institute of Technology, USA
Farzad Kamrani	KTH Royal Institute of Technology, Sweden
Helen Karatza	Aristotle University of Thessaloniki, Greece
Sye Loong Keoh	University of Glasgow, UK, and Singapore Campus, Singapore
Yun Bae Kim	Sungkyunkwan University, South Korea
Bohu Li	Beijing University of Aeronautics and Astronautics, China
Ge Li	National University of Defence Technology, China
Liang Li	Ritsumeikan University, Japan
Zengxiang Li	Institute of High Performance Computing, A*STAR, Singapore
Malcolm Low	Singapore Institute of Technology, Singapore
Linbo Luo	Xidian University, China
Imran Mahmood	National University of Science & Technology, Pakistan
Yahaya Md Sam	Universiti Teknologi Malaysia, Malaysia
Zaharuddin Mohamed	Universiti Teknologi Malaysia, Malaysia
Navonil Mustafee	University of Exeter, UK

Bhakti Stephan Onggo	University of Southampton, UK
Ravi Seshadri	Singapore-MIT Alliance for Research and Technology, Singapore
Xiao Song	Beihang University, China
Yuen Jien Soo	National University of Singapore, Singapore
Claudia Szabo	The University of Adelaide, Australia
Sun Teck Tan	National University of Singapore, Singapore
Satoshi Tanaka	Ritsumeikan University, Japan
Wenjie Tang	National University of Defense Technology, China
Yifa Tang	Chinese Academy of Sciences, China
Simon Taylor	Brunel University, UK
Yong Meng Teo	National University of Singapore, Singapore
Georgios Theodoropoulos	Southern University of Science and Technology, China
Stephen John Turner	Vidyasirimedhi Institute of Science and Technology, Thailand
Bimlesh Wadhwa	National University of Singapore, Singapore
Yiping Yao	National University of Defense Technology, China
Allan N. Zhang	Singapore Institute of Manufacturing Technology, Singapore
Lin Zhang	Beihang University, China
Jinghui Zhong	South China University of Technology, China

Best Paper Chair

Axel Lehmann	Universität der Bundeswehr München, Germany

Best Paper Sub-committee

Yun-Bae Kim	Sung Kyun Kwan University, South Korea
Yahaya Md Sam	Universiti Teknologi Malaysia, Malaysia
Satoshi Tanaka	Ritsumeikan University, Japan
Yong Meng Teo	National University of Singapore, Singapore
Lin Zhang	Beihang University, China

Finance Chair

Sun Teck Tan	National University of Singapore, Singapore

Local Arrangement Chairs

Bimlesh Wadhwa	National University of Singapore, Singapore
Yuen Jien Soo	National University of Singapore, Singapore

Publications Chair

Muhammad Shalihin bin
Othman

National University of Singapore, Singapore

Web Masters

Chengxin Wang
Muhammad Shalihin bin
Othman

National University of Singapore, Singapore
National University of Singapore, Singapore

ASIASIM Council 2019

President

Gary Tan (President)　　　　　SSAGSG

Council Members

Bo Hu Li (President)　　　　　CSF
Lin Zhang (Vice President)　　CSF
Xiao Song (Board Member)　　CSF
Satoshi Tanaka　　　　　　　JSST
  (Chair of Foreign
  Affairs)
Kyoko Hasegawa　　　　　　JSST
  (Board Member)
Liang Li (Board Member)　　　JSST
Yun-Bae Kim　　　　　　　　SKKU
Kang Sun Lee (Vice　　　　　KSS
  President)
Soo-Hyun Park (Board　　　　KSS
  Member)
Yong Meng Teo (Board　　　　SSAGSG
  Member)
Yahaya Md Sam (President)　　MSS
Rubiyah binte Yusof　　　　　UTM
Zaharuddin Mohamed　　　　UTM

Honorary Member

Axel Lehmann　　　　　Universität der Bundeswehr München, Germany

Sponsors

ASIASIM: Federation of Asia Simulation Societies
Society of Simulation and Gaming of Singapore
Advent2 Labs Consultation Pte Ltd
Tezos Southeast Asia

Technical Co-sponsors

China Simulation Federation (CSF)
Japanese Society for Simulation Technology (JSST)
Korea Society for Simulation (KSS)
Malaysian Simulation Society (MSS)
Society for Modeling and Simulation International (SCS)

Organisers

Society of Simulation and Gaming of Singapore
National University of Singapore, Singapore
Nanyang Technological University, Singapore

Keynote Speakers

Keynote I: The Challenges of Repeatability and Fidelity of Cyber-Physical Digital Twins

David M. Nicol
Franklin W. Woeltge Professor of ECE
University of Illinois, Urbana-Champaign

Director, Information Trust Institute
Director, Advanced Digital Sciences Center
Director, Critical Infrastructure Resilience Institute

Abstract. A digital twin of a cyber-physical system is a simulation whose execution mimics the behavior of both the physical and cyber components of the system. While the idea of co-joining or federating simulations has been considered for quite a long time, the rise in interest of cyber-physical systems, coupled with increased computational power has brought the idea to the forefront under the labeling of 'digital twin'. Uses include exploration of how cyber malfeasance might negatively impact the physical system, how the physical system may react to unusual inputs or boundary conditions, whether a particular control applied to the system will push it into a region of unsafe behavior. Fidelity of digital twins is clearly a desirable attribute, as is repeatability. In the former case we want confidence that the digital twin faithfully (enough) captures the behavior of interest, in the latter case we need to be able to understand, by replying the simulation, how a particular behavior observed in the simulation came to occur. This talk focuses on the challenges of repeatability and fidelity in a cyber-physical digital twin, when that twin combines classical simulation with emulation of executing software.

Biography

David M. Nicol is the Franklin W. Woeltge Professor of Electrical and Computer Engineering at the University of Illinois in Urbana-Champaign, where he also serves as the Director of the Information Trust Institute, and Director of the Advanced Digital Sciences Center (Singapore). He has a B.A. in Mathematics from Carleton College (1979), and M.S. and Ph.D. degrees in Computer Science (1985) from the University of Virginia. Professor Nicol's research interests encompass high performance computing, discrete system modeling and simulation, and end-to-end modeling/analysis of cyber-security, resilience, and trust in complex systems. He served as Editor-in-Chief of ACM Transactions on Modeling and Computer Simulation (1997-2003) and since 2018 has served as Editor-in-Chief of IEEE's flagship publication on cyber-security, IEEE Security and Privacy. He was elected Fellow of the IEEE in 2003, Fellow of the ACM in 2006, and in 2007 was the inaugural recipient of the ACM SIGSIM Distinguished Contributions award.

Keynote II: Blockchain Safety and Smart Contract Simulation

Jun Furuse
Chief Executive Officer (CEO)
DaiLambda, Inc.

Scientific Director,
Tezos Japan

Abstract. Blockchain is a distributed database in an open network, where anyone can join by running a node without permission. As far as we know, such a system can be maintained only by incentivizing the participants to behave honestly at its resolution of the conflicts. Consequently, blockchain must handle a huge amount of rewards as cryptocurrencies and any bugs may become attack vectors for theft. Therefore, safety is the first concern for blockchain developers.

Smart contracts are programs associated with blockchain accounts and executed at transactions. Since the execution happens on all the nodes, the caller must pay a fee to the network. To estimate the cost, the caller must simulate each transaction before sending it to the network. This simulation is also important to secure the smart contracts along with formally verifying their safety properties, since any bug or misspecification may turn them to automatic stealing machines. Several existing works of this smart contract simulation in Tezos blockchain and its future directions will be discussed.

Biography

Jun is working for Tezos blockchain technology as one of the few Asian core developers since its mainnet launch in September 2019. He is also a scientific director of Tezos Japan, an NPO to promote Tezos technology in Japan to the industry and the academia. Being a researcher of functional programming and its static type system (Ph. D., Université Paris Diderot), his interests are always in applying programming language theory and formal verification methods to provide better security to mission-critical systems. He has started his own company DaiLambda in the last year, after 10 years of career as a quantitative developer for systems for derivative product modeling (LexiFi, Standard Chartered Bank) and high-frequency trading (Jane Street Capital).

Contents

Simulation Applications: Blockchain, Deep Learning and Cloud

Simulation and Visualization

Simulation Applications

Short Papers

Best Paper Nominees

Digital Twin Technology for Aquaponics: Towards Optimizing Food Production with Dynamic Data Driven Application Systems

Ayyaz Ahmed[1,2], Shahid Zulfiqar[2], Adam Ghandar[1(✉)], Yang Chen[1], Masatoshi Hanai[1], and Georgios Theodoropoulos[1]

[1] Southern University of Science and Technology,
Shenzhen, People's Republic of China
{aghandar,yajun,gtheodoropoulos}@sustc.edu.cn, aghandar@sustech.edu.cn,
11849250@mail.sustech.edu.cn

[2] Al-Khawarizmi Institute of Computer Science, University of Engineering
and Technology (UET)- Lahore, Lahore, Pakistan
{ayyaz.ahmed,shahid.zulfiqar}@kics.edu.pk

Abstract. Aquaponics, or recirculating aquaculture production systems, harness the symbiotic relationship between plants and fish for food production. A large quantity of fish can be raised in a small volume of water by the effect of plants in removing toxic waste products excreted by fish; in turn the waste is broken down by microbial activity to obtain concentrated nutrients for intensive plant/crop growing. The concentration of nutrients generated is similar to hydroponic nutrient solutions. Water is conserved in the integrated process and may be reused. In this paper we consider an approach comprising self-contained aquaponics production units each of which is a closed system where the balance of fish stock and plants is monitored and controlled automatically. We provide empirical results of a simulation and a physical implementation. The design involves an online virtual production unit implemented with a simulation that is updated with data from the real system (a dynamic data driven application system). The virtual unit anticipates the performance of the real system and enabling what if analysis and optimization of the behavior of the whole system: for example to maximize production, minimize waste, conserve water and other resources, meet quality standards, and other production goals.

Keywords: Dynamic Data Driven Application System (DDDAS) ·
Simulation modelling · Digital twin · Cyber-physical system ·
Aquaponics

1 Introduction

Human society faces challenges in food security and sustainability due to factors such as urbanization, natural resource depletion and loss of biodiversity [11].

© Springer Nature Singapore Pte Ltd. 2019
G. Tan et al. (Eds.): AsiaSim 2019, CCIS 1094, pp. 3–14, 2019.
https://doi.org/10.1007/978-981-15-1078-6_1

Technological innovation is significant in efforts toward food system improvement that are guided for instance by intergovernmental organizations such as the United Nations Food and Agriculture Organization (FAO) [8] and the G20[1]. These efforts recognize that while in the past a focus was on boosting agriculture production quantity (for a survey of recent technological advances in this area see [26]) a new focus is needed to tackle basic causes of hunger and malnutrition. Efforts today focus on transformative changes across the entire value chain in the way food is produced, consumed and distributed[2] [25]. For examples of applications that involve innovation in agricultural value chains, see [27] which proposes a hydroponic planter for urban agriculture that is designed to support a novel service industry and value chain configuration through local production in an urban environment; [9] looks at the linking producers of different scales, traditional and non-traditional with customers through a network interface and gateway so as to attain necessary attributes of volume, traceability, and consistency that are important in mass production food systems but also gain benefits of small scale production such as customized produce and local production.

According to the FAO, agricultural innovation needs to encompass diverse stakeholders including small family farmers and local industry taking into account unique cultural and geographic constraints (technological as well as policy, organizational and social aspects). Aquaoponics [7], can provide fish and fresh produce that is produced, potentially, co-located with consumers in urban environments such as rooftops thus reducing necessity for transportation and storage. It can facilitate intensive farming for high yields in limited space with efficient use of resources. Aquaponics has been applied to produce food in difficult and constrained conditions, for instance the FAO describes application in the Gaza strip [1]: an arid, urban area in protracted crisis[3]. The potential for aquaponics to provide food security and sustenance in difficult constrained environments sustainably with limited resources, and to form a component of an innovative sustainable value chain with diverse stakeholder participation, has resulted in recent research interest.

Aquaponics combines hydroponics (growing plants without soil) and aquaculture (raising fish). Fish excrete waste, these dissolved nutrients accumulate in the water and provide plants with nutrition [24]. Water is recirculated between fish and plants resulting in a much lower requirement for water than traditional soil based agriculture. In effect aquaponics is a holistic farming technology where a controlled ecosystem is formulated where plants and fish live in symbiotic relation supported by microbial activity (to break down waste and generate nutrients) [16,19].

From a whole system point of view, aquaponic implementations are complex systems. Combining natural and human elements interacting together in complex dynamics that result from factors such as heterogeneity of plants and fish, non linear dynamics with thresholds relating to parameters (such as concentrations

---

[1] http://www.g20.utoronto.ca/2018/2018-07-28-agriculture.html.
[2] http://www.fao.org/3/CA2460EN/ca2460en.pdf.
[3] http://www.fao.org/3/a-i5620e.pdf.

of nutrients and water quality), feedback loops, and other factors resulting from combining human and natural systems that are fundamentally highly challenging to model accurately [14]. Due to the complexity of the aquaponic system, it is very challenging first to accurately model and then to predict or optimize the whole system toward system goals such as to maximize production, minimize waste, conserve water and other resources, meet quality standards, or other performance criteria. Possibly as a result, the current state-of-the-art cyber-physical aquaponic systems proposed in the literature do not attempt optimization of the whole system [23,30]. Rather, silos or components, are controlled by local optimization processes or decision rules based on prior assumptions. We investigate a new approach using a dynamic data driven application system (DDDAS) [6,15,21].

The main contributions of the paper are as follows:

- *Cyber-physical Aquaponic System.* We describe a cyber-physical aquaponics system based on Internet-of-Things (IoT) sensors for monitoring system and environmental conditions.
- *Digital Twin of an Aquaponic System.* A virtual aquaponic system is implemented as a simulation and validated.

The rest of the paper is organized as follows: technological innovations in aquaponics are reviewed in Sect. 2; Sect. 3 describes our IoT enabled physical system; Sect. 4 describes the virtual replica; Sect. 5 evaluates and validates both; Sect. 6 concludes the paper.

2 Background and Literature Review

Digitization has been applied to obtain benefits in many spheres of society including developing state-of-the-art production systems, see Industry 4.0 [12]. In digital twin, real time data acquisition from physical entities are connected to simulated representations. The approach was anticipated by the concept of Dynamic Data Driven Application Systems [4]. The uptake of digital twin technology has been slower in small enterprises although the potential benefits are very large [28]. In other sectors apart from agriculture real time data acquisition combined with simulation has also proven beneficial. For a selection see [5,20,22].

IoT-Based Aquaponic Systems. For a recent survey of work applying automation and IoT technology for aquaponic production see [2]. Real time data and IoT sensors enable data relating to various system parameters to be obtained and analyzed. A control loop is completed when based on the data tasks in the operation of the system are performed, for example: add fish food, alter the water level in the fish tank, recirculate water between fish tank and grow bed, turn on/off the grow lights, adjust the PH level, etc. Recent research reports implementation of networked sensors to support monitoring key variables such as water quality in aquaponic systems that are designed to provide locally grown organic food in smart city concept and reduce reliance on traditional agriculture [18].

Many recent applications have a context of providing local high quality produce in urban settings and can implement low cost integrated monitoring and control using micro devices such as the Arduino, Rasberry Pi and Intel Edison to coordinate various network components and sensor feeds. For instance, in [17] an implementation uses Rasberry Pi to monitors PH, temperature and dissolved oxygen levels. In [23] there is a focus on the PH and its application to control plant and fish growth rates. In [30] a mobile application to monitor temperature and humidity and on the basis of readings control a fan, water pump and mist maker is described. A somewhat related implementation which uses Intel Edison as a processor is described in [29].

Analytics and Simulation Enhanced Aquaponic Systems. Various analytic techniques can be combined with real time data to provide decision support and automated management capabilities. There is limited research in modeling the behavior of aquaponics as a complex system. There is however work that describes development of mathematical techniques to predict important system variables. In [13] analytics supports a model based management strategy and determines optimized nutrient management strategies for producing tomato and Nile perch (Tilapia) fish by predicting and mitigating excess concentration of total suspended solids and sodium and ammonia concentrations and balance the concentration of nutrients for plant growth versus the water quality required for raising fish.

3   Cyber-Physical Aquaponic System

This section provides overview of the aquaponic system and implementation of sensor hardware.

3.1   System Overview

The cyber-physical aquaponic system consists of hydroponics, aquaculture and an IoT sensor system.

Figure 1 shows the complete schematic cycle of the aquaponics system. Water flows from the fish tank into a mechanical filtration where solid waste is removed. Solid waste is removed but ammonia is dissolved in water, water then enters a bio-filter where nitrifying bacteria convert ammonia to nitrates. Ammonia is dangerous for both fish and plants, therefore we have to convert it into nitrates which are a fertilizer for plants. Nitrate rich water is then moved into grow bed and plants absorb the nitrates. Cleaned water with reduced amonia and nitrates finally returns back to the fish tank. Grow lights were installed above the grow bed as the system is installed indoors. Multiple sensors were installed in both the fish tank and grow bed. Air is introduced in system for the fish. It also helps the nitrification process in bio-filter. Details of the hardware and software components are provided in Fig. 2.

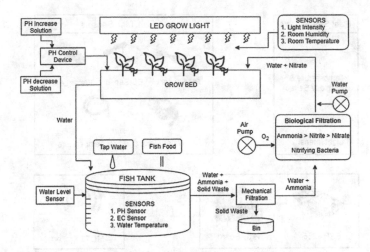

Fig. 1. Architecture of aquaponics system.

3.2 Hardware Implementation

The IoT sensor system that was implemented consists of 3 main components or modules: sensor units, networking units, and computational units, see Fig. 2. The sensor data is communicated through the networking units to the computational units for analysis in computational units.

Sensor units measure temperature, light intensity, water flow, dissolved salts (TDS/EC sensor), and PH. The data feed is transferred through networking components for analysis and actuation. Networking Units include an ESP8266 device for transferring data over WiFi to MQQT broker. A 4 channel mechanical coil relay board is used to control the air and water pumps and the growth lights. Energy saving features include switching off growth lights when ambient light is sufficient for growth (greater than 50 lumens). MQQT Broker[4] is used to gather topics sent by ESP8266, it is able to send back messages for control and actuation. A secure MQQT broker is situated on the local IP on Rasberry Pi. A Raspberry Pi device provides computation. It collects data from ESP8266 via broker and we use NODE-RED to handle results and perform logging. Thingspeakis[5] provides analytics functionality and visualization, it also includes functionality for back storage. Further data storage is through MangoDB and MyPHP for back-end processing of data. Other physical units include a water pump (15 L/min), air pump (3.5 L/min). A secondary air pump provides redundancy in case of failure (crucial component for fish survival). We placed our system near a window which provides natural light still we need grow lights as direct sunlight is not available. We used two 12 watt white led panel light and one 30 watt grow light. An automatic fish feeder for dispensing food (4 times/day) is an important part as fish are sensitive to over eating.

---

[4] http://mqtt.org/.
[5] https://thingspeak.com/.

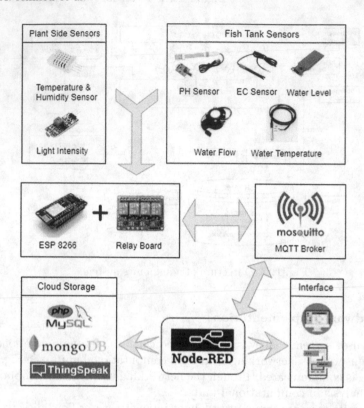

Fig. 2. Implementation of the sensor system.

4 Simulation

The simulation code is accessible at the following url: https://github.com/ Monsooooon/AquaponicSim. The main simulation modules include: fish feed, TDS, fish weight gain, PH, Nitrates and plant growth are modeled. The feed rate depends on feed conversion ratio, fish weight and number of fish. For the type of fish in the system we set the FCR to 0.6, this means that if fish eats one kg of feed, it will convert 60% of it in its body weight. Figure 4 illustrates the interaction between the system variables as modeled. The conversion rate between them are determined by multiple environment factors, including pH, light strength and temperatures, and will also influence the growth rate of the plants and fish.

$$F_r = F_{cr} w_f N_f, \tag{1}$$

where F_r is fish feed rate, F_{cr} is feed conservation ratio, w_f is fish weight gain and N_f is the number of fish in the system per meter cubic (Fig. 3).

Fish weight gain depends on fish initial weight, water temperature, the fish growth co-efficient is as prescribed by Goddek [10]:

$$W_f(t)_i = [W_0^{1-\beta_f} + (1 - \beta_f)\alpha_f e^{\gamma_f T_w} \Delta t]^{\frac{1}{1-\beta_f}} \tag{2}$$

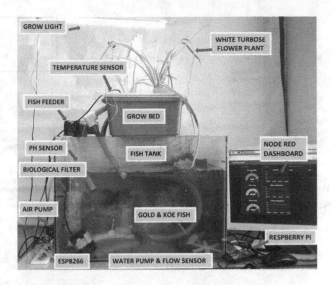

Fig. 3. Cyber physical aquaponics system

where W_f (g) is the fish weight at a specific time increasing, W_0 (g) is the initial fish weight, T_w is the water temperature (°C), and α_f, β_f and γ_f are species-specific growth-coefficients ($\alpha_f = 0.0277$, $\beta_f = 0.4071$ and $\gamma_f = 0.0697$), and i denotes for accumulation of W_f in time (i.e. changing biomass with each simulation step).

TDS of water depends on fish feed, EC (electrical conductivity) and their co-relation factor which is different for each fish species:

$$TDS = F.EC.KE \tag{3}$$

Water PH depends on hydronium $HO_3{}^-$, nitrates and water temperature.

$$pH = HO_3{}^- \cdot NO_3 \cdot T_w \tag{4}$$

Nitrates which is essential for plants and not toxic for fish. It is modeled by the following equation:

$$Nitrates(ppm) = Ammonia(NH_3) \cdot Nitrification\ Coefficient \tag{5}$$

The current assumption is to keep water temperature constant. The plant growth model contains factors of CO_2, nutrients, sunlight and oxygen dissolved in water. We apply a model presented by Akyol [3] extended with factors for BOD and nitrates.

$$X_{new} = (i, It + 1) + y + \beta + BOD\ mg/L \tag{6}$$

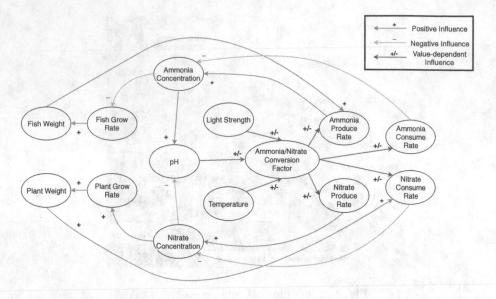

Fig. 4. The simulation models variables

Water is re-circulated again and again in our system with water loss because of evaporation and solid waste removal. We model total water loss in four-week time as described by Wetzel [31]

$$g_h = \Theta A(y_s - y), \tag{7}$$

where, gh: amount of evaporated water per hour (kg/h), $\theta = (25 + 19\,v)$ evaporation coefficient (kg/m²h), v: velocity of air above the water surface (3 m/s), A: water surface area (1 m²), S: Dissolved solid quantity removed from system kg/h, ys: maximum humidity ratio of saturated air (0.51), and y is humidity ratio air (0.43 kg H2O in kg Dry Air).

5   Results and Empirical Analysis

This section provides results of implementation of the aquaponic system described in the previous sections. The results discussed in this section were obtained during a four-week experiment with physical system.

The humidity of our system ranges between 32–51%, room temperature varied from 24–30 °C. Fish aquarium water temperature was a little lower than room temperature. Water temperature was 24–29 °C. Humidity and temperature levels are both in a good range for plant and fish growth. We have not observed any significant problems due to temperature and humidity changes.

Fish feed was set at 20 grams per day. As shown in Fig. 5a, after one week feed was reduced as the TDS level increases. After another week the feed was increase 10% again as the TDS and PH become stable. After the third week the feed was decreased again as the nitrates are high. Compared with the real fish weight with simulation as in Fig. 5b, actual fish weight gain is lower. Feed was reduced to keep the ammonia and nitrates level stable.

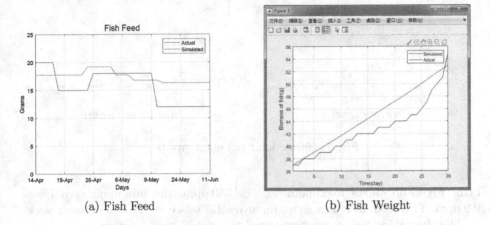

(a) Fish Feed   (b) Fish Weight

Fig. 5. Fish Feed and fish weight.

There is very little difference between the PH of physical with digital twin, as shown in Fig. 6a. Actual PH increases in the first two weeks, becomes stable as the nitrifying bacteria start converting the ammonia into nitrates. The simulation also predicted PH and TDS both dependent on fish feed and bio-filtration.

The total dissolved solids (TDS) is shown in Fig. 6. TDS decreases when the plants start to grow at full speed. TDS is correlated with the amount of food introduced to the system. In the simulation, TDS was a linear trend, ranging from 400 to 472 in 4-week time. Fish can thrive with conditions up to 600 ppm

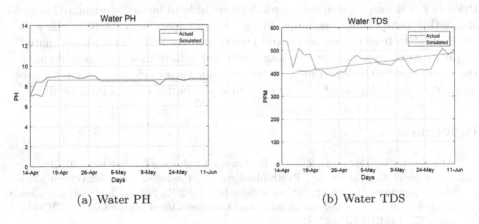

(a) Water PH   (b) Water TDS

Fig. 6. Water PH and TDS

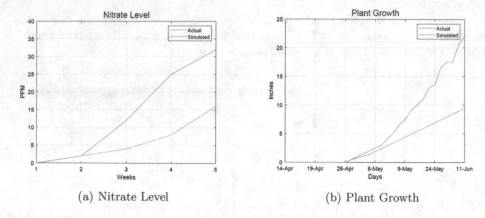

(a) Nitrate Level   (b) Plant Growth

Fig. 7. Nitrate level and plant growth.

TDS. Figure 6b shows maximum TDS is 550 ppm, the minimum actual was 389 ppm. TDS also decreases as we remove solid waste at the end on each week.

The simulation fails to predict actual nitrates. Actual nitrates rise in weeks 3 and 4 (Fig. 7a). It reaches at 32 mg/l at the end of week 4. Two plants are not sufficient to absorb all nitrates from water. As shown in Fig. 7b actual plant growth is greater than expected by the simulated one as the nitrates levels increases unexpectedly and the plant grows faster. We have also controlled the plant growth by changing the fish feed rates. This is an effective method to control plant production in aquaponics system.

6   Conclusion

This paper described implementation and validation of a physical IoT aquaponic system and a simulated representation. Empirical results showed that some quantities (e.g. PH and total dissolved solids) were able to be easily estimated in the simulation but others were more difficult to anticipate accurately in the approach used such as nitrate levels and growth rates which were underestimated. In future work coupling the simulation and real system more closely will enable the simulation variables to be updated in order to provide more accurate predictions of the behavior of the system and hence better control functionality.

References

1. Abdelnour, S., Tartir, A., Zurayk, R.: Farming palestine for freedom (2012)
2. Aishwarya, K., Harish, M., Prathibhashree, S., Panimozhi, K.: Survey on automated aquponics based gardening approaches. In: 2018 Second International Conference on Inventive Communication and Computational Technologies (ICICCT), pp. 1377–1381. IEEE (2018)

3. Akyol, A.: Plant intelligence based metaheuristic optimization algorithms. Artif. Intell. Rev. (2013). https://doi.org/10.1007/s10462-016-9486-6
4. Blasch, E., Seetharaman, G., Reinhardt, K.: Dynamic data driven applications system concept for information fusion. Procedia Comput. Sci. **18**, 1999–2007 (2013)
5. Bubak, M., van Albada, G.D., Dongarra, J., Sloot, P.M.A. (eds.): ICCS 2008. LNCS, vol. 5103. Springer, Heidelberg (2008). https://doi.org/10.1007/978-3-540-69389-5
6. Chhetri, S.R., Faezi, S., Faruque, M.: Digital twin of manufacturing systems. Center for Embedded & Cyber-Physical Systems (2017)
7. Diver, S., Rinehart, L.: Aquaponics-Integration of hydroponics with aquaculture. Attra (2000)
8. Food, FAO: Agriculture: key to achieving the 2030 agenda for sustainable development. Rome: Food and Agriculture Organization of the United Nations (2016)
9. Ghandar, A., Theodoropoulos, G., Zheng, B., Chen, S., Gong, Y., Zhong, M.: A dynamic data driven application system to manage urban agricultural ecosystems in smart cities. In: 2018 4th International Conference on Universal Village (UV), pp. 1–7. IEEE (2018)
10. Goddek, S.: A fully integrated simulation model of multi-loop aquaponics: a case study for system sizing in different environments. Agric. Syst. **171**, 143–154 (2019)
11. Godfray, H.C.J., et al.: Food security: the challenge of feeding 9 billion people. Science **327**(5967), 812–818 (2010)
12. Lasi, H., Fettke, P., Kemper, H.G., Feld, T., Hoffmann, M.: Industry 4.0. Bus. Inf. Syst. Eng. **6**(4), 239–242 (2014)
13. Lastiri, D.R., et al.: Model-based management strategy for resource efficient design and operation of an aquaponic system. Aquac. Eng. **83**, 27–39 (2018)
14. Liu, J., et al.: Complexity of coupled human and natural systems. Science **317**(5844), 1513–1516 (2007)
15. Madey, G.R., et al.: Enhanced situational awareness: application of DDDAS concepts to emergency and disaster management. In: Shi, Y., van Albada, G.D., Dongarra, J., Sloot, P.M.A. (eds.) ICCS 2007. LNCS, vol. 4487, pp. 1090–1097. Springer, Heidelberg (2007). https://doi.org/10.1007/978-3-540-72584-8_143
16. Mamatha, M., Namratha, S.: Design & implementation of indoor farming using automated aquaponics system. In: 2017 IEEE International Conference on Smart Technologies and Management for Computing, Communication, Controls, Energy and Materials (ICSTM), pp. 396–401. IEEE (2017)
17. Mandap, J.P., Sze, D., Reyes, G.N., Dumlao, S.M., Reyes, R., Chung, W.Y.D.: Aquaponics ph level, temperature, and dissolved oxygen monitoring and control system using raspberry pi as network backbone. In: TENCON 2018–2018 IEEE Region 10 Conference, pp. 1381–1386. IEEE (2018)
18. Manju, M., Karthik, V., Hariharan, S., Sreekar, B.: Real time monitoring of the environmental parameters of an aquaponic system based on internet of things. In: 2017 Third International Conference on Science Technology Engineering & Management (ICONSTEM), pp. 943–948. IEEE (2017)
19. Munguia-Fragozo, P., et al.: Perspective for aquaponic systems: "omic" technologies for microbial community analysis. BioMed Res. Int. **2015** (2015)
20. Mustafee, N., Powell, J.H.: From hybrid simulation to hybrid systems modelling. In: 2018 Winter Simulation Conference, WSC 2018, Gothenburg, Sweden, 9–12 December 2018, pp. 1430–1439 (2018)

21. Onggo, B.S.: Symbiotic simulation system (S3) for industry 4.0. In: Gunal, M.M. (ed.) Simulation for Industry 4.0. SSAM, pp. 153–165. Springer, Cham (2019). https://doi.org/10.1007/978-3-030-04137-3_10

22. Onggo, B.S., Mustafee, N., Smart, A., Juan, A.A., Molloy, O.: Symbiotic simulation system: hybrid systems model meets big data analytics. In: 2018 Winter Simulation Conference, WSC 2018, Gothenburg, Sweden, 9–12 December 2018, pp. 1358–1369 (2018)

23. Pasha, A.K., Mulyana, E., Hidayat, C., Ramdhani, M.A., Kurahman, O.T., Adhipradana, M.: System design of controlling and monitoring on aquaponic based on internet of things. In: 2018 4th International Conference on Wireless and Telematics (ICWT), pp. 1–5. IEEE (2018)

24. Rakocy, J.E., Masser, M.P., Losordo, T.M.: Recirculating aquaculture tank production systems: aquaponics–integrating fish and plant culture. SRAC Publ. **454**(1), 16 (2006)

25. Rockström, J., et al.: Sustainable intensification of agriculture for human prosperity and global sustainability. Ambio **46**(1), 4–17 (2017)

26. Ruan, J., et al.: A life cycle framework of green iot-based agriculture and its finance, operation, and management issues. IEEE Commun. Mag. **57**(3), 90–96 (2019)

27. Satoh, A.: A hydroponic planter system to enable an urban agriculture service industry. In: 2018 IEEE 7th Global Conference on Consumer Electronics (GCCE), pp. 281–284. IEEE (2018)

28. Uhlemann, T.H.J., Schock, C., Lehmann, C., Freiberger, S., Steinhilper, R.: The digital twin: demonstrating the potential of real time data acquisition in production systems. Procedia Manuf. **9**, 113–120 (2017)

29. Valiente, F.L., et al.: Internet of things (IoT)-based mobile application for monitoring of automated aquaponics system. In: 2018 IEEE 10th International Conference on Humanoid, Nanotechnology, Information Technology, Communication and Control, Environment and Management (HNICEM), pp. 1–6. IEEE (2018)

30. Vernandhes, W., Salahuddin, N.S., Kowanda, A., Sari, S.P.: Smart aquaponic with monitoring and control system based on IoT. In: 2017 Second International Conference on Informatics and Computing (ICIC), pp. 1–6. IEEE (2017)

31. WETZEL: Encyclopedia of soils in the environment. In: Water Evaporation, pp. 141–183 (2015). Science direct

On Evaluating Rust as a Programming Language for the Future of Massive Agent-Based Simulations

Alessia Antelmi[1](✉), Gennaro Cordasco[2](✉), Matteo D'Auria[1](✉),
Daniele De Vinco[1](✉), Alberto Negro[1](✉), and Carmine Spagnuolo[1](✉)

[1] ISISLab, Dipartimento di Informatica,
Università Degli Studi di Salerno, Fisciano, Italy
{aantelmi,matdauria,alberto,cspagnuolo}@unisa.it,
d.devinco@studenti.unisa.it
[2] Dipartimento di Psicologia,
Università degli Studi della Campania "Luigi Vanvitelli", Caserta, Italy
gennaro.cordasco@unicampania.it

Abstract. The analysis of real systems and the development of predictive models to describe the evolution of real phenomena are challenging tasks that can improve the design of methodologies in many research fields. In this context, Agent-Based Model (ABM) can be seen as an innovative tool for modelling real-world complex simulations. This paper presents Rust-AB, an open-source library for developing ABM simulation on sequential and/or parallel computing platforms, exploiting Rust as programming language. The Rust-AB architecture as well as an investigation on the ability of Rust to develop ABM simulations are discussed. An ABM simulation written in Rust-AB, and a performance comparison against the well-adopted Java ABM toolkit MASON is also presented.

Keywords: Rust language · Agent-Based Model · Simulation · Framework

1 Introduction

Identifying fundamental rules that govern complex systems and developing predictive models to describe the evolution of real phenomena are challenging tasks that can improve the design of approaches and methodologies in many research fields [18]. The analysis of real systems has revealed several interesting emergent behaviours both in terms of structural features [10] and dynamic behaviours [17]. However, a full understanding of the dynamic behaviour generated by complex systems is extremely hard and requires innovative study methodologies. Recently, computational scientists have proposed the analysis of these phenomena through the exploitation of simulations based on Agent-Based Model (ABM). ABM simulations denote a class of models that, simulating the behaviour of multiple agents, aim to emulate and/or predict complex phenomena. An ABM consists of

© Springer Nature Singapore Pte Ltd. 2019
G. Tan et al. (Eds.): AsiaSim 2019, CCIS 1094, pp. 15–28, 2019.
https://doi.org/10.1007/978-981-15-1078-6_2

three components: agents, relations, and rules. The agents model a population; the relations define potential interactions among agents; the rules describe the behaviour of an agent as a result of an interaction.

Motivation. The success of computational sciences has led to increasing demand for computation-intensive software implementations. Hence, the need to improve the performance of ABMs simulations - successfully adopted in many sciences [8] - in terms of both size (number of agents) and quality (complexity of interactions). Complex ABMs very often require the continuous computation of global data during the simulation [11]. In such cases, the problem consists in ensuring good performance and a high-level of effectiveness in simulation modelling. However, frameworks for distributed simulations are not able to compute global information efficiently (for instance, the total number of agents that satisfy a given property) [6]. The computation of a global parameter represents a bottleneck for distributed simulations, which jeopardise the performance due to the communication overhead. In such cases, the use of a parallel and/or sequential simulation framework provides better performances [7]. Moreover, to achieve performance, distributed simulations often require expensive hardware that is usable only by distributed computing experts. Providing efficient and effective software for developing ABM simulations in sequential computing allows the user to effortlessly execute simulations. This makes simulations more suitable for a "what-if" scenario, where the user needs to frequently change the simulation parameters and rapidly observe the results.

High-performance ABM simulations are built upon performance-critical operation, and interactions exhibit multiple levels of concurrency. Implementing an efficient framework for the development of ABM simulations is extremely challenging, and the choice of the implementation language is a crucial aspect to consider. It is common to use a language like C to gain performance, as it enables the programmer to exploit low-level memory operations (e.g. deallocating memory) thanks to its low level of abstraction (e.g. no object-oriented support). On the other hand, the usage of such languages turns out to be quite difficult, especially for domain experts with limited knowledge of computer programming and systems. In this work, we exploit Rust as programming language for the next generation of ABM simulation. Rust is a multi-paradigm system programming language with performance comparable to C. Its main feature lies in its memory model, designed to be both memory and thread safe. This aspect can be recognised as the core advantage of using Rust over languages as C++ and Java as it allows the user to write correct code, particularly in the presence of concurrency and parallelism. We will describe Rust key concepts in Sect. 3.

Outline and Paper Contributions. We present an overview of the current state-of-art of the ABM frameworks/libraries for developing simulation (see Sect. 2). In Sect. 3, we analyse Rust features with a focus on its peculiarity for writing ABM simulation. The main contribution of this work is the description of a novel library, **Rust-AB**, for writing ABM simulations. The Alpha 1.0 version of the library is released on a public GitHub repository [3] and is presented in Sect. 4. In Sect. 5, we present a case study: we developed an ABM simulation using Rust-AB, and we present a performance comparison with the same model on MASON.

2   Related Work

This Section outlines some existing tools - commonly, designed either as a framework or a library (or both) - for developing and running ABM simulations with a particular emphasis on their peculiarities, as described by Abar et al. [1].

   ABM software tools can be easily classified into two categories according to the underlying architecture: software for sequential computing architectures and software for distributed computing architectures. Table 1 describes the most important frameworks and libraries for ABM simulations according to the simulation engine programming language, user programming language, computing platform, application domain, and release license. First six rows of Table 1 summarise as many frameworks suitable for sequential computing simulations and that are fully described by Abar et al. [1]. Several frameworks are designed to develop large-scale simulations and provide good performance exploiting parallel/distributed computing architectures. The bottom part of Table 1 presents three frameworks for developing ABM simulations in distributed and parallel computing architecture.

   This work focuses on improving the simulation performance, when the computation of global data is required, on sequential or parallel architectures, avoiding the complexity and the limitations introduced by distributed computing. We will further focus on the effectiveness and the expressiveness of the produced software in developing ABM.

Table 1. ABM frameworks/software comparison.

ABM tool	Source Language	Applications language	Computing platform	Application domain	License
SWARM [12]	Java, Objective-C	Objective-C, Swarm code, Java	Personal computer, Workstation, Large-scale scientific computing clusters and HP supercomputers	Simulation of complex adaptive systems in social or biological sciences	Open source, GPL, Free
StarLogo [14]	Java/YoYo	StarLogo scripting	Desktop computer	Simulation in social and natural sciences, education	Closed source, Clearthought Software License version 1.0, Free
NetLogo [20]	Scala	NetLogo language	Desktop computer	2D/3D simulation in social and natural science, teaching/research	Open source, GPL, Free
REPAST [13]	Java / C#	Java; C#, C++, Lisp, Prolog Visual Basic.Net, Python scripting	Desktop and vast-scale distributed computing clusters	Simulation of social networks and integrates support for GIS, genetic algorithms	Open source, BSD, Free
MASON [19]	Java	Java	Desktop computer, Workstation	General multi-purpose 2D/3D simulation	Open source, Academic Free License version 3.0
FLAME [9]	C	Graphical user interface, visualiser and validation tools	Laptop, Workstation, HPC supercomputers	General multi-pupose simulation	Open source, GNU Lesser General Public License, Free
REPAST-HPC [4]	C++ with MPI	Standard or Logo-style C++	Large-scale distributed clusters and HP supercomputer	Simulations in computational social sciences, cellular automata, complex adaptive system	Open source, BSD, Free
D-MASON [5]	Java	Java	Desktop computer, Workstation, Clusters, Cloud architectures	General multi-purpose 2D/3D simulation	Open souce, Apache License version 2.0
FLAME-GPU [16]	C for CUDA OpenGL	C-based scripting and optimized CUDA code	Laptop, Workstation, HPC	3D simulation for emergent complex behaviours in biology/ medical domains with multi-massive amount of agent on GPU	Open source, FLAME GPU Licens Agreement, Free

3   Rust Background

Rust is a multi-paradigm system programming language, originally designed at Mozilla Research in 2009. Rust first stable release was launched in 2015, and since 2016 it figures as the *most loved programming language* in the yearly Stack Overflow Developer Survey. The Rust compiler is a free and open-source software dual-licensed under the MIT License and Apache License 2.0. The reasons why Rust is so widely used must be sought in its design principles. Rust, in fact, guarantees both memory and thread safety, thanks to its rich type system and its ownership model.

Ownership. Ownership is Rust's central feature: memory is managed through a system of ownership that the compiler checks at compile time. This means that there is no need for a garbage collector that constantly looks for no longer used memory. In addition, Rust programmers do not have to explicitly allocate and free the memory. Ownership is translated into practice with the following concept: each value in Rust has a variable called its *owner*. The owner is unique and when it goes out of scope, the value is dropped.

References and Borrowing. These two concepts are strictly related to Rust's ownership model. As in other programming languages, a given variable x can be passed either by *value* or by *reference*. When a value is passed by reference, it can be passed either by immutable reference using &x or by mutable reference using &mut x. The &x syntax creates a reference that refers to the value of x, but does not own it. For this reason, the value it points to will not be dropped when the reference goes out of scope. Similarly, the signature of the function uses & to indicate that the type of the parameter x is a reference. Using references as function parameters is known as *borrowing*. References, as Rust variables, are immutable by default. If a reference to a variable x needs to be modified, it has to be declared as *mutable* using &mut x. The benefit of having this restriction is that Rust can prevent data races at compilation time.

Furthermore, the Rust compiler guarantees that *dangling* references, i.e. a pointer that references a location in memory that may have been given to someone else, will never happen. Every reference in Rust has a *lifetime*, which is the scope for which that reference is valid. Most of the time, lifetimes are implicit and inferred, but they must be annotated when the lifetimes of references could be related in a different way. The main aim of lifetimes is to prevent dangling references.

Rust Object-Oriented Programming. Rust is a programming language influenced by many programming paradigms, including object-oriented (OO) programming (OOP). Therefore it shares certain common characteristics with OO languages:

- *Rust Objects.* Rust enables the definition of objects using structures, enums and impl blocks. A struct is a custom data type that packs together multiple related values that make up a meaningful group. As it happens with structs, enums can be defined to hold generic data types in their variants. The impl keyword is primarily used to define implementations on types.

- *Encapsulation* means that the implementation details of an object are not accessible to code using that object. Rust defines the pub keyword to let the programmer decide which modules, types, functions, and methods should be public. By default, anything else is private.
- *Inheritance* is a mechanism whereby an object can inherit from another object's definition, thus gaining the parent object's data and behaviour without having to define them again. Rust does not allow the user to define a struct that inherits the parent struct's fields and method implementations.
- *Polymorphism* means that your multiple objects can be substituted for each other at running time if they share certain characteristics. In Rust, this feature is enabled through *traits*. A trait tells the Rust compiler about functionalities a particular type has and can share with other types. Traits can be used to define shared behaviours in an abstract way, in which a type's behaviour is defined by the methods we can call on that type.

4   Rust-AB: Programming Agent-Based Models in Rust

Rust-AB is a discrete events simulation engine designed to be a ready-to-use ABM simulation library, suitable for the ABM community. To reduce the learning curve and simplify its usage, we adopted the same modular and standard architectural layout of the Java library MASON, based on the Model-View-Controller design pattern. More in detail, a MASON simulation is made up by three fundamental players: (i) the simulation agents, specified by the Java interface Steppable; (ii) the simulation scheduler, defined by the Scheduler object; (iii) the simulation state, represented by the SimState object. The implementation of a MASON simulation has to extend the SimState object, while its agents are represented through a Java class, which implements the Steppable interface.

Even though Rust-AB resembles MASON in its architecture, we have re-engineered the simulation engine to exploit Rust's peculiarities. Furthermore, Rust-AB has been designed to provide the programmers an easy and standard simulation framework for developing ABM, thus enabling an easier adoption of a new language as Rust. The Alpha 1.0 version of the Rust-AB simulation engine library is fully developed and released under MIT license on a public GitHub repository [3]. Section 4.1 describes Rust-AB architectural concepts and functionalities.

4.1   Rust-AB Architecture

Agent. An Agent is the most important concept of Rust-AB. According to the OO model of Rust, an agent is a trait of a Rust struct, which means that every Rust struct implementing the trait Agent is considered a simulation agent. Similarly to the MASON toolkit, the Agent implementation must provide a step method where the agent logic should be placed.

Schedule. Being Rust-AB a discrete event simulation engine, the `Schedule` is its core object as it provides all functionalities to manage a simulation according to event-based scheduling. It provides the same interface defined by MASON. The simulation proceeds by scheduling the agents time-by-time. A schedulable agent is a Rust struct that implements the Rust-AB trait `Agent` and the Rust trait `Clone`. To obey to the Rust programming model, the scheduler has to mandatory clone the agents before each simulation step. The scheduler works as a priority queue (FIFO), where the agents are sorted according to their scheduled time and a priority value - an integer. The simulation time - a real value - starts from the scheduling time of the first agent. At each discrete simulation step, all agents scheduled in the current simulation time perform a simulation step according to their scheduling priority. In the Alpha 1.0 version of Rust-AB, the scheduler provides two scheduling options:

- `schedule_once` inserts an agent in the schedule for a specific simulation step. The scheduling time and the priority are given as parameters. The priority is used to sort all agents within the same simulation time.
- `schedule_repeating` acts like *schedule_once*, with the difference that the agent will be scheduled for all subsequent simulation steps.

The schedule provides the `step` method which allows executing one simulation step. In this way, the programmer can easily design his/her simulation by looping for a certain number of step or for a given amount of CPU time.

Location2D. `Location2D` is a Rust-AB `trait`, defining a Rust struct exposing a position in a 2-D space. An agent can be placed in a field struct, thus enabling the programmer to easily model agents neighbourhood interactions. Every Rust struct that implements this trait can be placed in a Rust-AB field. A position in a 2-D space is modelled as a Rust-AB struct `Real2D`. A given `Location2D` implementation must provide two functionalities: (i) `get_location`, that provides the current position in the space - a Real2D, and (ii) `set_location`, which allows to move an object.

Field2D. `Field2D` is a sparse matrix structure modelling agent interactions on a 2-D space. The `Field2D` structure is parameterized on a given type implementing: `Location2D` Rust-AB trait, and Rust `Clone`, `Hash`, and `Eq` (equivalence relation) traits. `Location2D` defines the structure on which the field operates, while the remaining traits allow a more efficient implementation of the field functionalities. It is worth mentioning that the field structure is useful not only for the agents, but for any kind of Rust type that implements the described traits. This designing aspect allows the programmer to easily model interactions with any kind of simulation environment. The `Field2D` structure provides the following methods:

- `set_object_location` inserts/updates an object in a field in a given position.
- `get_neighbors_within_distance`, returns a vector of objects contained in the circle centered at a given position with a radius equal to the

distance parameter. An optimized radial searching method is used to compute the neighborhood.

- `get_object_location`, returns the position of a Location2D object.
- `get_objects_at_location`, returns a vector of objects stored in a given position.
- `num_objects`, returns the total number of objects stored in the field.
- `num_objects_at_location`, returns the number of objects at a given `Real2D` object position.

Simulation State. `Simulation State` is the state of a Rust-AB simulation. A Rust-AB simulation is composed by an agent definition (i.e., a Rust struct that implements the trait *Agent*), a Rust-AB scheduler instance (declared for the agent implementation), and a set of fields and variables. The simulation logic is implemented in the step function of the agent. For this reason, the programming environment must provide a mechanism to access the simulation state from the agent's step function.

The simulation state is defined using a Rust struct, containing all fields and variables. To access this struct, the programmer has to declare the struct itself as a static reference and initialise it at running time. Moreover, to ensure the Rust memory model accesses to this struct must be done using a lock (or mutex), which secure safe memory access in the agent step function. This procedure is better described in Sect. 5.

Limitations. The main design limitations of Rust-AB are due to the basic Rust OOP model and its memory model. The first limitation concerns the multi-agents capabilities of Rust-AB: the current version Rust-AB does not support multiple definitions of an agent. Nevertheless, it is still possible to implement a multi-agents model by defining different behaviours in the same agent definition. The second limitation lies in the fact that the field environment can only accommodate objects of the same type. To model interactions between objects of a different type, it is necessary to use multiple field environment instances (one for each type).

5   A Case Study: The *Boids* Simulation

To analyse the effectiveness and efficiency of Rust-AB, we implemented a well-known ABM on which we performed several benchmarks varying the model scale parameters. The performance of Rust-AB have been compared against the MASON toolkit running the same ABM. We developed the Boids model [15] by Raynolds (1986), which is a steering behaviour ABM for autonomous agents simulating the flocking behaviour of birds. The agent behaviour is derived by a linear combination of three independent rules: (1) *Separation*: steer in order to avoid crowding local flock-mates; (2) *Alignment*: steer towards the average heading of local flock-mates; (3) *Cohesion*: steer to move towards the average position (centre of mass) of local flock-mates.

We developed the Rust-AB Boids model following the same strategy adopted for the *Flocker* MASON simulation, which implements the same model. First, we defined the agent code and its logic by implementing the `Agent` trait. Then, we defined the simulation state by providing the simulation parameters and the environment definitions. Finally, the main simulation function is defined, where the scheduling policy for agents and the fields initialisation are provided.

5.1   Agent Definition

A Rust-AB agent is a struct containing all the local agent data. For our purposes, we defined a new struct named *Bird* that emulates the concept of a bird in a flock. As stated in Sect. 4.1, a Rust-AB agent has to implement the traits `Agent`, `Eq` and `Hash`. According to the model specification, at each simulation step, every agent has to compute three steering rules according to the position of its neighbouring agents. For this reason, all the agents are placed in a Rust-AB *Field2D* environment. As a consequence, the agent definition must implement the trait *Location2D*, as well as the traits *Clone* and *Copy* (that can be automatically computed using the Rust macro `#derive[(_)]`). The steering behaviour model can be implemented by storing the position of the agent in the previous and current simulation steps. The agent position can be modelled using a `Real2D` Rust-AB struct. To easily develop the trait *Hash*, an unique identifier is stored in the agent. Listing 1.1 shows the Rust-AB agent struct definition.

Rust Code 1.1: Rust-AB Agent Struct.

```
1   #[derive(Clone, Copy)]
2   pub struct Bird{
3       pub id: u128,
4       pub pos: Real2D,
5       pub last_d: Real2D,
6   }
```

The agent logic is defined in the `step` function. We designed the agent logic using three sub-functions defined in the agent implementation. Listing 1.2 shows the agent implementation code. Lines 1–8 define the object `Bird` by providing a constructor and three functions: `avoidance`, `cohesion`, and `consistency`, which implement the steering model rules. Each function takes as input parameter a reference to a vector of agents (the current agent neighbourhood) and returns a new `Real2D`, which is the force computed according to the position of flock-mates. Lines 9–12 show the implementation of the `Location2D` trait, which enables to place the agent in the `Field2D` environment. Lines 13–20 define the implementation of the traits `Hash` and `Eq`. Lines 21–39 implement the agent `step` function describing the agent logic, which simulates the steering behaviour of the model. The agent computes its neighbourhood (line 23) and, using the sub-functions, evaluates its new position. The computed position is then used to update the status of the environment (line 37), exploiting a lock mechanism.

Rust Code 1.2: Rust-AB Agent Implementation.

```rust
1   impl Bird {
2       pub fn new(id: u128, pos: Real2D, last_d: Real2D) -> Self {
3           Bird {id, pos, last_d}
4       }
5       pub fn avoidance (self, vec: &Vec<Bird>) -> Real2D {..}
6       pub fn cohesion (self, vec: &Vec<Bird>) -> Real2D {..}
7       pub fn consistency (self, vec: &Vec<Bird>) -> Real2D {..}
8   }
9   impl Location2D for Bird {
10      fn get_location(self) -> Real2D { self.pos }
11      fn set_location(&mut self, loc: Real2D) { self.pos = loc; }
12  }
13  impl Hash for Bird {
14      fn hash<H>(&self, state: &mut H) where H: Hasher,
15      { state.write_u128(self.id); state.finish();}
16  }
17  impl Eq for Bird {}
18  impl PartialEq for Bird {
19      fn eq(&self, other: &Bird) -> bool {self.id == other.id}
20  }
21  impl Agent for Bird {
22      fn step(&mut self) {
23          let vec = GLOBAL_STATE.lock().unwrap().field1.
↪       get_neighbors_within_distance(self.pos,10.0);
24          let avoid = self.avoidance(&vec);
25          let cohe  = self.cohesion(&vec);
26          let rand  = self.randomness();
27          let cons  = self.consistency(&vec);
28          let mom   = self.last_d;
29          let mut dx = COHESION*cohe.x + AVOIDANCE*avoid.x + CONSISTENCY*cons.x +
↪       RANDOMNESS*rand.x + MOMENTUM*mom.x;
30          let mut dy = COHESION*cohe.y + AVOIDANCE*avoid.y + CONSISTENCY*cons.y +
↪       RANDOMNESS*rand.y + MOMENTUM*mom.y;
31          let dis = (dx*dx + dy*dy).sqrt();
32          if dis > 0.0 { dx = dx/dis*JUMP; dy = dy/dis*JUMP;}
33          let _lastd = Real2D {x: dx, y:dy};
34          let loc_x = toroidal_transform(self.pos.x + dx, WIDTH);
35          let loc_y = toroidal_transform(self.pos.y + dy, HEIGHT);
36          self.pos = Real2D{x: loc_x, y: loc_y};
37          GLOBAL_STATE.lock().unwrap().field1.set_object_location(*self, Real2D{x:
↪       loc_x, y: loc_y});
38      }
39  }
```

5.2   Model Definition

We define the Boids simulation state by declaring a new struct **State**. Listing 1.3 shows the code of the *State* struct (lines 1–6). According to the model and the agent definitions, we defined the agents' interactions through the **Field2D** environment. For this reason, the state struct contains only a *Field2D* declaration. As described in Sect. 3, the memory model of Rust does not allow data sharing across several function invocations. Thus, to access the simulation state inside the agent **step** function, the **State** instance has to be a global variable, accessed though a lock (or a mutex) to safely read it. The **State** struct has to be initialised at running time using the macro **lazy_static!** (lines 8–10).

Rust Code 1.3: Rust-AB Simulation State.

```
1   pub struct State{
2       pub field1: Field2D<Bird>,
3   }
4   impl State {
5       pub fn new(w: f64, h: f64, d: f64, t: bool) -> State { State {field1:
    ↪   Field2D::new(w, h, d, t),}}
6   }
7   //Global variables definition
8   lazy_static! {
9       static ref GLOBAL_STATE: Mutex<State> = Mutex::new(State::new(WIDTH, HEIGHT,
    ↪   DISCRETIZATION, TOROIDAL));
10  }
```

The main simulation function is shown in Listing 1.4. At line 2, a new Rust-AB `Schedule` is defined, while from line 3 to 11 a given number of agents are randomly initialised, placed in the `Field2D` (line 9), and scheduled using the `schedule _repeating` method (line 10). At line 12 the schedule step is called for a given number of times.

Rust Code 1.4: Rust-AB Main Simulation Function

```
1   fn main() {
2       let mut schedule: Schedule<Bird> = Schedule::new();
3       let mut rng = rand::thread_rng();
4       for bird_id in 0..NUM_AGENT{
5           let r1: f64 = rng.gen();
6           let r2: f64 = rng.gen();
7           let last_d = Real2D {x: 0.0, y: 0.0};
8           let bird = Bird::new(bird_id, Real2D{x: WIDTH*r1, y: HEIGHT*r2},last_d);
9           GLOBAL_STATE.lock().unwrap().field1.set_object_location(bird,bird.pos);
10          schedule.schedule_repeating(bird,0.0,0);
11      }
12      for _ in 1..STEP{ schedule.step(); }
13  }
```

5.3   Results

We performed several tests to assess Rust-AB ability to run simulations with different model scale properties. As benchmark simulation, we used Rust-AB *Boids* compared with MASON and NetLogo *Flockers*. Both simulations implement the same model. All experiments have been performed on a desktop machine equipped as follow: $1\times$ CPU i-7-8700T 12×2.40 MHz; 16 GB of RAM; Ubuntu Linux 18.04 LTS; Oracle Java Virtual Machine 1.7; Rust 1.31. We evaluated several simulation configurations by changing the simulation environment and the number of agents. The experiments were conducted in different settings: i) *constant agent density*, varying both number of agents and the dimensions of the simulation field; ii) *constant field size*, chancing only the number of agents; iii) *constant number of agents*, varying only the dimensions of the simulation field. The agent density of a simulation field can be easily computed by $\frac{w \times h}{A}$, where w and h denotes respectively the width and the height of the simulation field and A denotes the number of agents.

Constant Agent Density. In these experiments, we tested the simulation engine's ability to simulate an increasing number of agents, while maintaining the same scaling proprieties. Results are depicted in Fig. 1(a). The x-axis shows the number of agents - ranging from 100 to 1638400 - while the y-axis shows the performance in terms of average simulation step per second (log scale), during a 10 min of simulation. As shown in the plot on the left, Rust-AB and MASON obtain almost the same performance when the agent density is constant. On the other hand, the performance of NetLogo is always significantly smaller than the other simulators. It is worth highlighting that NetLogo was not able to execute the last three experiments due to memory requirements.

Constant Field Size. We evaluated the simulation engine's ability to simulate an increasing number of agents laying on a field of fixed size (200×200). Increasing the number of agents implies increasing the agent density and, consequently, the computational cost of computing the neighbourhood and the new position of each agent. Figure 1 shows how Rust-AB simulation scales much better than MASON and NetLogo simulations. In particular, MASON achieves the same performance of Rust-AB when the number of agents is low. However, at the increasing of the number of agents, and consequently of the total computational load, Rust-AB performs better. This behaviour may be due to Rust's ability to efficiently manage a high computational workload, mainly thanks to its memory system. Further analysis are needed to asses this hypothesis. On the contrary, NetLogo initially provides the worst results, while at the end, its performance is comparable to MASON. Again it is worth mentioning that neither MASON and NetLogo were able to execute the last two simulation configurations.

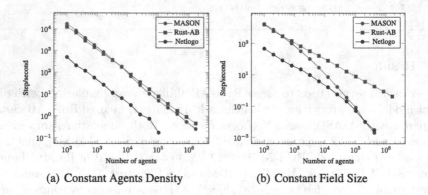

(a) Constant Agents Density   (b) Constant Field Size

Fig. 1. Rust-AB performance comparison.

Constant Number of Agents. With these tests, we evaluated the simulation engine's ability to simulate a constant number of agents (102400) varying the field dimension. Figure 2 presents the results. The x-axis describes the field size - ranging from 200×200 to 20298×20298 - while the y-axis represents the performance obtained in terms of average simulation step per second. As shown in the plot, Rust-AB outperforms the MASON until the density of the field become small enough to decrease the total computation load. When the density of the simulation field is small, the performance of the two libraries does not differ significantly. These results can be motivated by the same explanation given in the previous paragraph. For this experiment, we do not show the results of NetLogo as it was not able to run the simulation using the experiment configurations.

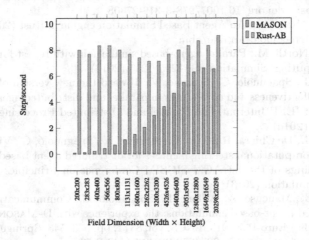

Fig. 2. Rust-AB vs MASON: constant number of agents.

6   Conclusion and Future Works

This work introduces the library *Rust-AB*, a discrete events simulation engine for ABM simulations written in Rust. Rust-AB is designed to be a *ready-to-use* tool for the ABM community and, for this reason, the architectural concepts of the well-adopted MASON library were re-engineered. We then described an example of Rust-AB simulation, implementing the Boids model, to investigate the performance of Rust-AB in comparison with MASON. Results, exploiting Rust-AB Alpha 1.0 release, are promising and exhibits a performance-enhancing compared to the MASON toolkit; in particular, for simulations with a high agent density. We consider this outcome as an important step ahead at disclosing the power of the Rust language to develop ABM simulations.

We plan to continue the development of the library to improve the simulation performance, through better exploitation of Rust peculiarities, such as safe concurrency capabilities. Moreover, we will experiment Rust-AB by developing more computing-intensive simulations, using models where the agent interactions are not only local but also exploits network-based interactions, as presented in [2].

References

1. Abar, S., Theodoropoulos, G., Lemarinier, P., O'Hare, G.: Agent based modelling and simulation tools: a review of the state-of-art software. Comput. Sci. Rev. **24**, 13–33 (2017)
2. Antelmi, A., Cordasco, G., Spagnuolo, C., Vicidomini, L.: On evaluating graph partitioning algorithms for distributed agent based models on networks. In: Hunold, S., et al. (eds.) Euro-Par 2015. LNCS, vol. 9523, pp. 367–378. Springer, Cham (2015). https://doi.org/10.1007/978-3-319-27308-2_30
3. Carmine, S.: Rust-AB: An Agent Based Simulation engine in Rust (2018). https://github.com/spagnuolocarmine/abm
4. Collier, N., North, M.: Parallel agent-based simulation with repast for high performance computing. Simulation **89**, 1215–1235 (2013)
5. Cordasco, G., Spagnuolo, C., Scarano, V.: Toward the new version of D-MASON: efficiency, effectiveness and correctness in parallel and distributed agent-based simulations. In: IEEE International Parallel and Distributed Processing Symposium Workshops (2016)
6. Cordasco, G., De Chiara, R., Raia, F., Scarano, V., Spagnuolo, C., Vicidomini, L.: Designing computational steering facilities for distributed agent based simulations. In: Proceedings of the 1st ACM SIGSIM Conference on Principles of Advanced Discrete Simulation (2013)
7. Cordasco, G., Mancuso, A., Milone, F., Spagnuolo, C.: Communication strategies in distributed agent-based simulations: the experience with D-MASON. In: an Mey, D., et al. (eds.) Euro-Par 2013. LNCS, vol. 8374, pp. 533–543. Springer, Heidelberg (2014). https://doi.org/10.1007/978-3-642-54420-0_52
8. Heath, B., Hill, R., Ciarallo, F.: A survey of agent-based modeling practices (January 1998 to July 2008). J. Artif. Soc. Soc. Simul. **12**(4), 9 (2009)
9. Holcombe, M., Coakley, S., Smallwood, R.: A general framework for agent-based modelling of complex systems. In: Proceedings of the European Conference on Complex Systems (2006)
10. Kleinberg, J.: The small-world phenomenon: an algorithmic perspective (2000)
11. Macal, C., North, M.: Tutorial on agent-based modeling and simulation Part 2: how to model with agents (2006)
12. Mahé, F., Rognes, T., Quince, C., de Vargas, C., Dunthorn, M.: Swarm: robust and fast clustering method for amplicon-based studies. PeerJ **2**, e593 (2014)
13. North, M.J., et al.: Complex adaptive systems modeling with repast simphony. Complex Adapt. Syst. Model. **1**(1), 3 (2013)
14. Resnick, M.: StarLogo: an environment for decentralized modeling and decentralized thinking. In: Conference Companion on Human Factors in Computing Systems (1996)
15. Reynolds, C.W.: Flocks, herds, and schools: a distributed behavioral model. Comput. Graph. (ACM) **21**, 25–34 (1987)
16. Richmond, P., Chimeh, M.K.: FLAME GPU: complex system simulation framework. In: 2017 International Conference on High Performance Computing Simulation (2017)
17. Tejaswi, V., Bindu, P., Thilagam, P.: Diffusion models and approaches for influence maximization in social networks (2016)
18. Thurner, S., Klimek, P., Hanel, R.: Introduction to the Theory of Complex Systems. Oxford University Press, Oxford (2018)
19. Wang, H., et al.: Scalability in the MASON multi-agent simulation system (2019)
20. Wilensky, U.: NetLogo 3.1. 3 (2006)

Conv-LSTM: Pedestrian Trajectory Prediction in Crowded Scenarios

Kai Chen[1], Xiao Song[1(✉)], and Hang Yu[2]

[1] School of Automation Science and Electrical Engineering, Beihang University, Beijing, China
Songxiao@buaa.edu.cn
[2] State Key Laboratory of Intelligent Manufacturing System Technology, Beijing Institute of Electronic System Engineering, Beijing 100854, China

Abstract. Pedestrian trajectory prediction is a challenging problem in the crowded and chaotic scenarios. Currently, the prediction error is still high because the input of Long Short-Term Memory (LSTM) network is a 1D vector, which cannot represent the spatial information of pedestrians. To tackle this, we propose to use tensors to represent the complex environmental information. Meanwhile, LSTM internal full connection is converted into full convolution to predict the spatiotemporal pedestrian trajectory sequences. The results show that our method reduces the displacement offset error better than recent works including Social-LSTM, SS-LSTM, CNN, Social-GAN, Scene-LSTM, providing more realistic trajectory prediction for the chaotic crowd.

Keywords: Convolutional neural network · Trajectory prediction · Pedestrian behavior

1 Introduction

The pedestrian trajectory prediction based on the deep learning method [1–5] has re-emerged in the area of computer vision and artificial intelligence in recent years. Existing pedestrian trajectory prediction algorithms can be divided into two categories: model-based methods and deep learning methods based on long-term and short-term memory (LSTM) architecture. The model-based approach [6–8] relies on manually designed behavioral model functions and manual pedestrian motion attributes rather than learning pedestrian movement behavior from training data. LSTM-based methods [1, 3, 4, 9] have attempted to incorporate information from the target neighborhood into the training process and use the scene context to predict the trajectory. However, the internal structure of LSTM is a one-dimensional vector, so must be the input of the model, which destroys the spatial information around the pedestrians. Therefore, this model cannot learn the spatial information around the pedestrians, especially in dense crowds.

In the field of object detection, CNN has been widely used in the field of image recognition [10, 11]. In [12], the author used CNN to get similar scene features for new scene images and used them as inputs to LSTM-based models for predicting human motion behavior. In [13], the author proposed and developed the scene model called

© Springer Nature Singapore Pte Ltd. 2019
G. Tan et al. (Eds.): AsiaSim 2019, CCIS 1094, pp. 29–39, 2019.
https://doi.org/10.1007/978-981-15-1078-6_3

Scene-LSTM, in which the scene is divided into equally sized grid cells that are further divided into sub-grids to provide more accurate space position within the unit. Based on this, the end-to-end convolution LSTM network is designed and trained to predict the time walker trajectory. Experiments were conducted to test the feasibility of the proposed network.

2   Related Works

Existing pedestrian model can be divided into two categories: social interaction models and social-scene models. Some social interaction models are characterized by social interactions features (e.g. grouping, obstacle avoidance, etc.) and calculate the next position of each pedestrian by minimizing the functions represented by these features. [14] calculates the desired speed of each pedestrian at the current frame with energy function that can minimize the collisions and directions toward the final destination of the pedestrian. [15] extended the model and social group behavior in [14], such as the use of energy functions for gravitation and group, used the gradient descent to minimize the final energy function. Recently, several LSTM-based methods have been proposed to model social interactions. Social-LSTM [16] assumes that the state (direction, speed) of each pedestrian is affected by nearby pedestrians in the rectangular area. The current state of these neighboring pedestrians is used as input to calculate the next state of the target. Social Attention [17] uses a structured RNN network [18] to simulate social interaction. Unlike [16, 17] considers social interactions throughout the scene. In particular, distant people may also have a social impact on the movement of the target. These social effects of other people on the primary goal are represented by attention vectors. This vector is calculated as the weighted sum of the current states of these people and is used as an input to predict the next position of the target.

Social-scene models [19–21] combine the scene features with social interactions [16] to predict pedestrian trajectories. [19] and [21] explore scene effects by using CNN to extract features of the scene layout and use them as input to the LSTM network to learn walking behavior. [20] assumes that the closer each target to the obstacles in the scene, the greater their impact on the walking behavior of the target. All of these studies focus more on the use of LSTM to learn spatio-temporal sequences, but few discuss how to extract the environmental characteristics of each pedestrian in a dense population while ensuring that the spatial information of these features remains the same. Therefore, we propose the spatial information representation of pedestrians and the deep convolution LSTM network to generate more realistic Track. At the same time, [19–21] simply added the scene features to the network model without considering the relationship between the scene features and the current target pedestrians so that the learning ability of the network has not been greatly improved. Our proposed deep convolution LSTM takes into account the interaction of humans and the overall spatial characteristics of the scene during the prediction process. Experimental comparisons show that our network can generate more realistic trajectories.

3 Design of the Proposed Conv-LSTM

We will briefly introduce the Conv-LSTM network and then outline our representation of pedestrian interaction and scene interaction features as well as the design and implementation of the deep network models.

3.1 Basic Design of Conv-LSTM

Considering that one prominent feature of convolution is its invariance in spatial characteristics, we use convolution operations to extend the fc-LSTM so that it has the transition function of the convolution structure.

The input and output of Conv-LSTM is shown in Fig. 1(a), and the proposed internal calculation structure is shown in Fig. 1(b). Corresponding mathematical expressions describing Conv-LSTM working mechanism are listed in Eqs. 1–6, where O represents Hadamard element-wise multiplication, * represents a convolution operation, and σ represents a Sigmoid function. X_t denotes the input received at time t. The long-term memory C_{t-1} and H_{t-1} (both are the same size 3D tensors) are transferred to update C_t and H_t. Meanwhile, the input X_t and the working memory H_{t-1} are combined to learn the forget gate. In Conv-LSTM, each element in the forget gate tensor determines to which extent a long-term memory element needs to be retained. Here, the value of these elements is [0, 1] where the greatest value 1 means completely saved and the smallest value, 0 means that completely forgotten. Mathematical modeling details of Conv-LSTM are as follows:

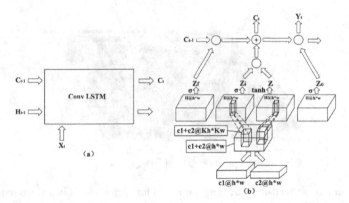

Fig. 1. (a) is the traditional design of LSTM. (b) is the proposed LSTM.

First, a convolutional neural network is employed to learn this forget gate Z_f:

$$Z_f = \sigma(W_{xf} * X_t + W_{hf} * H_{t-1} + b_f) \tag{1}$$

Second, we extract the information that can be learned from X_t, which is the candidate memory Z for long-term memory:

$$Z = tanh(W_x * X_t + W_h * H_{t-1} + b) \tag{2}$$

Third, we combine the above two steps. Our goal is to forget the memory that is no longer needed and save the useful part of the input. Then we get the updated long-term memory C_t:

$$Z_i = \sigma(W_{xi} * X_t + W_{hi} * H_{t-1} + b_i) \tag{3}$$

$$C_t = Z_f \circ C_{t-1} + Z_i \circ Z \tag{4}$$

Fourth, we update the working memory. The network needs to learn how to focus on the long-term memory that makes the most sense in the current step. Here we use the following formula to learn the focus vector Z_o:

$$Z_o = \sigma(W_{xo} * X_t + W_{ho} * H_{t-1} + b_o) \tag{5}$$

Lastly, the working memory H_t is calculated using the following formula. In other words, the network selects the element whose attention vector is 1 and ignores the element whose attention vector is 0.

$$H_t = Z_0 \circ \tanh(C_t) \tag{6}$$

3.2 Spatial Information Representation of Pedestrians and Scene

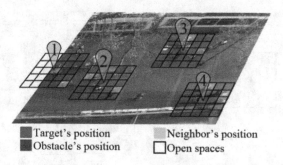

■ Target's position	■ Neighbor's position
■ Obstacle's position	□ Open spaces

Fig. 2. We learn the scene data by training our model for each grid-cell in a video sequence. The red dot represents the position of the subject pedestrian Yellow dot is his neighboring pedestrians. Purple dot denotes obstacles such as buildings and poles. White dot is reachable area. (Color figure online)

Through actual observation and questionnaire survey, we have found out that the following information mainly influences the pedestrians in the crowd: the location information, speed information and quantity information of the pedestrians within a certain range, the location information of fixed obstacles and spatial information of the whole scene. How to effectively represent these inputs is a very important issue when training the end-to-end pedestrian decision network model. In order to accurately represent the spatial information of pedestrians and scenes, according to the pixel area and neighborhood of the image occupied by a single pedestrian, we use 5 * 5 grid neighborhoods as shown in Fig. 2 (the grid size is set to 200 pixels and 40 pixels) to represent a 5 * 5 mesh map around the target pedestrian. Below we use the public dataset ETH-hotel [22] scenario as an example to introduce the input data format of our model.

(1) **Relative Position of Pedestrians in the Target Neighborhood**

Manh [13] shows that the number and relative position of pedestrians in the crowd have a great influence on the decision of their own trajectory. The pedestrian density information around the pedestrian in the scene is very important, and the relative position of other pedestrians will affect the specific movement direction of the pedestrian. In this study, we use the number of pedestrians in a single 40 * 40 (unit: pixel) size area to define the pedestrian density information of the unit grid. As shown in Fig. 2, taking the No. 2 pedestrian as an example, the relative position information of the pedestrians around No. 2 pedestrian is as shown in the Fig. 4(a). 1 means that there is a pedestrian at the current moment of the position, and 0 means that there is no one at the current moment of the position.

(2) **Speed Information of Pedestrians in the Target Neighborhood**

We use the horizontal and vertical speed scalars of pedestrians to express the pedestrian's speed vector. Figure 4(b) and (c) show the lateral and longitudinal velocities of Fig. 2. When pedestrians make sports decisions, they usually observe about 2 * 2 (unit: m) around them, about 200 in the ETH data set. * 200 pixels range. We take a 5 * 5 size network around a single pedestrian for valid data for a single pedestrian. In Fig. 4(b) and (c), the yellow number indicates the horizontal longitudinal velocity value of the pedestrian at the current time. When we add the valid data information of the target red pedestrian No. 2, the red square is taken as the center. Then, we obtain two 5 * 5 matrices as the pedestrian neighborhood speed information.

(3) **Obstacle Information in the Target Neighborhood**

There are many types of fixed obstacles. In Fig. 2, there are mainly trees, chairs, walls, telephone poles and trains. The area occupied by these obstacles is unreachable to pedestrians, so we use unreachable areas to indicate obstacles. We define the grid with obstacles as unreachable areas and set its value to 0 with 1; we define the grid without obstacles as reachable and set its value to 0. According to the above rules, we obtain the obstacle data information of the pedestrian No. 2 shown in the Fig. 4(e).

(4) **The Perception of the Entire Scene by the Target Neighborhood**

We use the neighborhood information around the target pedestrian and the entire image as a convolution operation to capture the perception of the entire neighborhood by the target neighborhood. Another motivation for using scene scales is that while social scales focus more on the local pedestrian's neighborhoods, such perceptual information is very valuable when the scene features capture global information for the scene for long trajectory prediction.

The deep features of the convolutional network have been shown to accurately locate the target, so we used the pre-trained 1,000 categories of VGG-16 [23] networks on ImageNet to extract deep image features. As shown in Fig. 3, we can see the more prominent information of pedestrians and obstacles in the deep features of the network, the shallow features contain more texture information of the image. In the upper part of Fig. 3 we extract the convolutional features of the entire scene and in the lower part we extract the deep convolutional features of the range of 200*200 (unit: pixels) in the 2nd pedestrian neighborhood in Fig. 2. Then in the middle of Fig. 3, we take the feature of 14 * 14 size in the deep feature of the target neighborhood as the convolution kernel and the features of the panoramic deep feature with 56 * 56 size and convolution (padding = 4, stride = 5). Then, the Max Pooling operation is followed by 5 * 5 output. The corresponding output thus obtained can weaken the open space information in the panorama while highlighting the significant information such as trains, crowds, and walls in the scene. Take the No. 2 pedestrian in Fig. 2 as an example, and the final data obtained is normalized to the Fig. 4(e).

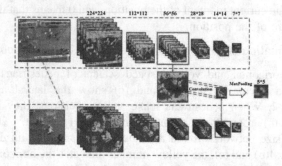

Fig. 3. Flowchart for extracting target neighborhood perception of the entire scene based on the VGG net.

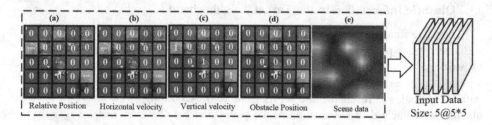

Fig. 4. Pedestrian comprehensive data information.

As shown in Fig. 4, we combine the above information to represent the effective data information of the pedestrians in the scene at this time. This information can be combined to return the speed information of pedestrians in the horizontal and vertical directions at the next moment.

3.3   Model Structure

Although LSTM has RNN structure and is good to predict sequence, the traditional FC-LSTM cannot fully present spatial information of pedestrians. So we try to use Conv-LSTM to replace full connection operation of FC-LSTM to ensure that the spatial characteristics of the input information are unchanged.

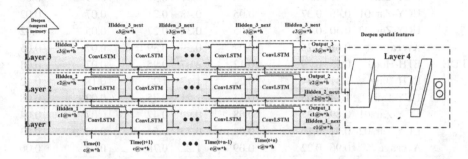

Fig. 5. Structure of the proposed deepened conv-LSTM network.

As shown in Fig. 5, the proposed network consists of Layers 1–3. Each layer has 8 convolutional LSTMs, whose inputs are the 8 observed pedestrian trajectory sequences from time t to $t + 8$. The output is the predicted speed v_x, v_y of the subject pedestrian at time t + 9. The 1st layer receives 8 sequential 5@5 * 5 tensors and 32@5 * 5 initial hidden layer input and each conv-LSTM outputs a hidden layer tensor of 32@5 * 5 and a cell tensor of 32@5 * 5. The 2nd layer receives 8 sequential 32@5 * 5 hidden layer tensors and 64@5 * 5 initial hidden layer input, and each conv-LSTM outputs a hidden layer tensor of 64@5 * 5 and a cell tensor of 64@5*5. The 3rd one receives 8 sequential 64@5 * 5 hidden layer tensors and 128 * 5 * 5 initial hidden layer input, and each conv-LSTM outputs a hidden layer tensor of 128@5 * 5 and a cell tensor of 128@5 * 5. The main role of Layer 4 is to deepen the spatial information, improve the network complexity, and return to the speed information of the target in the horizontal and vertical directions.

4   Experiments

We evaluate our model on two publicly available datasets: ETH [22], and UCY [24]. These two datasets contain 5 crowd sets with a total of 1,536 pedestrians exhibiting complex interactions such as walking together, groups crossing each other, joint collision avoidance and nonlinear trajectories as shown in [22]. These datasets are recorded at 25 frames per second, annotated every 0.4 s and contain 4 different scenes.

Similar to [1], we use a leave-one-out approach where we train and validate our approach on 4 sets, and test on the remaining set. We repeat this for all the 5 sets. For validation, within each set we get 20% of the set of trajectories as validation data. Social- LSTM has also been trained in the same manner. We observe the trajectory for

Table 1. The quantitative results on 5 different video sequences. All methods predict human trajectories in 12 frames and using 8 observed frames [12, 13, 19, 25, 26].

Metrics	Sequences	SF	Social-LSTM	SS-LSTM	CNN	Social-GAN	Scene-LSTM	OUR
ADE	ETH-Hotel	0.25	0.25	0.07	1.04	0.48	0.06	0.03
	ETH-Univ	0.41	0.18	0.10	0.59	0.75	0.10	0.07
	UCY-Univ	0.57	0.25	0.08	0.57	0.36	0.09	0.06
	UCY-Zara01	0.40	0.37	0.05	0.43	0.21	0.07	0.02
	UCY-Zara02	0.40	0.19	0.05	0.34	0.27	0.05	0.02
	Average	0.61	0.25	0.07	0.59	0.39	0.07	0.05
FDE	ETH-Hotel	0.55	0.29	0.12	2.07	0.95	0.07	0.04
	ETH-Univ	1.31	0.34	0.24	1.17	1.22	0.18	0.12
	UCY-Univ	1.14	0.03	0.13	1.21	0.75	0.02	0.08
	UCY-Zara01	0.89	0.32	0.08	0.90	0.42	0.07	0.04
	UCY-Zara02	0.91	0.10	0.08	0.75	0.54	0.02	0.03
	Average	0.96	0.22	0.09	1.22	0.78	0.07	0.06

8 time-steps and predict the trajectory for the next 12 time-steps. The quantitative results in Table 1 show that our model outperforms the others on two metrics on most video sequences. We achieve better ADE [22] and FDE [22] in most sequences compared to other methods. Results in Table 1 confirm that our model is more efficient in predicting the trajectory (ADE) of each target than Scene-LSTM and also performs well in predicting the final position.

Figure 6. shows examples of the predicted human trajectories from three methods plus ground truth. Figure 6(a) shows that all three methods perform well for predicting the pedestrian trajectory of a nearly uniform linear motion. Figure 6 (b) shows that our model correctly predicts the trajectories of the target to bypass the tree and turn left. In Fig. 6(c, d), the pedestrians move in two directions, respectively, and our network model learns such a rule where the road is spacious and there are few people around, pedestrians are more inclined to walk in the middle of the road. Figure 6 shows that our model accurately predicts the trajectory of the trajectory along the head of the car. Social-LSTM fails to bypass the car because the model did not contain obstacle information. Although the social force succeeded to avoid the car, it drives the target away from the original destination. Figure 6(f) is a more complicated scene where two people walking on the front left side of the target, several people on the right side stood still and there is one person behind. The result of social force prediction is that target act in situ. Our model and Social-LSTM accurately predict the target across the crowd, but our model predicts the final position of the target more accurately.

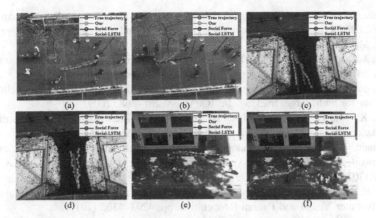

Fig. 6. Some examples of the predicted trajectories from different methods in various video sequences: (a, b) ETH-Hotel, (c, d) ETH-Univ, (e, f) UCY-Zara02.

5 Conclusion

This study proposes a multi-channel tensor to express the information needed for pedestrians. This tensor includes relative position, speed and the number of pedestrians within a certain range, as well as the location of fixed obstacles, the perceptual information of the entire scene. Using this data we trained an end-to-end neural network model to simulate the flow of pedestrians in the crowd. Our network makes full use of the invariance of the convolutional space. Replace the fully connected network inside the traditional LSTM with the volume network, so that the space motion information of pedestrians is not lost while ensuring network complexity and discriminating ability. Our results show that our method is superior to existing methods. In future work we will study the integration of scene models with social models to improve the quality of predictions. We intend to further explore the social interaction between humans and other static or moving objects. Our goal is to use our human trajectory prediction methods to solve computer vision problems such as multi-target and multi-camera multi-target tracking systems.

References

1. Alahi, A., Goel, K., Ramanathan, V., Robicquet, A., Li, F.-F., Savarese, S.: Social LSTM: human trajectory prediction in crowded spaces. In: CVPR, pp. 961–971, June 2016
2. Song, X., Han, D., Sun, J.: A data-driven neural network approach to simulate pedestrian movement. Physica A-Stat. Mech. Appl. **509**(11), 827–844 (2018)
3. Lee, N., Choi, W., Vernaza, P., Choy, C.B., Torr, P.H.S., Chandraker, M.: DESIRE: distant future prediction in dynamic scenes with interacting agents. In: CVPR (2017)
4. Su, H., Zhu, J., Dong, Y., Zhang, B.: Forecast the plausible paths in crowd scenes. In: IJCAI, pp. 2772–2778 (2017)

5. Vemula, A., Muelling, K., Oh, J.: Modeling cooperative navigation in dense human crowds. In: 2017 IEEE International Conference on Robotics and Automation (ICRA), pp. 1685–1692, May 2017

6. Song, X., Xie, H., Sun, J., Han, D.: Simulation of pedestrian rotation dynamics near crowded exits. IEEE Trans. Intell. Transp. Syst. **20**(8), 3142–3155 (2019)

7. Pellegrini, S., Ess, A., Schindler, K., van Gool, L.: You'll never walk alone: modeling social behavior for multi-target tracking. In: ICCV, pp. 261–268 (2009)

8. Song, X., Ma, L., Ma, Y.: Selfishness- and selflessness-based models of pedestrian room evacuation. Physica A-stat. Mech. Appl. **447**(4), 455–466 (2016)

9. Fernando, T., Denman, S., Sridharan, S., Fookes, C.: Soft + hardwired attention: an LSTM framework for human trajectory prediction and abnormal event detection. arXiv preprint arXiv:1702.05552 (2017)

10. Nam, H., Han, B.: Learning Multi-domain convolutional neural networks for visual tracking. In: Computer Vision and Pattern Recognition, pp. 4293–4302 (2016)

11. Simonyan, K., Zisserman, A.: Very deep convolutional networks for large-scale image recognition. In: Proceedings of the International Conference on Learning Representations (2015)

12. Nikhil, N., Tran Morris, B.: Convolutional neural network for trajectory prediction. In: Proceedings of the European Conference on Computer Vision (ECCV) (2018)

13. Manh, H., Alaghband, G.: Scene-lstm: a model for human trajectory prediction. arXiv preprint arXiv:1808.04018 (2018)

14. Pellegrini, S., Ess, A., Schindler, K., van Gool, L.: You'll never walk alone: Modeling social behavior for multi-target tracking. In: IEEE 12th International Conference on Computer Vision (ICCV), pp. 261–268 (2009)

15. Yamaguchi, K., Berg, A.C., Ortiz, L.E., Berg, T.L.: Who are you with and where are you going? In: CVPR, pp. 1345–1352 (2011)

16. Alahi, A., Goel, K., Ramanathan, V., Robicquet, A., Fei-Fei, L., Savarese, S.: Social LSTM: human trajectory prediction in crowded spaces. In: IEEE Conference on Computer Vision and Pattern Recognition (CVPR), pp. 961–971 (2016)

17. Vemula, A., Muelling, K., Oh, J.: Social attention: modeling attention in human crowds. arXiv:1710.04689 [cs] (2017)

18. Jain, A., Zamir, A.R., Savarese, S., Saxena, A.: Structural-RNN: deep learning on spatio-temporal graphs. In: CVPR 2016, pp. 5308–5317 (2016)

19. Xue, H., Huynh, D.Q., Reynolds, M.: SS-LSTM: a hierarchical LSTM model for pedestrian trajectory prediction. In: IEEE Winter Conference on Applications of Computer Vision (WACV), pp. 1186–1194 (2018)

20. Bartoli, F., Lisanti, G., Ballan, L., Del Bimbo, A.: Context-Aware Trajectory Prediction, arXiv:1705.02503 [cs], May 2017

21. Varshneya, D., Srinivasaraghavan, G.: Human Trajectory Prediction using Spatially aware Deep Attention Models. arXiv:1705.09436 [cs], May 2017

22. Pellegrini, S., Ess, A., Schindler, K., et al.: You'll never walk alone: Modeling social behavior for multi-target tracking. In: 2009 IEEE 12th International Conference on Computer Vision, pp. 261–268. IEEE (2009)

23. Simonyan, K., Zisserman, A.: Very deep convolutional networks forlarge-scale image recognition. In: Proceedings of the International Conference on Learning Representations (2015)

24. Lerner, A., Chrysanthou, Y., Lischinski, D.L: Crowds by example. In: Computer Graphics Forum, vol. 26, no. (3), pp. 655–664. Blackwell Publishing Ltd, Oxford (2007)

25. Gupta, A., Johnson, J., Fei-Fei, L., et al.: Social GAN: socially acceptable trajectories with generative adversarial networks. In: Proceedings of the IEEE Conference on Computer Vision and Pattern Recognition, pp. 2255–2264 (2018)
26. Song, X., Shi, W., Ma, Y.: Impact of informal networks on opinion dynamics in hierarchically formal organization. Physica A-stat. Mech. Appl. **436**(10), 916–924 (2015)

Simulation and Modeling Methodology

A Framework for Joint Simulation of Distributed FMUs

Hang Ji[1,3,4], Junhua Zhou[1,3,4], Luan Tao[1,3,4], Xiao Song[2(✉)],
Guoqiang Shi[1,3,4], Chao Ruan[1,3,4], Tingyu Lin[1,3,4],
and Xiang Zhai[1,3,4]

[1] State Key Laboratory of Intelligent Manufacturing System Technology,
Beijing Institute of Electronic System Engineering, Beijing 100854, China
jihangchn@163.com
[2] School of Automation Science and Electrical Engineering,
Beihang University, Beijing, China
songxiao@buaa.edu.cn
[3] Beijing Complex Product Advanced Manufacturing Engineering Research
Center, Beijing Simulation Center, Beijing 100854, China
[4] Science and Technology on Space System Simulation Laboratory,
Beijing Simulation Center, Beijing 100854, China

Abstract. In this study we designed a joint simulation framework for distributed Functional Mock-up Interfaces (FMUs), which could be regarded as an extension of FMI criterion. The proposed framework includes remote procedure call to exchange data in distributed network efficiently. Meanwhile, a node management is designed to monitor and manage connection status and invocation procedures. In addition, the I/O Management module is used to ensure global consistency of data and interfaces. Moreover, a Time Management module is created to provide time advance function. An electro-hydraulic brake system is taken as an example to show feasibility of this framework.

Keywords: Distributed framework · FMI for Co-Simulation · RPC

1 Introduction

Distributed Interactive Simulation (DIS) is an advanced simulation technology that integrates simulation systems distributed in different locations with the support of high-speed computer networks and carries out parallel simulation experiments in space-time consistent human-computer interaction environment through data exchange between simulation entities [1]. With the rapid development of computer technology and the rapid increase of network transmission speed, the development of hardware and software technology of multiprocessor system is slow. In addition, the scale of problems faced by simulation technology becomes increasingly larger, and the types of problems increase day by day. Distributed simulation technology begins to show its advantages [2, 3, 13–15].

Nowadays, Functional Mock-up Interface (FMI) is an emerging modeling and simulation criterion. FMI defines an interface to be implemented by an executable

G. Tan et al. (Eds.): AsiaSim 2019, CCIS 1094, pp. 43–53, 2019.
https://doi.org/10.1007/978-981-15-1078-6_4

called FMU (Functional Mock-up Unit) [4]. FMI makes multi-model-instance-interaction possible by adopting XML based model description file and dynamic link libraries. It enables encapsulating dynamic models into simulators and running numerous simulators under single federation [5].

FMI 1.0, the first version, was published in 2010, followed by FMI 2.0 in July 2014. The FMI development was initiated by Daimler AG with the goal to improve the exchange of simulation models between suppliers and OEMs. As of today, development of the standard continues through the participation of 16 companies and research institutes under the roof of the Modelica Association as a Modelica Association Project [6]. FMI is supported by over 100 tools and is used by automotive and non-automotive organizations throughout Europe, Asia and North America.

FMI for Co-simulation is designed for the coupling of two or more simulation models in a co-simulation environment. Co-simulation is a rather general approach to the simulation of the coupled technical systems and coupled physical phenomena in engineering with focus on unstationary problems [7, 8]. In its general form, FMU models are gathered in one process and the master invokes them using standard interfaces. However, in other occasions such as the case when the FMU providers prefer their models being deployed in their own tool environment or FMU developers produce their models in distributed locations and the centralization of the models is not easy to implement. It would lead to the different models as well as the master not being always in the same processes, sometimes may even not be in the same computers.

Several successful cases of applying communication middleware to distributed FMI simulation have been made. High Level Architecture (HLA) is a widely used distributed collaborative simulation standard that can provide basic technical support for modeling and simulation of the complex systems and handle the heterogeneous, distributed, and synergetic simulation scenes. [9–11] all tried to employ HLA as the master component of FMUs and provided a complete, generic and standalone master algorithms. However, the HLA is a rather heavy and difficult structure, building HLA-based framework could be really hard to implement and expand. [11] uses RCOSIM approach to allow the parallelization on multi-core processors of Co-Simulations using the FMI standard, but it places more emphasis on the algorithm rather than framework arrangement. [12] proposes DACCOSIM to support distributed architectures of FMI simulation, moreover, it implements the algorithm to perform the complex initialization of the various components of the multi-simulation, which gave us a great revelation in designing the simulation framework.

In this context, the study designed a simulation framework of making distributed FMUs interact in a unified environment, the framework provides Remote Procedure Call (RPC) to exchange data in network efficiently, Node Management to monitor and manage connection status and invocation procedures, I/O Management to ensure global consistency of data and interfaces, Time Management to provide convening time advance algorithm, Sect. 2 gives the overview of our framework, Sects. 3, 4, and 5 elaborate three core contents separately. Finally, a case study and conclusion are provided.

2 Overview of Framework Design

According to the FMI standard for Co-Simulation, the data exchange and communication between the subsystems can be typically done using one of the network communication technologies such as MPI or TCP/IP. Nevertheless, the definition of the communication layer is not part of the FMI standard; it just provides Fig. 1 to characterize the distributed Co-Simulation infrastructure. Otherwise, the design of application server and master should be fulfilled by framework planners.

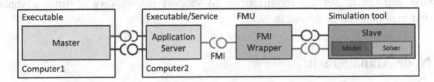

Fig. 1. Distributed Co-Simulation infrastructure provide by FMI

The traditional TCP/IP communication technology is rather fundamental and simple, it does not provide a sound and robust framework to support complex simulation scenes. The Internet Communication Engine (ICE) developed by ZeroC Inc., is an object-oriented RPC framework that helps users build distributed applications with minimal efforts. ICE allows developers to focus on application logic, and it takes care of all interactions with low-level network programming interfaces. With ICE, there is no need to worry about details such as opening network connections, serializing and DE serializing data for network transmission or retrying failed connection attempts.

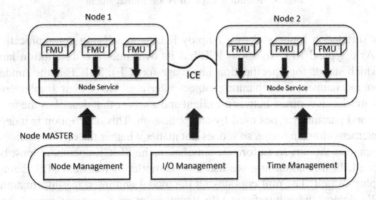

Fig. 2. Overall architecture of the framework

The Fig. 2 depicts the framework of how to make FMUs in different computers and processes run together. The Node Management, I/O Management and Time Management are planted in master node and provide background supports for node services in each distributed terminals.

More specifically, Node Management is in charge of node and connection conditions, it supervises all the network operations, distributes remote proxies and monitors CPU loads on each node, detailed working mechanism can be found in Sect. 3. I/O Management abstracts the data structures among FMUs into topics so that the system can transmit information by publish/subscribe pattern, which would decouple the constraint relationships between models. It provides synchronization mechanism and inspection mechanism to assure the stability of interface invocation, detailed running logic can be found in Sect. 4. Time management decides the communication step and the system behavior in the communication points, it provides conservative time progression and list of service requirements to support the validity of time advance, detailed methods can be found in Sect. 5.

3   Node Management

The implementation logic of Node Management is shown in Fig. 3. Three modules: registry, node admin and load balance are included.

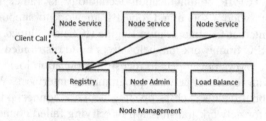

Fig. 3. Running logic of Node Management

In our simulation framework, we employ ICE as underlying communication middleware. As a typical RPC solution, ICE has its own interface description language-SLICE (which stands for Specification Language for ICE). SLICE is the fundamental abstraction mechanism for separating object interfaces from their implementations. SLICE establishes a contract between a client and a server that describes the interfaces, operations and parameter types used by an application. This description is independent of the implementation language, so it does not matter whether the client is written in the same language as the server. Before the simulation, the SLICE document must be made and compiled. In this condition, we use C++ compiler to translate SLICE into C++-standard plug-in unit. The unit contains all the model and interface information in our system. We deploy these interfaces into target nodes as a service; record the correspondence relations of services and endpoints into registry.

As a result, the registry maintains a map of services and endpoints. When a client call comes from another node service, the master node intercepts it, obtains its service requirements and establishes the connection for client and server by looking up the mapping table, and finally, it passes this information on node admin to monitor the connection conditions.

The node admin is responsible for several properties. First, it manages each node service's connection status. When a new connection is about to be established, the node admin would start the necessary node services if needed (on-demand server activation), set up TCP/IP network, store the relative information and handle the proxy to a client; when a connection is expired, the node admin would close the network, shut down the node services if needed. In addition, the node admin could require for each node's CPU load information by pre-set gateway. This information is the base of the load balance algorithm. Last but not least, it synchronizes its data with registry to make sure that the services registry information is complied with services management information.

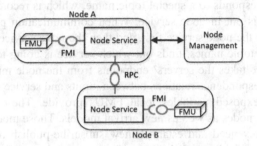

Fig. 4. Invoking process supported by Node Management

The process of the function call and data transmission using Node Management is described in Fig. 4: FMU in *node A* needs inputs at a communication point, it invokes functions using FMI standard interfaces provided by local node service. Node service will extract the required service name and send it to Node Management, the Node Management finds the endpoint that can provide corresponding service and handle the token back to *node A*, the *node A* uses this token as a remote proxy and calls the *node B* service. Finally, node service in *node B* picks up the needed data and answers the remote procedure call.

The advantage of above-mentioned process is as follows: the FMI-based invoking only occurs inside nodes, FMUs interacts with each other just like local procedure call, the network process is done by middleware automatically; node management provides rather robust service management, ensures that services are available and up to date; load balance structure is open for user to guarantee the high performance of the simulation system.

4 I/O Management

FMI for Co-Simulation provides an interface standard as a solution of time dependent coupled systems made of subsystems that are continuous in time (model components that are described by unstationary differential equations) or time-discrete ones (model components that are described by difference equations like, for example discrete controllers). Figure 5 shows block representation of the coupled system, u represents the inputs of the system, y represents the outputs, while v is all exposed variables.

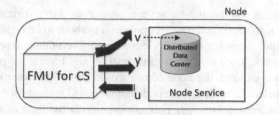

Fig. 5. Data exchange between FMU and node service

Every input corresponds to a special topic name, which is recorded in a local data center. Data center is put in node service. When communication point comes, FMU requires inputs from the node service first, and then the node service looks up the data center using inputs' topic names, finds out which service is going to be requested. At last, the node service takes the servers' endpoints from the node management.

Besides the correspondence relations between inputs and service names, data center also maintains all exposed variables local FMUs provide. These variables can be proposed to existing nodes as well as new arrival models. Those models can select and decide what data they need and establish new subscribe-publish relationships. As a result, the exposed variables and the inputs/outputs can be converted based on the models' demands.

Because all the node services have their own data center, the data centers are distributed inside the system. As a result, the distributed data centers must ensure data consistency. For example, when input is changed, the update information has to be sent to other node services that are related to this input. Therefore, we put an association table in I/O Management to save publish and subscribe information, each publish data has one topic and several subscribers. Every distributed data center has a special RPC gateway to communicate with a node admin in order to receive and send changes in time and guarantee the interface relations are up to time.

A complete process of how I/O Management works can be described as follows: When a new FMU joins the simulation, the I/O Management analyzes its XML description file first and extracts inputs, outputs and exposed variables. Then, the synchronization mechanism is triggered and every distributed data center will receive the information and decide whether they are about to connect with these variables. When the simulation is running and this FMU requires some inputs in next step, node service would release service request to node management first, then the inspection mechanism is triggered, node service sends publisher name, subscriber name and topic name to I/O Management to verify if these properties match. If yes, the real RPC service call is executed.

5 Time Management

FMI defines the communication points $tc(i)$, the communication steps $tc(i) \rightarrow tc(i + 1)$, the communication step sizes $hc = tc(i + 1) - tc(i)$ and the term "communication point" as the communication between subsystems in a Co-Simulation environment. The most common master time management algorithm stops at each communication point $tc(i)$, collects the outputs from all subsystems, evaluates the subsystem inputs, distributes these subsystem inputs to the slaves and continues the Co-Simulation with the next communication step $tc(i) \rightarrow tc(i + 1)$ with fixed communication step size hc. In each slave, an appropriate solver is used to integrate one of the subsystems for a given communication step. FMI for Co-Simulation is designed to support a very general class of master algorithms but it does not define the master algorithm itself.

As a basis, our time management is responsible for implementing above conservative time progression method. Before the simulation begins, the time management will select a proper number as a step size by finding the greatest common divisor among all FMU XML description documents. Once the simulation begins, time management will act as the master and distribute the advance tokens, gathering the grant signals. Time management module interacts directly with node service in each node. This node service controls the time advance function of FMUs.

Conservative time progression is a rather safe algorithm to manage the time accuracy of simulation, but it lacks efficiency to some degree. In our framework, we implemented another more effective method, which is based on the list of service requirements.

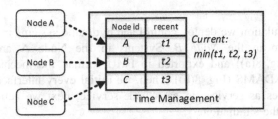

Fig. 6. Time advance based on the list of service requirements

The running logic can be seen in Fig. 6. In Time Management we deploy a map to depict the relationships between nodes and their recent service demand points called the list of service requirements. The communication framework is based on service invoking, every node can decide which service is about to use according to the FMU internal parameters. When the simulation is running, nodes keep sending the recent service demand point to Time Management, tacitly approving that its time has advanced to this point and waiting for the service invoking command. The Time Management will gather all nodes' recent points and schedule the table to calculate the minimum of these time points. Once it finds the next points, the Time Management will adjust the system current time to this point and give the right to relevant node to execute the procedure call. Finally, Time Management reclaims new recent point of this node and does the calculation again.

The advantage of this method is that there is no need for each node to keep track of its local and global time. It only stops when the input data is necessary, applies for the service invoking token, fetches the data and goes on, which can reduce the traffic and improve the robustness of the simulation system.

6 Case Study

To give further explanation of our framework, we implemented a simple electro-hydraulic brake system. Three subsystems and two nodes are included, the subsystems and interactions are shown in Fig. 7. Basically, the control system handles its expected rotation angle to hydraulic system, the hydraulic system calculates the hydraulic thrust based on current parameters and gives it to mechanism system, the latter loads the force to mechanisms and makes the hatch door rotate.

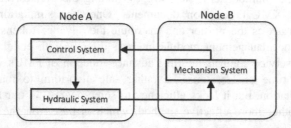

Fig. 7. System construction of the electro-hydraulic brake system

Before the simulation we deploy control and hydraulic systems in the *Node A* and mechanism system in the *Node B*. Systems in the Node A are developed in OpenModelica (Fig. 8(a)) and exported in FMU format, the mechanism system is developed using ADAMS (Fig. 8(b)). Then, we initial every interface as a topic and register these topics as services in each node service; next we activate these node services and start the simulation.

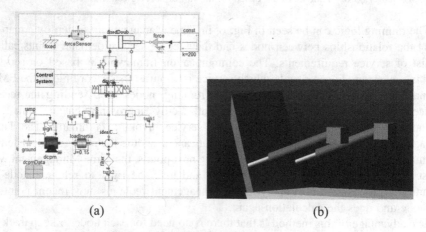

(a)   (b)

Fig. 8. Subsystems of the electro-hydraulic brake system

Figure 9 illustrates the running process of the *Node A*. When generating data it transfers them out with local advancement without stopping. When data is needed, it applies for service invocation token from the Time Management first, once the grant signal comes, it submits the interface message to I/O Management to get and verify the service detail. Finally, it requires the remote proxy from the Node Management by service name; it does the procedure call and goes on.

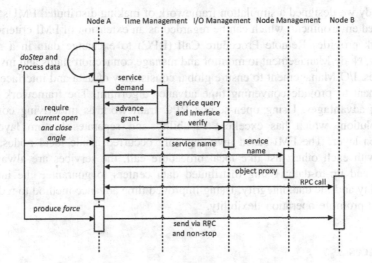

Fig. 9. Running process of *Node A* in the case study

Finally, we collect the rotation angle and force to make the result diagram. As the Fig. 10(a) shows, the simulation lasts 7.5 s and the max force is almost 2,000 N, which increases first and then decreases. As the Fig. 10(b) shows, the open and close angle increases first and decreases with the magnitude of the force in 7.5 s, the max angle being pi/2, 90°.

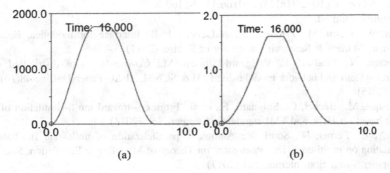

Fig. 10. Hydraulic force and rotation angle of the case system

As a result, we successfully applied our framework on the electro-hydraulic brake system, made FMUs in distributed nodes that interacted in a unified environment, obtained accurate results and supported the simulation with sound Node Management, I/O management and Time Management.

7 Conclusion

In the study we designed a simulation framework of making distributed FMUs interact in a unified environment, which can be regarded as an extension of FMI criterion. The framework provides Remote Procedure Call (RPC) to exchange data in a network efficiently, Node Management to monitor and manage connection status and invocation procedures, I/O Management to ensure global consistency of data and interfaces, Time Management to provide convening time advance algorithm. The framework has the following advantages. Using open-source RPC framework as underlying communication solution, which has excellent capability and separates bottom layer from application layer; The FMI-based invoking only occurred inside local nodes, FMUs interact with each other just like local procedure call, the services are always high available and up-to-date; Using distributed data centers to guarantee the interfaces accessibility and the data integrity; Using improved time advance method to reduce the traffic and promote operation flexibility.

References

1. IEEE Standard for Distributed Interactive Simulation - Communication Services and Profiles. IEEE Std. IEEE (2002)
2. Fullford, D.: Distributed interactive simulation: its past, present, and future. In: Conference on Winter Simulation. IEEE Computer Society (1996)
3. Taylor, S.J.E.: Distributed simulation: state-of-the-art and potential for operational research. Eur. J. Oper. Res. 2018:S0377221718303357 (2018)
4. Balda, P.: Real-time simulator of component models based on Functional Mock-up Interface 2.0. In: 2017 21st International Conference on Process Control (PC). IEEE (2017)
5. Fritzson, P.: Principles of object oriented modeling and simulation with modelica 3.3 (A Cyber-Physical Approach) ‖ Appendix G: FMI - Functional Mockup Interface (2014). https://doi.org/10.1002/9781118989166:1159-1169
6. https://fmi-standard.org/
7. Chen, W., Huhn, M., Fritzson, P.: A Generic FMU interface for modelica. Faculty of Graduate Studies & Research University of Regina (2011)
8. Pedersen, N., Madsen, J., Vejlgaard-Laursen, M.: Co-simulation of distributed engine control system and network model using FMI & SCNSL. IFAC-PapersOnLine 48(16), 261–266 (2015)
9. Lévesque, M., Béchet, C., Suignard, E., et al.: From co- toward multi-simulation of smart grids based on HLA and FMI standards. Comput. Sci. (2014)
10. Saidi, S.E., Pernet, N., Sorel, Y.: Automatic parallelization of multi-rate fmi-based co-simulation on multi-core. In: Symposium on Theory of Modeling & Simulation. Society for Computer Simulation International (2017)

11. Awais, M.U., Palensky, P., et al.: The high level architecture RTI as a master to the functional mock-up interface components. In: International Conference on ICNC 2013 (2013)
12. Galtier, V., Vialle, S., Dad, C., et al.: FMI-based distributed multi-simulation with DACCOSIM. In: Symposium on Theory of Modeling & Simulation: Devs Integrative M&S Symposium. Society for Computer Simulation International (2015)
13. Ji, H., Zhai, X., Song, X., et al.: HLA-based federation development framework supporting model reuse. In: AsiaSim: Asian Simulation Conference (2018)
14. Song, X., Zhang, L.: A DEVS based modelling and methodology-COSIM. Appl. Math. Inf. Sci. 6(2), 417–423 (2012)
15. Song, X., Ji, H., Tang, W.J., et al.: A simulation-language-compiler-based modeling and simulation framework. Int. J. Ind. Eng.-Theory Appl. Pract. 24(2), 134–145 (2017)

Interactive Modeling Environment Based on the System Entity Structure and Model Base

Han Wool Kim and Changbeom Choi(✉)

Handong Global University, 558 Handong-ro Buk-gu,
Pohang-si, Gyeongsangbuk-do, Republic of Korea
{21400229, cbchoi}@handong.edu

Abstract. The modeling and simulation tool must be intuitive so that the users can easily model the problem and simulate the simulation model to develop a solution for engineers who have a different level of knowledge. The person who wants to solve the problem must have prior knowledge to model, simulate, and execute the simulation model. Unfortunately, most modeling and simulation tools require such prior knowledge to the users. This research utilizes the chatbot services to help the simulationists who does not have enough modeling and simulation knowledge. By utilizing the chatbot services, a simulationist may compose a simulator and simulate the system anytime, anywhere.

Keywords: System Entity Structure · Model Base · Inquiry-based modeling · Chatbot

1 Introduction

The problems of modern society are complicated and interrelated through various domains. As a result, various researchers should participate in multi-disciplinary research to describe the phenomenon of the system and develop a solution to the problem. The Modeling and Simulation (M&S) theory has been introduced to support such multi-disciplinary research [1]. In general, a simulationist model a system that describes the phenomenon of the real system based on the simulation objective. Then, the simulationist develops the simulation model using a programming language to simulate the model on the computing environment. Therefore, the simulationists should be an expert on the problem domain, so that the simulationists should capable of deciding the abstraction level of the problem to capture the simulation objectives. At the same time, the simulationist should have a knowledge of the modeling theory, such as the Discrete Event System (DEVS) Formalism [2], the Petri-net [3], or the Unified Modeling Language (UML) to expose the characteristics of the problem, and the simulationists should have skills to develop their model into computer simulation models. Unfortunately, it is rare for a simulationist to be a domain expert and have both modeling knowledge and development abilities at the same time. Therefore, a user may not perform modeling and simulation when the user does not have enough prior knowledge or programming skills.

This research proposes an alternative M&S environment based on the System Entity Structure (SES) to help the simulationist who does not have modeling and

© Springer Nature Singapore Pte Ltd. 2019
G. Tan et al. (Eds.): AsiaSim 2019, CCIS 1094, pp. 54–64, 2019.
https://doi.org/10.1007/978-981-15-1078-6_5

simulation knowledge and development skills. The alternative M&S environment provides a familiar interface, a chatbot service from a social network service (SNS), to the users so the user may build a simulation, simulate, and get the modeling or simulation results through SNS. By utilizing the chatbot service, the users can easily access simulation models from a simulation model repository without having programming knowledge, and they can quickly get the simulation results by typing a few commands.

This paper is organized as follows. Section 2 introduces the related works in brief. To help the engineer with different levels of knowledge, we introduce the M&S environment based on the System Entity Structure and DEVS Formalism in Sect. 3. A case study and conclusion are presented in Sect. 4 and Sect. 5, respectively.

2   Related Works

2.1   UML

The Unified Modeling Language (UML) is a modeling language developed by Grady Booch, James Rumbaugh, and Ivar Jacobson in 1994. The UML is a de facto standard for developing computer software. The UML may specify and visualize the characteristics of a system and may capture the requirements and constraints of the system easily [4]. Since the UML is a well-known standard to develop computer software, many simulationists utilized the UML to develop simulators. They utilize the UML notation to capture the requirements of the simulation model, describe the structure of the simulation model and illustrate the interaction between simulation models by utilizing the use case diagram, class diagram and sequence diagram.

The use case diagram is a behavior diagram that defines the relations between actors and a set of use cases. The class diagram is a diagram that shows the structure of a system as a class. Unlike the class diagram, the sequence diagram illustrates the interaction among objects in the system.

Several studies are introduced to design the simulation system and develop the simulators using UML diagrams [5–7]. However, simulationists should develop a simulation model by themselves or find programming experts to develop their model. Also, the UML is just a framework to capture the requirements and constraints of the system, and it does not develop the simulation model automatically, the simulationist should understand the meaning of the diagrams and use them to design the simulation.

2.2   DEVS Formalism

The DEVS Formalism is the set-theoretical framework that has a modular form developed by Zeigler. Since the DEVS formalism allows simulationists to model the system in the hierarchical form, they can model the system from scratch or compose simulation models by selecting simulation models and define the relationship among the model. Therefore, the DEVS formalism is one of the well-known simulation theory that can develop complex simulation models [8].

The DEVS Formalism uses two models to develop the simulation model, the Atomic Model, and the Coupled Model. An atomic model is the basic model and has specifications for the dynamics of the model. The coupled model utilizes 7-tuple to depict the structure of a system. In Coupled model, a simulationist may use several atomic or coupled models to build complex systems hierarchically.

There are several simulation environments to support the instantiate the Atomic Model and Coupled Model in the DEVS formalism [9–11]. Some simulation environments require programming skills to develop a simulation model, and another simulation environment requires background knowledge to develop a simulation model. However, those simulation environments may not be enough to simulationists, who do not have enough knowledge to develop a model from scratch or do not want to build a simulation model using programming language.

2.3   System Entity Structure and Model Base

The System Entity Structure and Model Base (SES/MB) framework is used to find various alternative solutions in M&S fields [12–14]. The SES/MB consists of the SES Base and Model Base. The SES Base stores structure information of the system as a tree form, the SES tree. The SES tree has multiple entity nodes and attributes nodes to specify the structure and the alternatives of the system entities. The Model Base (MB) stores the simulation templates, which can be instantiated during the simulation. The simulation model represents the behavioral knowledge of the system entity.

In the SES/MB framework, a simulationist may synthesize a simulator using the SES tree and simulation model. During the synthesizing process, the simulationist may select the alternative of a system, which is called pruning, then the SES/MB framework automatically synthesis a simulation model.

This research adopts the strong points of the SES/MB structure and chooses different interfaces as other simulation environments. Mainly, this research utilizes the chatbot service of the SNS. By utilizing the chatbot services, any simulationist may use their phone or PCs to compose a simulation, synthesize the simulation, and simulate it, rather than using special simulation tools.

3   Proposed Environment and M&S Method

This section introduces the proposed environment based on the SES/MB and the M&S method using chatbot service. The proposed environment is implemented using Python [15] and Telegram Chatbot Application Programming Interface (API) [16].

3.1   Proposed Environment

Since the proposed environment is based on the SES/MB framework, the proposed environment has three managers, Entity Manager, Model Manager, and Execution Manager, to support the modeling and simulation of a system based on the SES/MB. Following Fig. 1 shows the architecture of the proposed M&S environment.

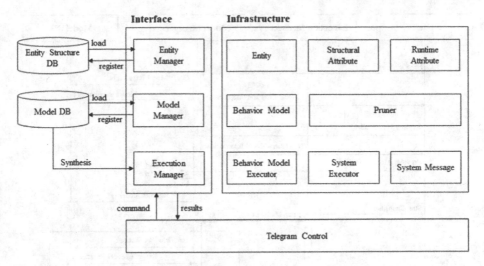

Fig. 1. The architecture of the proposed environment

The proposed environment has two databases to store the structure of an entity and the simulation model instances in Fig. 1. The Entity Structure DB manages the SES, which is consist of Entity and Attribute nodes. The Entity node denotes the name of the components and manages the attributes nodes. There are two types of an attribute node in the proposed environment, the structural attribute and runtime attribute. The structural attribute contains the input/output event ports, sub-components, and relationship among input/output event ports and the ports of the sub-components. On the other hand, the Runtime Attribute contains the necessary information to instantiate the entity. It contains the model information of a simulation model in the Model DB. The Behavior Model of the proposed environment is the basis of the simulation model that generates the behavior of the simulation model. Mainly, the Behavior Model adopts the form of the Atomic Model so that the simulationist who has prior knowledge of the DEVS formalism can easily insert and modify the model using Model Manager.

When simulationists want to build their simulation model using the proposed environment, the simulationist may select the SES from the Entity Structure DB. Then, the simulationist may decide to use the SES from the Entity DB or develop a new SES by composing the entities and models in the DBs. Since the SES may have various alternatives, the simulationist may prune the alternative based on the SES. Also, this research proposes the inquiry-based modeling method using chatbot service to handle the pruning process. Also, the simulationist may want to execute the simulation model, and the proposed environment provides an interface to control the simulations. Following Fig. 2 shows the sequence of actions among users, Execution Manager, Model Manager, and Model DB.

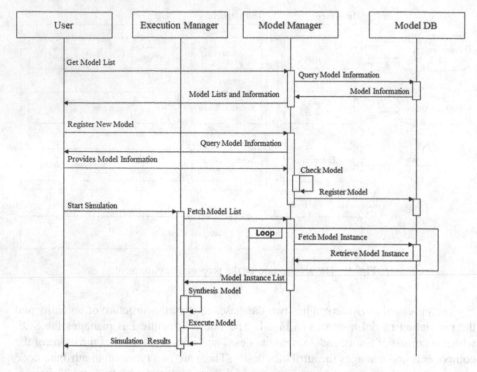

Fig. 2. The sequence of actions of the Model Manager

As shown in Fig. 2, the Model Manager handles the requests from the user and the Execution Manager. Especially when a user wants to register a new model into the Model DB, the Model Manager should get complete information from the user to define and instantiate the simulation model. To help the user, the Model Manager may generate the queries to develop a simulation model step by step. Also, when the users want to execute the simulation, they will trigger a start simulation event. Then, the Execution Manager receives the event and sends a fetch event to the Model Manager to retrieve the simulation model instances. After retrieving all model instances, the Execution Manager synthesizes the simulation model into a simulator and starts the simulation model.

3.2   Inquiry-Based Modeling and Simulation Method

A chatbot service in the SNS is a service that conducts a conversation with a user via speech or text to achieve a specific goal. Therefore, a chatbot can easily acquire information from a user step by step in a dialog system. This research adopts the strong points of the chatbot. Since users may have a different level of capabilities, the proposed system may generate inquiry based on the state. For example, when a user wants to select alternatives to a system, the user may start modeling by entering a command. Then, the system replies and ask what the user wants. Following Fig. 3 shows the inquiry-based modeling method using SNS.

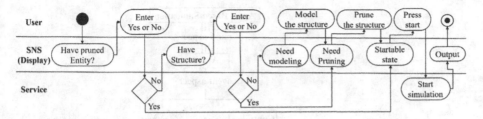

Fig. 3. Inquiry-based modeling using SNS

Inquiry-based modeling is modeling where the service system first asks a question and finds the level of the user. As shown in Fig. 3, the SNS chatbot generates the inquiry to the users during the modeling process. Inquiry-based service system asks the user if the pruning process is necessary, and if the user has already done the pruning process, the simulation can be performed immediately. Afterward, the service system can help the user to perform the necessary processes by identifying and modeling whether the modeling process or the pruning process is required. If the user already has a modeled structure, the service system helps the user to go through the pruning process and select the model configuration. If the user has no modeled structure, the service system guides the user so that the user can go through the basic modeling of creating an entity or port. After the previous steps have been completed, the service system will help the user proceed to the next step to derive the simulation results.

4 Case Study

This section illustrates the usability of the proposed M&S environment and its inquiry-based M&S method by introducing the agent-based evacuation model.

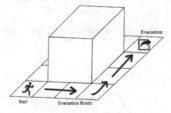

Fig. 4. Concepts of the Agent-Based Simulation model

In this section, the Agent-Based Simulation (ABS) Model is used as an example of the inquiry-based M&S method. ABS Model is a model that can analyze the path to move to each target. Figure 4 shows the concept of the example.

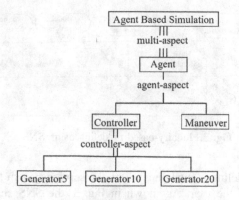

Fig. 5. SES structure of agent model

Figure 5 shows the ABS concept using the SES structure. ABS Entity is a structure that selects one of the generators from the Controller when pruning. ABS entity can be configured to include various Agents. The Agent consists of a Controller and a Maneuver. The Controller delivers the target point, and a Maneuver makes Agent moving to the specified destination. The Controller can have Generators that create the target point. For this case study, the structure of the Controller is defined to have various Generators. Therefore, anyone who can develop a simulation model can make and synthesize various kinds of Maneuver and Controller by using the ABS model. Even people who are not able to model simulation can select the desired Generator during the pruning process, synthesize it, and then see the simulation result by using the ABS model.

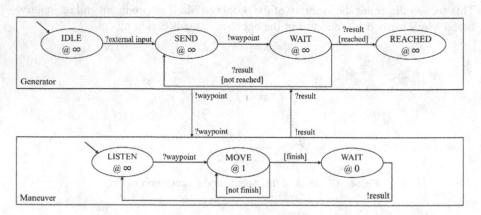

Fig. 6. DEVS diagram of ABS model

Figure 6 shows the relationship between the Generator and Maneuver in the DEVS diagram. The Generator is a model that generates waypoints, passes waypoints, and receives results. Init state of Generator is IDLE, and when it is input from outside, it becomes SEND state and outputs waypoint and waits for the next input in a WAIT state. If Generator receives an input event again, Generator checks for the remaining waypoint, and if it remains, Generator returns to the SEND state. If not, Generator stops with the REACHED state. Maneuver expresses the Agent's location in a model that performs movement per unit time to move to the waypoint created by the Generator. Maneuver has states LISTEN, MOVE, and WAIT. The initial state, LISTEN, waits until it receives a waypoint. If Maneuver receives a waypoint, it moves to the waypoint once in the MOVE state and checks if the current position has reached the waypoint. If the waypoint is not reached, Maneuver stays in the MOVE state and executes the movement once again. When the waypoint is reached, it is in the WAIT state and sends the result to the Generator.

Fig. 7. Actual program execution using an inquiry-based algorithm

Figure 7 shows the sequence of actions of the Model Manager in the proposed environment. When a user starts a chat and sends a sequence of commands, the chatbot invokes operations of the managers in the proposed environment. Figure 7 is a screenshot of the process of creating generators after creating an agent with a root entity. As shown in Fig. 7, the chatbot asks the user to complete the simulation model even if the user does not know what to do.

Figure 8 shows the modeling results using the proposed environment. When the user enters the model name in the Telegram, then telegram automatically generates a picture and shows it, as shown in Fig. 8. By viewing the automatically generated picture, the user can quickly check that there is nothing wrong. If anything goes wrong, the user can use Telegram again to modify the model's structure.

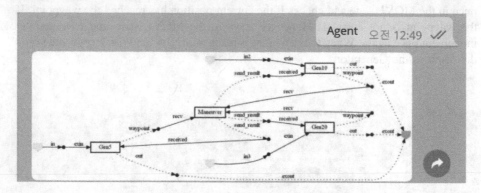

Fig. 8. Visualization of the proposed environment

Figure 9 shows the simulation execution and the simulation results using the proposed environment. After inputting and requesting a simulation output, the Telegram delivers the output directly to the user in the Telegram environment, as shown in Fig. 9. Since the proposed environment is implemented in Telegram, the user can use the Telegram application of the smartphone anytime, anywhere to insert multiple inputs and get the result with a simple operation.

Fig. 9. Sending simulation results to the users

The text file received in Fig. 9 is arranged, as shown in Fig. 10. Figure 10 shows the result of running the ABS model. The waypoints created by the Agent are listed at the top, and the left side shows the time of the simulation environment, next is agent ID, and next is the Agent's current position according to the time.

waypoint Agent5: [(70, 40), (50, 45), (30, 60), (20, 70), (40, 90)]
waypoint Agent5: [(95, 42), (90, 45), (70, 52), (55, 42), (55, 42), (40, 50), (30, 60), (20, 70), (22, 73), (40, 80)]
waypoint Agent20: [(80, 8), (70, 15), (60, 17), (57, 11), (50, 13), (46, 18), (30, 22), (20, 26), (10, 29), (7, 30), (10, 38), (13, 50), (15, 60), (17, 70), (19, 75), (20.5, 80), (2*
0 Agent5   current location 79.10557280900008 44.5527864045004
0 Agent10 current location 95.0 56.0
0 Agent20 current location 79.16439898730536 2.986393928321437
1 Agent5   current location 78.21114361800016 44.10557280900008
1 Agent10 current location 95.0 55.0
1 Agent20 current location 79.32879797461072 3.9727878476642875
2 Agent5   current location 77.31671842700024 43.6583592135012
2 Agent10 current location 95.0 54.0
2 Agent20 current location 79.49319896191608 4.959181771496431
3 Agent5   current location 76.42229123600032 43.21114561800016
3 Agent10 current location 95.0 53.0
3 Agent20 current location 79.65759594922143 5.945575695328576
4 Agent5   current location 75.52786404500004 42.7639320225002
4 Agent10 current location 95.0 52.0
4 Agent20 current location 79.82199493652679 6.931963861916072
5 Agent5   current location 74.63343685400048 42.3167184270024
5 Agent10 current location 95.0 51.0
5 Agent20 current location 79.98639392383214 7.918363542992864

Fig. 10. Simulation results of the echo protocol model

Figure 11 shows the result of Fig. 10 using the visualization tool. Users may not have development capability to build a simulation model to get results of the simulation model. Moreover, the user may not have a simulation environment and computing resources to conduct the simulation. However, the user may not consider the simulation environment and the computing resources because the chatbot service enables users to utilize a remote simulation environment. Therefore, even a user who has little experience in manipulating the simulation environment can get the result based on the model made by a simple operation.

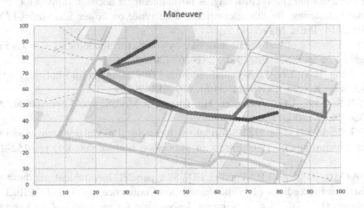

Fig. 11. Simulation results visualization of the agent model

5 Conclusion

As society and its problem become complicated, the need for the M&S increases. The simulation environment should provide an intuitive method to the users who may not have prior knowledge, such as modeling theory or development capability to simulate the simulation model.

This research introduced the M&S environment to help the users to conduct the simulation by utilizing the SES/MB and SNS chatbot. By utilizing the SES/MB framework, a user may build a simulation model quickly by selecting simulation model instances. The chatbot service enables inquiry-based modeling and simulation of a system to the users. Also, the chatbot services allow the users to access the remote simulation environment and the computing resources, so that the users may execute their simulation model and get the simulation results quickly. This environment may be extended by providing a web-based interface.

Acknowledgement. This work was supported by Electronics and Telecommunications Research Institute (ETRI) grant funded by the Korean government [19ZH1100, Development of Flexible Simulation Learning Management Platform for Mixed Real-Virtual Data].

References

1. Park, H.C., Kim, T.G.: A relational algebraic framework for VHDL models management. Trans. Soc. Comput. Simul. **15**(2), 43–55 (1998)
2. Sarjoughian, H.: Inductive modeling of discrete event systems: a TMS-based non-monotonic reasoning approach. The University of Arizona (1995)
3. Murata, T.: Petri nets: properties, analysis and application. Proc. IEEE **77**(4), 541–580 (1989)
4. Booch, G.: Unified Modeling Language User Guide, 2nd edn. Pearson Education, Noida (2005)
5. Colak, I., Kabalci, E., Yesilbudak, M., Kahraman, H.T.: A novel intelligent decision support tool for average wind speed clustering. A novel intelligent decision support tool for average wind speed clustering. In: 8th International Conference on Power Electronics-ECCE Asia, pp. 2010–2014. IEEE, May 2011
6. Viana, T.: A catalog of bad smells in design-by-contract methodologies with Java modeling language. J. Comput. Sci. Eng. **7**(4), 251–262 (2013)
7. Park, J., Kang, H.Y., Lee, J.: A spatial-temporal POI data model for implementing location-based services. Korean J. Geomat. **34**(6), 609–618 (2016)
8. Zeigler, B.P., Kim, T.G., Praehofer, H.: Theory of Modeling and Simulation. Academic Press, San Diego (2000)
9. Kim, T.G., Park, S.B.: The DEVS formalism: hierarchical modular systems specification in C++. In: Proceedings of 1992 European Simulation Multiconference, pp. 152–156, June 1992
10. Chow, A.C.H., Zeigler, B.P.: Parallel EDVS: a parallel, hierarchical, modular modeling formalism. In: Proceedings of Winter Simulation Conference, pp. 716–722. IEEE (1994)
11. Vangheluwe, H.L.: DEVS as a common denominator for multi-formalism hybrid systems modelling. In: IEEE International Symposium on Computer-Aided Control System Design (cat. no. 00th8537), CASCSD, pp. 129–134. IEEE (2000)
12. Kim, B.S., Choi, C.B., Kim, T.G.: Multifaceted modeling and simulation framework for system of systems using HLA/RTI. In: Proceedings of the 16th Communications & Networking Symposium, p. 4. Society for Computer Simulation International, April 2013
13. Hagendorf, O., Pawletta, T.: A framework for simulation-based structure and parameter optimization of discrete-event systems. In: Discrete-Event Modeling and Simulation, pp. 199–222. CRC Press (2018)
14. Deatcu, C., Folkerts, H., Pawletta, T., Durak, U.: Design patterns for variability modeling SES ontology. In: Proceedings of the Model-driven Approaches for Simulation Engineering Symposium, p. 3. Society for Computer Simulation International, April 2018
15. Python. https://www.python.org/. Accessed 30 June 2019
16. Telegram Chatbot document. https://github.com/python-telegram-bot/python-telegram-bot/wiki/Code-snippets#post-an-image-from-memory. Accessed 14 June 2019

A Generic Maturity Model
for Verification and Validation
of Modeling and Simulation Applications

Zhongshi Wang[1(✉)] and Axel Lehmann[2]

[1] ITIS GmbH, 85577 Neubiberg, Germany
zhongshi.wang@unibw.de
[2] Bundeswehr University Munich, 85577 Neubiberg, Germany
axel.lehmann@unibw.de

Abstract. As a consequence of the increasing complexity and variety of modeling and simulation (M&S) applications, the demand for demonstrating the credibility and acceptability of M&S and its results by introducing appropriate quality measures, techniques, and tools is obvious. Verification and validation (V&V) is used as an instrument to obtain sufficient confidence in credibility of M&S results. The sufficient confidence is dictated not only by the amount of the invested V&V efforts, but rather by the maturity of the V&V efforts and quality of the collected V&V evidences, such as their completeness and strength. This paper presents a generic V&V maturity model, which (1) can be used (or with slight modifications) for any simulation study with structured M&S and V&V processes; (2) takes different influence factors into consideration: levels of independent V&V, intensity of V&V efforts, and significance of V&V techniques; (3) defines and describes the V&V maturity and its levels in a comprehensible and self-explanatory manner, so that no specialized skills and expertise are required for application of this approach.

Keywords: Maturity assessment · Quality and credibility assurance · Modeling and simulation (M&S) · Verification and validation (V&V)

1 Introduction

The permanently increasing performance of information and communication technologies (ICT) enables a permanently increasing complexity of all kinds of technical systems, on one hand, and the development and effective application of increasingly complex modeling and simulation (M&S) for manifold purposes, on the other hand. Besides benefits of M&S innovations and advances, increasing risks with respect to quality – especially correctness and validity of M&S specification, design, development and operation as well as regarding credibility and utility of simulation results and their interpretation become an urgent concern.

For the purpose of M&S credibility assessment, verification and validation (V&V) can be generally considered as a supporting process to develop an acceptance recommendation by means of collecting information, building evidence,

© Springer Nature Singapore Pte Ltd. 2019
G. Tan et al. (Eds.): AsiaSim 2019, CCIS 1094, pp. 65–76, 2019.
https://doi.org/10.1007/978-981-15-1078-6_6

and improving M&S confidence [8,11,19,21]. As illustrated in Fig. 1, the following information sources are of particular importance:

- documents or specifications about M&S goals, capabilities, requirements, and constraints;
- M&S (intermediate) products, such as specified acceptability goal, criteria, conceptual model, executive model, design of experiments, results presentation and interpretation etc.;
- referent, e.g. data of real or similar/comparable systems, historical records, experts estimations, or theoretical considerations.

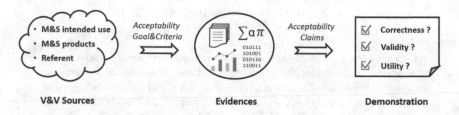

Fig. 1. V&V as process of collecting evidences.

In the process of assessing the collected information and its satisfaction with the defined acceptability criteria, pieces of evidence demonstrating correctness, validity and utility of models, simulations, and data are accumulated. Using various V&V measures and techniques, such as inspections, evaluations and tests, this process continues or repeats itself until sufficient confidence in credibility and acceptability of M&S results is obtained [2,20]. The extent of sufficient confidence, on the one hand, is determined by M&S characters and objectives, on the other hand it is typically limited by the available M&S project resources and therefore has to be adapted according to specified cost, time and application constraints [25,26]. In addition, the sufficiency of the confidence is not only dictated by the amount of the invested V&V efforts, but rather by the manner how and what kinds of evidences are collected, namely quality of the gained evidences, such as their completeness and strength. Thus, measuring maturity of the V&V efforts and quality of the evidences is the crucial issue for the confidence building process.

Based on the investigation of several exiting approaches relating M&S maturity measurement, such as Balci's M&S quality indicators [2], the application of the Capability Maturity Model [7] in the M&S context, the Predictive Capability Maturity Model [13,14], and the Simulation Validation Process Maturity Model (SVPMM) [8], this work introduces a generic maturity model measuring quality of V&V evidence from multiple perspectives: levels of independent V&V, intensity of V&V efforts, and significance of V&V techniques. The remainder of the article includes (1) a brief review of the related work; (2) definition and description of the V&V maturity and its levels; and (3) demonstration and discussion of the application potentials.

2 Measuring Maturity in the Context of Modeling and Simulation

Balci [2,4] proposes an approach to assessing the overall M&S quality, consisting of indicators to measure the quality characteristics from the viewpoints: product, process, project, and people. In this work, however, the significance and weighting of the individual indicators with respect to the overall quality assessment are not described. On the other hand, how to use the defined quality indicators to establish different M&S and V&V maturity levels (improvement over time) is also not discussed.

For conducting maturity assessment compatible with the Capability Maturity Model (CMM) [17], Conwell et al. [7] suggest a direct use of the Software Capability Maturity Model (SW-CMM) and the Software Acquisition Capability Maturity Model (SA-CMM) in assessing M&S development and acquisition processes. As stated in [8], this approach discusses the importance of V&V to M&S development and acquisition processes in general, but does not describe how to structure and conduct V&V and its maturity assessment explicitly. In addition, a potential application of this approach in practice is also not reported.

As a stand-alone maturity measurement tool, the Predictive Capability Maturity Model (PCMM) [13,14] is focused on assessing the quality levels of the computational aspects of M&S efforts. In PCMM the following six elements are objectives of the maturity assessment:

- Representation and geometric fidelity;
- Physics and material model fidelity;
- Code verification;
- Solution verification;
- Model validation;
- Uncertainty quantification and sensitivity analysis.

For each of the six elements, PCMM defines an assessment ranking scale with four levels (0–3) of maturity. A higher maturity level indicates the increasing quality as well as quantity of the gathered information about the improvement of M&S and V&V efforts. One limitation of PCMM is its restricted application area. As already explained by the six elements above, PCMM is specially used for physics and engineering modeling. According to the analysis of [6], PCMM is primarily applicable to M&S efforts dealing with nonlinear Partial Differential Equations (PDE), and is commonly used within Computational Fluid Dynamics (CFD). In addition, the assessment ranking scale of PCMM only descriptively specifies the quality characteristics to be fulfilled in each maturity level (approximately: no/little, some, significant, or detailed and complete evidence of maturity). How to reach a higher maturity level, namely which V&V measures and activities are needed to improve the quality of evidences, so that they become more complete, more accurate, or even more objective, is however not part of PCMM.

The Simulation Validation Process Maturity Model (SVPMM) [8] has been developed based on the consideration that validation is a process generating information about validity of simulation models (in form of validation evidences) as its solo product. In SVPMM the quality properties of information (or items of evidence) are defined by (1) completeness of the information, (2) correctness of the information, and (3) confidence that the information is complete and correct enough for the intended use of models. In order to produce validation evidence, SVPMM uses five contribution elements as inputs, consisting of typical artifacts relating to M&S development and its validation processes:

- Validation criteria;
- Referents;
- Conceptual models;
- Verification results of development products, examples of development products are software designs, implementation components and their documentation etc.;
- Simulation results.

By means of a six level assessment scale, each of the five input elements is ranked from no validation conducted to an automated validation process. With the increasing maturity levels, quality and objectivity of the gathered validation evidences increase. The defined process maturity levels are explained as the following informal validity statements:

- Level 0: I have no idea of the maturity (no assessment);
- Level 1: It works, trust me (subjective validation only);
- Level 2: It represents the right entities and attributes (objective requirements);
- Level 3: It does the right things, its representations are complete enough (objective results sampling);
- Level 4: For what it does, its representations are accurate enough (objective referents);
- Level 5: I'm confident that this simulation is valid (automated/formal validation).

A possible point of confusion in this maturity model could be the use of term "validation". SVPMM considers simulation validation as a whole process instead of using verification and validation. This implies on the one hand a separate consideration of V&V processes, on the other hand, verification is in fact regarded as an integrated part of the simulation validation process, such as verification of (intermediate) development products. According to the common understanding, verification and validation are corresponding and complementary processes. Not only development products defined in this approach, but also definition of M&S intended use, specification of M&S requirements, conceptual models are subject to M&S verification as well as validation.

In comparison with PCMM, which, as an object-oriented approach, specifies the descriptive quality characteristics of maturity levels to be reached by an M&S element or product, SVPMM defines V&V measures using increasing objectivity for a higher quality level from the perspective of V&V processes.

Each of the object-oriented and process-oriented approaches only separately consider one aspect related to maturity assessment of V&V efforts. The following section describes the development of a generic V&V maturity assessment with a combined consideration of multiple influencing factors.

3   Generic V&V Maturity Assessment Model

3.1   Factors Influencing Maturity of V&V Evidences

Figure 2 illustrates a general description of structured M&S V&V [22]. From the development's point of view, a simulation study is initiated by presenting sponsor needs and consists of a set of ordered development phases. In each phase a defined work product is developed such as specifications of intended use and M&S requirements, conceptual model, executable model, and simulation results. A work product consists of several content-related subjects, each of which represents a specific issue or a model element. From the V&V point of view, each model development activity is coupled with a corresponding V&V effort throughout the M&S life cycle. Thus, V&V evidences are results of evaluations and tests performed by using appropriate V&V techniques with respect to each M&S work product. In addition, V&V evidences should be collected and investigated in an independent manner, namely the application of independent V&V (IV&V) [1,12,26] is an essential consideration of this work.

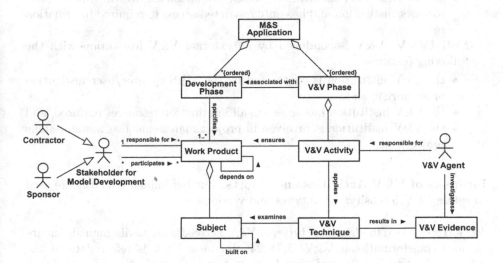

Fig. 2. Influence factors of V&V maturity assessment

3.2   Definition of the V&V Maturity

The Generic V&V Maturity (GVVM) is defined by the triple (L, I, S), where:

- L: Level of independent V&V (IV&V);
- I: Intensity of V&V activities and efforts;
- S: Significance of V&V techniques.

Level of Independent V&V (IV&V). Typically, IV&V can be measured and classified from the perspectives [3,9]: (1) technical independence, (2) management independence, and financial independence. Oberkampf and Roy [15] define a five level IV&V sliding scale from no independence to high IV&V. On the basis of this approach, the following three IV&V levels are considered in GVVM:

- **No IV&V**: V&V is conducted either by the M&S developer or by a V&V team within the M&S developer institution;
- **Limited IV&V**: V&V is conducted by:
  - an external V&V institution, which is contracted by the M&S developer institution as a subcontractor; or
  - a V&V team within the M&S sponsor/user institution; or
  - an external V&V institution, which is contracted by the M&S sponsor/user institution and is not involved in V&V planning and management; or
  - an external V&V institution, which is contracted by the M&S sponsor/user institution and has only restricted access to required information resources.
- **Full IV&V**: V&V is conduced by an external V&V institution with the following features:
  - the V&V institution is contracted by the M&S sponsor/user institution or authority; and
  - the V&V institution has access to all information resources required; and
  - the V&V institution is involved in project management as a stand-alone project role.

Intensity of V&V Activities and Efforts. Further influence factors are used to refine V&V intensity: V&V types and versions.

V&V Types. Two fundamental types of V&V activities are to distinguish: intrinsic and transformational V&V [5,18,24]. Intrinsic V&V is referred to as the self-contained examination of a work product, namely evaluation of consistency with respect to itself. Transformational V&V, on the other hand, is conducted by examination of the consistency with previously created work products. The two types of V&V can be used in a complementary manner for collecting V&V evidences from different perspectives.

V&V Versions. From the development's point of view, M&S errors, deficiencies, or ambiguities identified by V&V efforts motivate a revision of the existing work products, so that a new M&S version is created, which could in turn require further and in-depth V&V efforts. Thus, with increasing V&V versions, more quantitative as well as more qualitative V&V evidences can be gathered.

V&V Intensity Matrix. By means of a matrix, the two factors: V&V types and V&V versions are mutually combined. Table 1 shows the definition of the three intensity levels: **initial**, **advanced**, and **extensive**.

Table 1. Levels of V&V intensity.

V&V intensity	V&V type	V&V version
Initial	Intrinsic only	Single version
	Transformational only	
Advanced	Intrinsic only	Multiple versions
	Transformational only	
	Intrinsic and Transformational	Single version
Extensive	Intrinsic and Transformational	Multiple versions

Significance of V&V Techniques. Quality of V&V evidences also depends primarily on, which level of formality and objectivity the applied V&V techniques exhibit. Compared to ad hoc techniques, a V&V technique with high level of formality defines a well structured examination process, clear responsibilities of the participants involved, and therefore high reproducibility of V&V results.

Unlike subjective techniques, which rely heavily on individual's insights and intuitions, particularly opinions of subject matter experts (SMEs), objective V&V techniques are either based on comparisons of M&S results with the real data or theoretical considerations, or are conducted by means of statistical methods or mathematical procedure. Subjective techniques are used in a readily comprehensible manner, and can be regarded as the only possibility, when no objective methods are applicable. However, assumptions and estimates of SMEs are not always reliable [16], or experts may differ in their opinions about the model estimation. On the other hand, objective techniques can provide the unique V&V evidence, but their application is usually presupposed by specific conditions (availability of referent data) or requires the mastery of particular knowledge or skills for testing personnel (V&V agents). More details about formality and objectivity of V&V techniques are discussed in [10,23]. This work defines the following three levels of V&V significance:

- **Subjective:** Application of subjective V&V techniques with low or middle formality;
- **Semi-objective:** Application of subjective V&V techniques with high formality (e.g. inspections); or application of objective V&V techniques on the basis of sampling;
- **Objective:** Application of objective V&V techniques for comparison of M&S results; or application of mathematical procedures; or application of automated proof processes.

3.3 Maturity Levels Defined in GVVM

According to the respective extent of V&V independence, intensity, and significance, five maturity levels (form level 0 to level 4) are defined. As shown in Fig. 3, quality of V&V evidences, e.g. correctness, completeness, accuracy, and objectivity, increases with the increasing maturity levels.

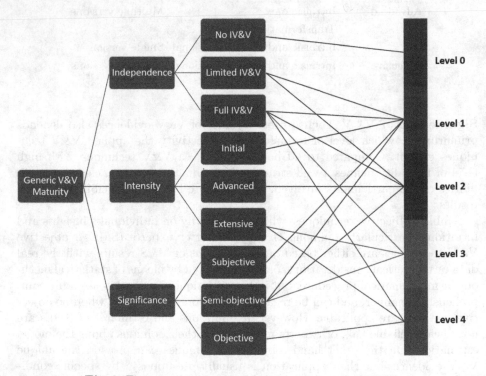

Fig. 3. Five maturity levels and their measures in GVVM.

Following a top down approach, each of the maturity levels is determined based on the decision sequence from levels of IV&V, intensity of V&V efforts to significance of V&V techniques (see Fig. 4). Thus, the maturity level 0 is determined, when the maturity factor *independence* is referred to as *No IV&V*

(namely: no V&V conducted or only internal testing available), regardless how the other two factors *intensity* and *significance* are measured. This means that the internal tests performed by the M&S developer or by a V&V team within the same organization are considered as the lowest maturity level because of the missing of independence.

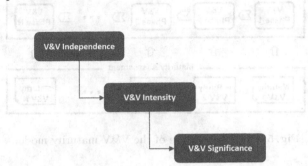

Fig. 4. Decision sequence for determining the maturity levels.

This consideration does not imply that internal tests are not relevant with respect to quality assurance. Indeed, they are the essential quality measures for any simulation study. In the context of credibility assessment however, the results of internal tests need to be analyzed and evaluated by an independent third party prior to the use as V&V evidence.

The maturity level 1 and level 2 are determined, when the factor *independence* can be referred to either as *Limited* or as *Full IV&V*. The two levels differ in their measurement of the factor *intensity*. While an initial V&V intensity is assigned to the level 1, the factor *intensity* of the level 2 is referred to as *Advanced*. Since mainly initial and early V&V efforts are assigned to the level 1 and level 2, the application of objective V&V techniques, such as formal methods, are practically not possible. Therefore, the combination of objective techniques is generally excluded for the two maturity levels.

The maturity level 3 and level 4 are determined, when the factor *independence* is exclusively referred to as *Full IV&V*. They have the same measurement of V&V intensity as well. The difference between the two levels is that while *Semi-objective* is assigned to the level 3, the factor *significance* of the level 4 is referred to as *Objective*.

4   Application of the Proposed V&V Maturity Model

Because of the generic nature in defining the V&V maturity and deriving its maturity levels, the proposed V&V maturity model (GVVM) can be applied to any simulation study with well defined and structured model development and V&V processes.

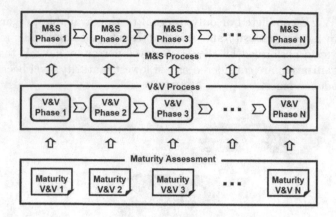

Fig. 5. Purpose and use of the V&V maturity model.

As illustrated in Fig. 5, for V&V of each work product defined in the M&S life cycle, a maturity level can be assessed. Thus, the V&V maturity of a complete simulation study is described by a vector M as follows:

$$M = (m_1, m_2, m_3, ..., m_N)$$

where an element $m_i \in \{0, 1, 2, 3, 4\}$ is the value of the maturity level of V&V results in phase i ($i = 1, ..., N$), and N is the number of M&S and V&V phases. For practical use, two types of maturity are of interest: the required/targeted V&V maturity $M_{required}$ and the actual maturity M_{actual} (assessed at a certain time of M&S development).

$M_{required}$ specifies the predefined V&V maturity levels to be reached for each V&V phase and can therefore serve as a contractual basis or as quality requirements for tailoring of M&S and V&V activities.

M_{actual} is the result of assessing the maturity levels based on the currently achieved V&V results for each M&S project milestone. Then a delta analysis between M_{actual} and $M_{required}$ should be performed by the project management, which typically consists of representatives from the M&S sponsor, M&S developer, and V&V institution. In case of not reaching the required level(s), further measures for improving the V&V maturity should be also developed jointly by the three parties. For example, the maturity of the ith V&V phase $m_{required(i)} = 3$ is prescribed in $M_{required}$, while the corresponding $m_{actual(i)} = 2$ is assessed in M_{actual}. In order to increase the maturity of $V\&V_i$ from the level 2 to level 3, the following improvement potentials could be applied:

1. From the management perspective: increasing the independence level of V&V, e.g. access to all required resources, integrated in the project management as a stand-alone role (if not yet);
2. From the M&S development perspective: revising and refining the work products and their documentation, so that more detailed and in-depth V&V becomes feasible;
3. From the V&V perspective: applying additional objective techniques.

5 Conclusion

The V&V maturity model proposed in this paper presents a generic way to measure quality of V&V efforts and their collected evidences for any type of M&S applications. By means of assessing the V&V independence, V&V intensity, and V&V significance respectively, five levels of the growing V&V maturity are specified, which indicate, on the one hand, methodical measures for improving V&V quality, on the other hand, also the required resources and expenses from the perspectives: project management, M&S development, and V&V. In addition, since the definition and description of the generic V&V maturity and its maturity levels are nearly self-explanatory, no special skills or trainings in assessment techniques are required for use of the V&V maturity model.

References

1. Arthur, J.D., Nance, R.E.: Verification and validation without independence: a recipe for failure. In: Joines, J., Barton, R., Kang, K., Fishwick, P. (eds.) Proceedings of the 2000 Winter Simulation Conference, pp. 859–865 (2000)
2. Balci, O.: Quality assessment, verification, and validation of modeling and simulation applications. In: Ingalls, R., Rossetti, M., Smith, J., Peters, B. (eds.) Proceedings of the 2004 Winter Simulation Conference, pp. 122–129 (2004)
3. Balci, O.: A life cycle for modeling and simulation. Simul. Trans. Soc. Model. Simul. Int. **88**(7), 870–883 (2012)
4. Balci, O.: Quality indicators throughout the modeling and simulation life cycle. In: Yilmaz, L. (ed.) Concepts and Methodologies for Modeling and Simulation. SFMA, pp. 199–215. Springer, Cham (2015). https://doi.org/10.1007/978-3-319-15096-3_9
5. Brade, D.: Enhancing modeling and simulation accreditation by structuring verification and validation results. In: Joines, J., Barton, R., Kang, K., Fishwick, P. (eds.) Proceedings of the 2000 Winter Simulation Conference (2000)
6. Carlsson, M., Andersson, H., Gavel, H., Ölvander, J.: Methodology for development and validation of multipurpose simulation models. In: 50th AIAA Aerospace Sciences Meeting Including the New Horizons Forum and Aerospace Exposition. American Institute of Aeronautics and Astronautics (2012)
7. Conwell, C.L., Enrigth, R., Stutzman, M.A.: Capability maturity models support of modeling and simulation verification, validation, and accreditation. In: Joines, J., Barton, R., Kang, K., Fishwick, P. (eds.) Proceedings of the 2000 Winter Simulation Conference, pp. 819–828 (2000)
8. Harmon, S.Y., Youngblood, S.M.: A proposed model for simulation validation process maturity. J. Def. Model. Simul. Appl. Methodol. Technol. (JDMS) **2**(4), 179–190 (2005)
9. IEEE: IEEE Standard for Software Verification and Validation. IEEE Computer Society (1998). IEEE std 1012–1998
10. Lehmann, A., Wang, Z.: Efficient use of V&V techniques for quality and credibiltiy assurance of complex modeling and simulation applications. Int. J. Ind. Eng. Theory Appl. Pract. **24**(2), 220–228 (2017)
11. Lehmann, A., Wang, Z.: Verification, validation, and accreditation (VV&A) - requirements, standards, and trends. In: Lin, Z., Zeigler, B.P., Laili, Y. (eds.) Model Engineering for Simulation, chap. 6, pp. 101–121. Elsevier Inc. (2019)

12. Lewis, R.O.: Independent Verification and Validation: A Life Cycle Engineering Process for Quality Software, 1st edn. Wiley, New York (1992)
13. Oberkampf, W.L., Pilch, M., Trucano, T.G.: Predictive capability maturity model for computational modeling and simulation. Technical report SAND2007-5948, Sandia National Laboratories Albuquerque, NM (2007)
14. Oberkampf, W.L., Roy, C.J.: Maturity assessment of modeling and simulation. In: Verification and Validation in Sceintific Computing, chap. 15, pp. 696–727. Cambridge University Press (2010)
15. Oberkampf, W.L., Roy, C.J.: Verification and Validation in Sceintific Computing. Cambridge University Press, Cambridge (2010)
16. Overstreet, C.M.: Model testing: is it only a special case of software testing. In: Yücesan, E., Chen, C.H., Snowdon, J., Charnes, J. (eds.) Proceedings of the 2002 Winter Simulation Conference, pp. 641–647 (2002)
17. Paulk, M.C., Curtis, B., Chrissis, M.B., Weber, C.V.: Capability maturity model for software, version 1.1. Technical report, Software Engineering Institute, Carnegie Mellon University, Pittsburgh, Pennsylvania 15213 (1993). CMU/SEI-93-TR-024, ESC-TR-93-177
18. Rabe, M., Spieckermann, S., Wenzel, S.: Verification and validation activities within a new procedure model for V&V in production and logistics simulation. In: Rossetti, M., Hill, R., Johansson, B., Dunkin, A., Ingalls, R. (eds.) Proceedings of the 2009 Winter Simulation Conference (WSC), pp. 2509–2519 (2009)
19. Sargent, R.G.: Verification and validation of simulation models. In: Jain, S., Creasey, R.R., Himmelspach, J., White, K.P., Fu, M. (eds.) Proceedings of the 2011 Winter Simulation Conference, pp. 183–198 (2011)
20. Sargent, R.G.: An introductory tutorial on verification and validation of simulation models. In: Yilmaz, L., Chan, W.K.V., Moon, I., Roeder, T.M.K., Macal, C., Rossetti, M.D. (eds.) Proceedings of the 2015 Winter Simulation Conference (WSC), pp. 1729–1740 (2015)
21. Simulation Interoperability Standards Organization (SISO): GM-VV Volume 1: Introduction and Overview, Guide for Generic Methodology for Verification and Validation (GM-VV) to Support Acceptance of Models, Simulations, and Data, October 2012. SISO-GUIDE-001.1-2012
22. Wang, Z.: Towards a measurement tool for verification and validation of simulation models. In: Jain, S., Creasey, R., Himmelspach, J., White, K., Fu, M. (eds.) Proceedings of the 2011 Winter Simulation Conference (2011)
23. Wang, Z.: Selecting verification and validation techniques for simulation project: a planning and tailoring strategy. In: Pasupathy, P., Kim, S.H., Tolk, A., Hill, R., Kuhl, M.E. (eds.) Proceedings of the 2013 Winter Simulation Conference (2013)
24. Wang, Z., Lehmann, A.: Verification and validation of simulation models and applications: a methodological approach. In: Ince, A.N., Bragg, A. (eds.) Recent Advances in Modeling and Simulation Tools for Communication Networks and Services, pp. 227–240. Springer, New York (2007). https://doi.org/10.1007/978-0-387-73908-3_11. Chap. 11
25. Wang, Z., Lehmann, A.: Quality assurance of models and simulation applications. Int. J. Model. Simul. Sci. Comput. 1(1), 27–45 (2010)
26. Wang, Z., Lehmann, A., Karagkasidis, A.: A multistage approach for quality- and efficiency-related tailoring of modelling and simulation processes. Simul. News Eur. 19(2), 12–20 (2009)

Numerical and Monte Carlo Simulation

Non-Local Fokker-Planck Equation of Imperfect Impulsive Interventions and its Effectively Super-Convergent Numerical Discretization

Hidekazu Yoshioka[1]([✉]) [iD], Yuta Yaegashi[2], Motoh Tsujimura[3] [iD],
and Masayuki Fujihara[2]

[1] Shimane University, Nishikawatsu-cho 1060, Matsue 690-8504, Japan
yoshih@life.shimane-u.ac.jp
[2] Kyoto University, Kitashirakawa Oiwake-cho, Kyoto 606-8502, Japan
yaegashi.yuta.54s@st.kyoto-u.ac.jp,
fujihara@kais.kyoto-u.ac.jp
[3] Doshisha University, Karasuma-Higashi-iru, Imadegawa-dori,
Kyoto 602-8580, Japan
mtsujimu@mail.doshisha.ac.jp

Abstract. Human interventions to control environmental and ecological system dynamics are efficiently described as impulsive interventions by which the system state suddenly transits. Such interventions in applications are imperfect in the sense that the state transition is not exactly controllable and thus uncertain. Mathematical description of the imperfect impulsive interventions, despite relevance in practical problems of environmental and ecological engineering, has not been addressed so far to the best of the authors' knowledge. The objectives and contributions of this research are formulation and numerical computation of single-species population dynamics controlled through imperfect impulsive interventions. We focus on a management problem of a waterfowl population as a model problem where the population dynamics follows a stochastic differential equation subject to impulsive harvesting. We show that the stationary probability density function of the population dynamics is governed by a 1-D Fokker-Planck equation with a special non-locality, which potentially becomes an obstacle in analyzing the equation. We demonstrate that the equation is analytically solvable under a simplified condition, which is validated through a Monte-Carlo simulation result. We also demonstrate that a simple finite volume scheme can approximate its solution in a stable, conservative, and super-convergent manner.

Keywords: Imperfect impulsive intervention · Non-Local Fokker-Planck Equation · Exponentially-fitted finite volume scheme

© Springer Nature Singapore Pte Ltd. 2019
G. Tan et al. (Eds.): AsiaSim 2019, CCIS 1094, pp. 79–91, 2019.
https://doi.org/10.1007/978-981-15-1078-6_7

1 Introduction

Human interventions are becoming more common in management of environmental and ecological system dynamics, such as extermination of invasive species [1] and harvesting regulation of biological resources [2]. Establishment of management policies of the system dynamics from the viewpoint of both cost-effectiveness and feasibility is an indispensable topic. To this end, we incorporate the imperfect interventions into the management problems because the human interventions do not always progress just as planned. The imperfectness is caused by uncertainties with respect to the magnitude of interventions.

The dynamics of environmental and ecological systems is described by stochastic differential equations (SDEs) [3], and management problems through human interventions to the system dynamics are described as stochastic control problems [4, 5]. Pesticide applications for exterminating natural enemies of crops [6] and harvesting of bird population as a predator of fishery resources [7, 8] are such examples. The impulse control approach provides a suitable analytical method if the intervention causes a discrete change in the system. Impulse control problems arise not only in environmental and ecological management problems but also in many other engineering research areas [9, 10]. The optimal intervention policies to control system dynamics have been mathematically studied in detail from the viewpoint of the optimality equations [9]. However, much less attentions have been paid for behavior of the controlled system dynamics.

A Fokker-Planck equation is a governing differential equation of a probability density function (PDF) of stochastic system dynamics [11]. Recently, Yaegashi et al. [12] approached this issue through derivation and analysis of a 1-D Fokker-Planck equation of the controlled single-species population dynamics, which is the governing differential equation of the PDF of the state variable. However, they assumed that human interventions are perfect and that there exists no uncertainty in the interventions, which is not consistent with the above-mentioned reality of environmental and ecological systems management. This motivates us to extend their approach to imperfect interventions, which is a topic not addressed so far to the best of the authors' knowledge.

The objectives and contributions of this research are formulation and numerical computation of single-species population dynamics controlled by imperfect impulsive interventions. A particular emphasis is put on the fish-eating waterfowl management problem [7, 8]: a serious ecological problem in many countries of Europe, America, Asia, and New Zealand. This is an engineering problem with a relatively simple dynamics following an SDE subject to impulsive harvesting [8, 12]. We show that the stationary PDF of the population is governed by a 1-D Non-Local Fokker-Planck Equation (NL-FPE) with a special non-locality, which is potentially an obstacle in its analysis and computation. We demonstrate that the NL-FPE is analytically solvable in a simplified case. The solution is physically validated through a Monte-Carlo simulation. We develop an exponentially-fitted (local exact solution-based) finite volume scheme to discretize the NL-FPE in a stable, conservative, and super-convergent manner; the last one implies second-order convergence despite the equation has an advection term.

2 Mathematical Model

2.1 Impulse Control Model

Controlled Population Dynamics. A long-term model stochastic impulse control problem for population management is reviewed [8]. The decision-maker managing the population dynamics can impulsively reduce the population through interventions, which are carried out in a much shorter timescale than that of the dynamics. The population in a habitat at time $t \geq 0$ is denoted as $X_t \geq 0$, which is right continuous with left limits as in the conventional impulse control models [10]. The population dynamics, namely temporal evolution of the process $(X_t)_{t \geq 0}$, is assumed to be governed by the Itô's SDE subject to interventions:

$$\begin{cases} dX_t = X_t(\mu dt + \sigma dB_t), & \tau_i \leq t < \tau_{i+1} \\ X_{\tau_i} = X_{\tau_{i-}} - \zeta_i \end{cases} \tag{1}$$

with the initial population $X_{0-} = x \geq 0$, where $\mu > 0$ is the deterministic growth rate, $\sigma > 0$ is a volatility with $2\mu > \sigma^2$, and B_t is the 1-D standard Brownian motion on a usual complete probability space [3]. The second line of (1) is the human interventions, where each τ_i ($i = 0, 1, 2, \cdots$, $\tau_0 = 0$) is the stopping time adapted to a natural filtration generated by the Brownian motion and represents the time at which the population is harvested, and ζ_i ($i = 0, 1, 2, \ldots$, $\zeta_0 = 0$) is the magnitude of harvesting at τ_i.

Human interventions $\eta = (\tau_i, \zeta_i)_{i=0,1,2,\ldots}$ to control the population dynamics (1), which is hereafter simply referred to as the policy, are determined so that a performance index considering both costs and benefits of the population management is minimized. The performance index $J = J(x; \eta)$ is a functional of the process $(X_t)_{t \geq 0}$ and a policy η. The performance index in this model is [7, 8]

$$J(x; \eta) = \mathrm{E}\left[\int_0^\infty e^{-\delta s}\left(-u X_s^M + d X_s^m\right) ds + \sum_{i=1}^\infty e^{-\delta \tau_i} K(\zeta_i) \right], \tag{2}$$

where E is the expectation, $\delta > 0$ is a sufficiently large discount rate as an inverse of the time-scale of the decision-making, $u > 0$, $d > 0$, $0 < M < 1$ and $m > 1$ are constants. The first term in the right-hand side of (2) is the discounted sum of the utility $(-u X_s^M)$ and disutility $(d X_s^m)$ that the population may provide during the management period. Notice that the disutility is considered to be a non-negative value because we will consider a minimization problem. As explained in Yaegashi et al. [7], this term gives a simplest lumped representation of the sum of the utility and disutility. The sum $-u X_s^M + d X_s^m$ is convex and unimodal, and thus takes a global minimum value with some positive $X_s > 0$. Its minimizer is considered as a desired state of the population to be achieved through human interventions. The second term of (2) is the discounted sum of the cost of each harvesting, where

$$K(\zeta) = k_1\zeta + k_0 \ (\zeta > 0). \tag{3}$$

Here, $k_1 > 0$ is the proportional cost and $k_0 > 0$ is the fixed cost.

Following the standard methodology for impulse control problems [13, 14], the following threshold type strategy turns out to be optimal:

(Optimal Policy)
There exists the two thresholds $\bar{x}$ and $\underline{x}$ ($0 < \underline{x} < \bar{x}$) whose values depend on values of the model parameters. At each time $t \geq 0$, if $X_{t-} < \bar{x}$, then no intervention is taken If $X_{t-} \geq \bar{x}$, then the intervention is immediately taken and X_{t-} is reduced to $\underline{x}$.

In this way, the optimal policy is characterized with the thresholds $\bar{x}$ and $\underline{x}$, and the population is confined in a compact interval $[0, \bar{x}]$ and is harvested only when the population hits the upper threshold $\bar{x}$.

Imperfect Interventions. A drawback of the above-presented model is that the human interventions are achieved exactly in the sense that paying the cost $K(\zeta)$ reduces the population by the amount of ζ. However, it is plausible to assume that such an exact intervention is not realized in practice, but there exists uncertainty between the cost and realization. Mathematically, this means that paying the cost $K(\zeta)$ reduces the population, but the effectively reduced population is $Z\zeta$ not ζ, where $Z > 0$ is a stochastic variable that is not predictable for the decision-maker. This means that the population truly reduced at τ_i is $(\bar{x} - \underline{x})Z_i$ because of the imperfectness of interventions, which equals to the perfect model only if $Z_i = 1$. In what follows, we call an optimal control with the uncertainty Z_i as an imperfect intervention.

Hereafter, for the sake of brevity of descriptions, we set the amount of reduced population at τ_i by the imperfect optimal control as $\bar{x} - Z_i$ with an abuse of notation, again it equals $\bar{x} - \underline{x}$ if $Z_i = \underline{x}$. We assume that each Z_i ($i = 0, 1, 2, \ldots$) is possibly related to $\underline{x}$, and is i.i.d. Furthermore, each Z_i is assumed to be generated by a PDF $q = q(z)$ of $z = Z$ supported on $[a, b]$ such that $0 < \bar{x} - Z_i < \bar{x}$. Figure 1 plots a sample path of the controlled process $(X_t)_{t \geq 0}$ by an imperfect intervention. Note that the impulsive intervention itself is deterministic here, and is different from the unpredictable ones that reset the process randomly [15].

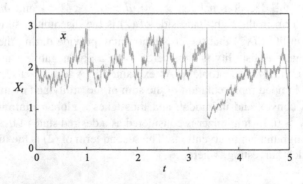

Fig. 1. A sample path of the controlled population dynamics (blue), the upper threshold $\bar{x}$ (red), and the uncertainty range $[a, b]$ (pink). (Color figure online)

2.2   Non-Local Fokker-Planck Equation

Derivation. The PDF of the controlled process $(X_t)_{t \geq 0}$ under imperfect interventions is denoted as $p(y)$ for $0 \leq y \leq \bar{x}$, where y represents the current value of the population. In general, a Fokker-Planck equation governs a PDF [11], and the equation is given as a conservative elliptic or parabolic differential equation subject to appropriate initial and/or boundary conditions. These equations are local like the conventional heat and wave equations. However, Yaegashi et al. [12] theoretically showed for the perfect impulse control model that the Fokker-Planck equation has a non-local term connecting the probability flux at $y = \bar{x}$ and that at $y = \underline{x}$, based on the physical consideration that the process is immediately and irreversibly transported $y = \bar{x}$ from to $y = \underline{x}$. In this research, we extend their approach to the model with imperfect interventions.

Now, we derive the NL-FPE based on a physical consideration. Since our focus in what follows is not the impulse control but rather the controlled population dynamics, we set $\bar{x} = 1$ without any loss of generality. Set $\Omega = [0, 1]$. The PDF p is non-negative and defined in Ω, and satisfies the conservation condition

$$\int_{\Omega} p(y) \mathrm{d}y = 1. \tag{4}$$

The flux $F = F(y)$ is assumed to belong to $C\left(\hat{\Omega}\right)$ with $\hat{\Omega} = [0, 1)$ and is defined as

$$F(y) = \mu y p - \frac{\mathrm{d}}{\mathrm{d}y}\left(\frac{\sigma^2 y^2}{2} p\right). \tag{5}$$

Set the left limit of F at $y = 1$ as

$$\bar{F} = \lim_{y \to 1-0} F(y). \tag{6}$$

As in Yaegashi et al. [12], the following boundary conditions are specified:

$$F(0) = 0 \text{ and } p(1) = 0. \tag{7}$$

The first boundary condition is the usual one meaning that the process $(X_t)_{t \geq 0}$ is non-negative and never approaches the boundary $y = 0$ if it has a positive initial condition. The second one means that the process $(X_t)_{t \geq 0}$ is immediately absorbed at the boundary $y = 1$, after that it is irreversibly transported to somewhere inside Ω according to the uncertainty Z.

What we have to find is the probabilistic relationship between the process $(X_t)_{t \geq 0}$ just before and after each intervention. From a physical consideration, the flux $\bar{F}$ is distributed in the interval $[a, b] \subset\subset \Omega$ according to the law q as

$$S(y) = \bar{F}q(y), \ a \leq y \leq b, \tag{8}$$

where $S(y)$ is the source of probability increase per unit length at y. In this way, the total distributed probability from the boundary $y = 1$ to the inside Ω is evaluated as

$$\int_a^b S(y)\mathrm{d}y = \int_a^b \bar{F}q(y)\mathrm{d}y = \bar{F} \int_a^b q(y)\mathrm{d}y = \bar{F}, \tag{9}$$

meaning that this non-local treatment of the transport of probability is conservative. Note that $\bar{F}$ is a constant and $\int_a^b q(y)\mathrm{d}y = 1$.

Considering the non-local relationship (8) combined with the standard derivation procedure for the other part of the domain, we get the complete description of the NL-FPE as a non-local two-point boundary value problem:

$$\frac{\mathrm{d}F}{\mathrm{d}y} = \chi_{[a,b]}q(y)\bar{F} \text{ inside } \Omega, \text{ subject to (4) and (7)}. \tag{10}$$

Here, $\chi_{[a,b]} = 1$ if $y \in [a, b]$ and $\chi_{[a,b]} = 0$ otherwise. This kind of non-locality through the boundary flux is not common in the conventional non-local diffusive transport problems. Our goal is to solve the NL-FPE, which is achieved exactly for a simplified case, and is carried out numerically for general cases.

The Exact Solution. For analytical tractability, we consider the uniform distribution

$$q(z) = \frac{1}{b - a} \ (a \leq z \leq b). \tag{11}$$

We briefly explain the derivation procedure of p in this case. Set $r = \mu - \sigma^2 > 0$ and $D = \sigma^2/2$. Firstly, the NL-FPE (10) is solved for $0 \leq y < a$ as

$$p(y) = C_1 y^m \tag{12}$$

with $m = r/D$ and an unknown constant C_1. Secondly, in $a \leq y \leq b$, (10) is solved as

$$p(y) = C_2 y^m - \frac{a\bar{F}}{(r+D)(b-a)}y^{-1} + \frac{\bar{F}}{r(b-a)} \tag{13}$$

with an unknown constant C_2. Thirdly, (10) is solved in $b < y < 1$ as

$$p(y) = C_3 y^m + \frac{\bar{F}}{r+D}y^{-1} \tag{14}$$

with an unknown constant C_3.

We have four unknown constants $\bar{F}$, C_1, C_2, and C_3, meaning that we have to impose four conditions to completely determine them. We explore a continuous solution p over the domain Ω. Then, we impose the three conditions

$$p(a-0) = p(a+0),\ p(b-0) = p(b+0),\ p(1) = 0, \tag{15}$$

and the remaining one is the conservation condition (4). The four conditions are independent with each other, and give a unique tetrad $(\bar{F}, C_1, C_2, C_3)$ whose representations are not presented here because of page limitations. Consequently, we get

$$p(y) = \begin{cases} C_1 y^m & (0 \leq y < a) \\ C_2 y^m - \frac{a\bar{F}}{(r+D)(b-a)} y^{-1} + \frac{\bar{F}}{r(b-a)} & (a \leq y \leq b) \\ \frac{\bar{F}}{r+D}(y^{-1} - y^m) & (b < y \leq 1) \end{cases} \tag{16}$$

and

$$F(y) = \begin{cases} 0 & (0 \leq y < a) \\ \frac{y-a}{b-a}\bar{F} & (a \leq y \leq b) \\ \bar{F} & (b < y < 1) \end{cases}. \tag{17}$$

By uniqueness of the construction method of the PDF p, we get the proposition below.

Proposition 1. *The NL-FPE* (10) *admits a unique continuous solution complying with the conservation condition* (4). *In addition, the flux F is continuous inside Ω.*

The exact solution has the regularity $C([0,1]) \cap C^2((0,a) \cup (a,b) \cup (b,1))$. Notice that the PDF of the perfect model [12] is derived from (16) under the limit $b \to a+0$, meaning that the present model considering the uncertainty is truly a generalization of the previous one. This solution is validated in the next section through a comparison with numerical solutions generated by a Monte-Carlo method and a finite volume scheme.

3 Numerical Computation

3.1 Finite Volume Scheme

Discretization. The finite volume scheme developed here is a generalization of the previous one [12]. The discretization starts from a time-dependent NL-FPE

$$\frac{\partial p}{\partial t} + \frac{\partial F}{\partial y} = \chi_{[a,b]} q(y)\bar{F} \text{ for } t > 0 \text{ and inside } \Omega, \text{ subject to (7)}, \tag{18}$$

integrated from an initial condition satisfying the conservation condition (4) and identifies the stationary PDF p with a steady solution to (18), which is numerically obtained with a sufficiently large $t > 0$ in (18).

The domain $\Omega = [0, 1]$ is divided into N cells and $N + 1$ nodes y_i as

$$0 = y_0 < y_1 < \ldots < y_L < \ldots < y_R < \ldots < y_{N-1} < y_N = 1 \tag{19}$$

so that $y_L = a$ and $y_R = b$. The nodes are located at the center of cells except at the boundaries $y = 0, 1$. For the sake of brevity, we assume the uniform discretization where the length between the nodes Δy are uniform: $\Delta y = 1/N$. The time increment for temporal integration is denoted as Δt. The PDF p approximated at the node i and the time step n is denoted as p_i^n. For the sake of brevity, set $y_{-1} = 0$.

The semi-discretized (18) in the cell i ($1 \leq i \leq N - 1$) is denoted as

$$\frac{dp_i}{dt} = -\frac{1}{\Delta x} \left(F_{i+\frac{1}{2}} - F_{i-\frac{1}{2}} \right) + S_i, \tag{20}$$

where S_i corresponds to the discretized S of (9) that is non-negative for $L \leq i \leq R$ and equals 0 otherwise. Each term of (20) is discretized as follows.

Following the fitting technique that evaluates a numerical flux from exact solutions to auxiliary two-point boundary value problems [12, 16], the numerical flux $F_{i+\frac{1}{2}}$ is evaluated through exponential functions as

$$F_{i+\frac{1}{2}} = -\frac{e^{\text{Pe}}}{1 - e^{\text{Pe}}} V_{i+\frac{1}{2}} p_i + \frac{1}{1 - e^{\text{Pe}}} V_{i+\frac{1}{2}} p_{i+1} = \alpha_i p_i + \beta_i p_{i+1} \tag{21}$$

with

$$\text{Pe} = \varepsilon_{i+\frac{1}{2}}^{-1} V_{i+\frac{1}{2}} \Delta y, \ V_{i+\frac{1}{2}} = \left(\mu - \sigma^2 \right) \left(\frac{y_i + y_{i+1}}{2} \right), \ \varepsilon_{i+\frac{1}{2}} = D \left(\frac{y_i + y_{i+1}}{2} \right)^2. \tag{22}$$

The source S_i is constructed so that the discretized system is conservative. Set $K = R - L$ and discretize the domain $[a, b]$ of q as

$$a = z_0 < z_1 < \ldots < z_{K-1} < z_K = b. \tag{23}$$

Set $z_{j+1/2} = (z_j + z_{j+1})/2$ and

$$Q_0 = \int_{z_0}^{z_{1/2}} q(z) dz, \ Q_j = \int_{z_{j-1/2}}^{z_{j+1/2}} q(z) dz \ (1 \leq j \leq K - 1), \ Q_K = \int_{z_{K-1/2}}^{z_K} q(z) dz. \tag{24}$$

which are exactly or numerically evaluated so that

$$\sum_{j=0}^{K} Q_j = 1. \tag{25}$$

Then, S_i is evaluated as

$$S_{j+L} = F_{N-\frac{1}{2}} Q_j \quad (0 \le j \le K). \tag{26}$$

Substituting (21) and (26) into (20) with an application of a fully-explicit discretization to the right-hand side yields

$$\frac{p_i^{n+1} - p_i^n}{\Delta t} = -\frac{1}{\Delta y}\left(\alpha_i p_i^n + \beta_i p_{i+1}^n - (\alpha_{i-1} p_{i-1}^n + \beta_{i-1} p_i^n)\right) + S_i^n. \tag{27}$$

Boundary conditions have to be specified to complete the discretization. At the boundary $y = 0$ ($i = 0$), we solve

$$\frac{p_0^{n+1} - p_0^n}{\Delta t} = -\frac{2}{\Delta y}\left(\alpha_0 p_0^n + \beta_0 p_1^n\right), \tag{28}$$

which is (27) with the boundary condition $F_{-\frac{1}{2}} = 0$. At the boundary $y = 1$ ($i = N$),

$$p_N^n = 0 \tag{29}$$

is directly specified. The system of linear equations containing (27), (28), and (29) is temporally evolved until the convergence condition

$$\max_i |p_i^{n+1} - p_i^n| < \omega \tag{30}$$

is satisfied for some $n \ge 1$, where $\omega = 10^{-12}$ in this paper. Then, p_i^{n+1} ($0 \le i \le N$) is taken as a numerical approximation to the NL-FPE (10).

Mathematical Properties. The present finite volume scheme has the several important mathematical properties. Firstly, the scheme is conservative in a discrete sense. Namely, if the initial condition satisfies

$$\Delta y\left(\frac{1}{2}\left(p_0^0 + p_N^0\right) + \sum_{i=1}^{N-1} p_i^0\right) = 1, \tag{31}$$

then

$$\Delta y\left(\frac{1}{2}\left(p_0^n + p_N^n\right) + \sum_{i=1}^{N-1} p_i^n\right) = 1 \quad (n \ge 1) \tag{32}$$

implying that numerical solutions are discrete analogue of the PDF. In addition, non-negativity of the numerical solution is satisfied for sufficiently small Δt [12], meaning that the scheme is stable. This stability is owing to the flux discretization (21). The scheme is simple and easy to implement, and furthermore conservative and stable as reviewed above. A drawback is that it may have at most first-order to second-order accurate, namely the error would decrease only linearly with respect to Δy in the worst case. This drawback can be efficiently mitigated through the modern dual-meshing technique [17], which is currently undergoing by the authors. Notice that uniqueness of numerical solutions at each computation is clearly guaranteed because of using a fully-explicit time discretization. An implicit discretization of our NL-FPE is also possible, but may be computationally inefficient because the coefficient matrix is dense.

3.2 Numerical Tests

The exact solution with a uniform distribution (11) is compared with numerical solutions generated with a standard Monte-Carlo method and the finite volume scheme. The Monte-Carlo method is based on a standard Euler-Maruyama discretization of the SDE(1) with the random numbers generated with Mersenne twisters. The total number of the sample points is 8×10^8 and the time increment for discretization of the SDE is 0.0001. Unless otherwise specified, the computational resolution of the finite volume scheme is set as $\Delta y = 1/600$ and $\Delta t = 0.00005$ with $N = 600$, $L = N/3$ ($a = 1/3$), and $R = 2N/3$ ($b = 2/3$). Considering the waterfowl management problem [7], the model parameters of the SDE are set as $\mu = 0.17$ (1/year) and $\sigma = 0.20$ (1/year$^{1/2}$). These computational conditions are used unless otherwise specified. The initial condition is a delta distribution concentrated at y_{50}.

Figure 2 demonstrates that the exact solution (16) and the two computational results agree well with each other, suggesting physical validity of the exact solution as a reasonable solution to the NL-FPE (10) and reasonable accuracy of the finite volume scheme. The convergence rate between the exact solution and numerical solutions with the scheme is then evaluated for different values of Δy. A four times finer temporal resolution was used for $N = 1,200$ to maintain numerical stability. The computational results of the error are summarized in Table 1, suggesting second-order convergence of the scheme despite the scheme is linear and the NL-FPE (10) has an advection term that often provides a source of first-order error. The second-order convergence is checked from the quadratic decrease of the maximum nodal errors. This kind of attractive convergence property is called super-convergence [17], and the present scheme is thus super-convergent. The largest deviations between the exact and numerical solutions occur near the points $y = a, b$ where the regularity of p decreases.

Finally, the scheme is applied to an advanced problem with $q(z) = (b - a)p((z - a)/(b - a))$, which leads to a nonlinear NL-FPE where the PDF p modulates the uncertainty itself. This problem can be considered as the simplest model problem of a feed-back learning of the uncertainty. Theoretically, more realistic nonlinearity would be possible, but they will be addressed in our future work and the present numerical computation serves as its starting point. Figure 3 shows the numerical solutions to the previous uniform q and that with the present p-dependent one, demonstrating that the PDF of the latter clearly has a more concentrated profile. The conservation property (32) is correctly satisfied in this case despite its non-linearity and non-locality. Notice that this is a non-linear case that Monte-Carlo methods potentially become less efficient.

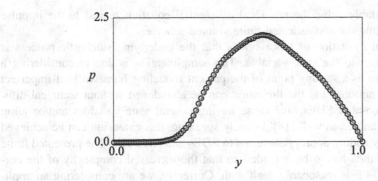

Fig. 2. Comparison of the exact solution (red line), a numerical solution generated by the Monte-Carlo method (black circles), and a numerical solution by the finite volume scheme (blue line). (Color figure online)

Table 1. The maximum nodal error of the finite volume scheme.

N	Error
75	3.584 E−03
150	8.988 E−04
300	2.249 E−04
600	5.623 E−05
1,200	1.408 E−05

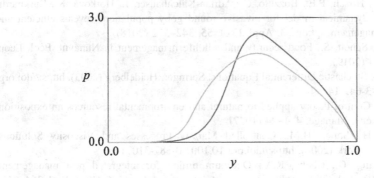

Fig. 3. Numerical solutions with the linear (red) and non-linear problems (blue). (Color figure online)

4 Conclusions

The NL-FPE was derived for the first time and its analytical solution was found under a simplified condition. An explicit exponentially-fitted finite volume scheme was then presented to discretize the NL-FPE in a stable and conservative manner. The scheme successfully generated numerical solutions converging super-linearly toward the exact solution, demonstrating its satisfactory computational performance. Overall, we could efficiently and stably solve the non-local differential equation related to the impulse control by utilizing the sophisticated finite volume scheme.

A theoretical limitation of this work is that the underlying stochastic process is linear with respect to the state variable. This simplification is due to considering a tractable problem as a starting point of the present modeling framework of imperfect impulsive interventions, and the limitation can be abandoned without technical difficulties. More complex SDEs, like those having several state variables and/or jump noises, can be handled as well [18]. Loosely speaking, this extension can be achieved through formally adding appropriate terms to SDEs and NL-FPEs. The presented finite volume scheme then has to be extended so that the increased complexity of the corresponding NL-FPE is reasonably dealt with. Currently, we are considering an application of the present mathematical framework to ecosystem management involving the population of waterfowl and small migratory fish as its prey. This non-linear and multi-dimensional problem is theoretically of interest as well as practically of importance in fisheries resource management [19]. Deeper mathematical analysis of NL-FPEs, such as their solvability and regularity, is also currently undergoing.

Acknowledgements. JSPS KAKENHI 17J09125, 18K01714, and 19H03073 support this research. The first author engaged this research as a member of Fisheries Ecosystem Project Center of Shimane University.

References

1. N'Guyen, A., Hirsch, P.E., Bozzuto, C., Adrian-Kalchhauser, I., Hôrková, K., Burkhardt-Holm, P.: A dynamical model for invasive round goby populations reveals efficient and effective management options. J. Appl. Ecol. **55**, 342–352 (2018)
2. Lysenko, D., Schott, S.: Food security and wildlife management in Nunavut. Ecol. Econ. **156**, 360–374 (2019)
3. Øksendal, B.: Stochastic Differential Equations. Springer, Heidelberg (2003). https://doi.org/10.1007/978-3-642-14394-6
4. Smith, V.L.: Control theory applied to natural and environmental resources an exposition. J. Environ. Econ. Manage. **4**, 1–24 (1977)
5. Fleming, W.H., Soner, H.M.: Controlled Markov Processes and Viscosity Solutions. Springer, New York (2006). https://doi.org/10.1007/0-387-31071-1
6. Tang, S., Tang, G., Cheke, R.A.: Optimum timing for integrated pest management: modelling rates of pesticide application and natural enemy releases. J. Theor. Biol. **264**, 623–638 (2010)
7. Yaegashi, Y., Yoshioka, H., Unami, K., Fujihara, M.: A singular stochastic control model for sustainable population management of the fish-eating waterfowl *Phalacrocorax carbo*. J. Environ. Manage. **219**, 18–27 (2018)
8. Yaegashi, Y., Yoshioka, H., Unami, K., Fujihara, M.: A stochastic impulse control model for population management of fish-eating bird *Phalacrocorax Carbo* and its numerical computation. In: Li, L., Hasegawa, K., Tanaka, S. (eds.) AsiaSim 2018. CCIS, vol. 946, pp. 425–438. Springer, Singapore (2018). https://doi.org/10.1007/978-981-13-2853-4_33

9. da Costa Moraes, M.B., Nagano, M.S., Sobreiro, V.A.: Stochastic cash flow management models: A literature review since the 1980s. In: Guarnieri, P. (ed.) Decision Models in Engineering and Management: Decision Engineering, pp. 11–28. Springer, Cham (2015). https://doi.org/10.1007/978-3-319-11949-6_2

10. Øksendal, B., Sulem, A.: Applied Stochastic Control of Jump Diffusions. Springer, Cham (2019). https://doi.org/10.1007/978-3-030-02781-0

11. Risken, H.: The Fokker-Planck Equation. Springer, Heidelberg (1996). https://doi.org/10.1007/978-3-642-61544-3

12. Yaegashi, Y., Yoshioka, H., Tsugihashi, K., Fujihara, M.: Analysis and computation of probability density functions for a 1-D impulsively controlled diffusion process. C.R. Math. **357**, 306–315 (2019)

13. Cadenillas, A.: Optimal central bank intervention in the foreign exchange market. J. Econ. Theor. **87**, 218–242 (1999)

14. Ohnishi, M., Tsujimura, M.: An impulse control of a geometric Brownian motion with quadratic costs. Eur. J. Oper. Res. **168**, 311–321 (2006)

15. Evans, M.R., Majumdar, S.N.: Diffusion with optimal resetting. J. Phys. A: Math. Theor. **44** (43), Paper No. 435001 (2011)

16. Yoshioka, H., Unami, K.: A cell-vertex finite volume scheme for solute transport equations in open channel networks. Prob. Eng. Mech. **31**, 30–38 (2012)

17. Angermann, L., Wang, S.: A super-convergent unsymmetric finite volume method for convection-diffusion equations. J. Comput. Appl. Math. **358**, 179–189 (2019)

18. Dang, D.M., Forsyth, P.A.: Better than pre-commitment mean-variance portfolio allocation strategies: a semi-self-financing Hamilton–Jacobi–Bellman equation approach. Eur. J. Oper. Res. **250**, 827–841 (2016)

19. Yoshioka, H., Yaegashi, Y.: Mathematical analysis for management of released fish. Optim. Control Appl. Method. **39**(2), 1141–1146 (2018)

Force Tracking Control of Nonlinear Active Suspension System with Hydraulic Actuator Dynamic

Erliana Samsuria$^{(\boxtimes)}$, Yahaya M. Sam, and Fazilah Hassan

Control and Mechatronic Engineering, School of Electrical Engineering,
Faculty of Engineering, Universiti Teknologi Malaysia, UTM Skudai,
Skudai 81310, Malaysia
erlianasha22@gmail.com

Abstract. This paper delivers findings on optimal control studies of two degree of freedom quarter car model. Nonlinear active suspension quarter car model is used which considering the strong nonlinearities of hydraulic actuator. The investigation on the benefit of using Sliding Mode Control as force tracking controller with the utilization of Particle Swarm Optimization is done in this paper. The controller is designed to improved trade-off performance between ride comfort and road handling ability. Comparison between proposed controller with PID control and conventional suspension system showed that performance of the proposed controller is significantly improved. Results illustrated via simulation runs using MATLAB.

Keywords: Active suspension system · Hydraulic actuator · Sliding mode control

1 Introduction

The suspension system provides a control towards the vehicles itself for having a good road handling and ride comfort in case facing an external disturbances and road irregularities while driving. Nowadays, most local automotive industry mostly implies conventional suspension system's design that usually having an issue with load carrying, passenger comfort and road handling [1]. It is difficult for traditional suspension system to achieve the trade-off between ride comfort and direction control of the vehicle. There are three main types of suspension that has been used/studied in vehicle systems, passive, semi-active and active suspension. Current automobile suspension system implies passive components also known as conventional suspension system that provide a non-controllable spring and damping coefficients with a fixed parameter. However, the trade-off between ride comfort, handling quality and load varying are difficult to achieve since the parameters are fixed. The difference for semi active suspension systems is the coefficient of dampers can be controlled [2]. In contrast to passive and semi-active, an active suspension system able to enhance energy externally by the use of force actuator to provide a closed loop response for the system rather than dissipates the energy by the use of springs in passive. Many researchers nowadays are

© Springer Nature Singapore Pte Ltd. 2019
G. Tan et al. (Eds.): AsiaSim 2019, CCIS 1094, pp. 92–102, 2019.
https://doi.org/10.1007/978-981-15-1078-6_8

interested in developed suspension with active control automobile systems. Previous works of automobile system focusing on linear model of active suspension are adopted to propose various control strategy for different components to be controlled [1–7]. The proposed controller in the mentioned references have greatly improved the suspension performance however the dynamical effect of the system's behaviors are being ignored. In fact, it is well known that the actuator behaves far from ideal in real life. The scopes for this paper is narrowed to hydraulic actuators for active suspension system model where the real implementation with its dynamic could easily be controlled to track a desired force with adequate techniques [8–13].

In this paper, the dynamic of an electro-hydraulic actuator is included in the design of non-linear active quarter car suspension system. The proposed control approach is designed based on sliding mode control algorithm to track the desired force trajectory generated by the skyhook damping dynamics. It has been proven that tuning the controlled parameters manually is a challenging task. Therefore, this paper proposed to utilized a particle swarm optimization (PSO) algorithm as tuning method in obtaining controllable gain and switching surface values that can minimise the effect of mismatched uncertainties.

2 Methodology

2.1 Non-linear Quarter Car Model

The car model studied in this paper comprises of one-fourth of the entire body with two degree of freedom, as illustrated in Fig. 1, The interconnection set-up using stiffness spring k_s, damper or shock absorber b_s, and a variable active force actuator F element which positioned between the sprung m_s and unsprung masses m_{us}.

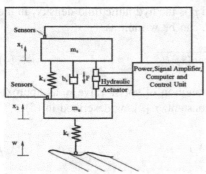
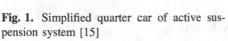
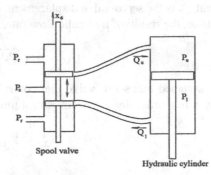

Fig. 1. Simplified quarter car of active suspension system [15]

Fig. 2. Schematic diagram of electro-hydraulic actuator

A state variable of x_1, x_2, and w represents the vertical displacement of car body (chassis), vertical displacement of wheel and road input disturbances, respectively. By applying a Newton's second law of motion, the governing equations that indicate nonlinear nature of the system model are derived as follows;

$$m_s \ddot{x}_1 = -F_s - F_b + F \tag{1}$$

$$m_u \ddot{x}_2 = F_s + F_b - F_w - F \tag{2}$$

Where F_s and F_b are spring and damping forces acting on the suspension respectively. The suspension components contain three different elements which are linear, symmetric and nonlinear as function of both suspension travel and velocity in each of applied forces [14]. Meanwhile, F_w is the force produced by road input disturbances and F is the generated force by actuator.

From Fig. 2, clearly showed the piston of the actuator is controlled by means of the voltage/current input to the electro-hydraulic servo valves in a three lane four-ways critical spool valve system [15, 16]. The hydraulic actuator force is produced through the high-pressure differences occur in the piston due to the movement of spool valve (P_L) multiplied with the cross-sectional area (A) of piston itself. The governing equations for the electro-hydraulic actuator can be structured into a simple form as modelled in [8, 14–16], where the derivatives of the load pressure is given by

$$\dot{P}_L = \alpha Q_L - \beta P_L - \alpha A \left(\dot{x}_1 - \dot{x}_2 \right) \tag{3}$$

By upon substitution of α, β, γ, which expressed as,

$$\alpha = \frac{4\beta_e}{V_t}; \quad \beta = \alpha C_{tm}; \quad \gamma = \alpha C_d w \sqrt{\frac{1}{\rho}}$$

where V_t is total volume of actuator, β_e is the effective bulb modulus, C_{tm} is the total leakage coefficient of piston, C_d is the discharge coefficient, w is the spool valve area gradient, x_v is the servo-valve displacement, and ρ is the hydraulic fluid density. In the meantime, the resulting hydraulic flow rate, QL can be written as,

$$Q_L = \gamma x_v \sqrt{P_s - sgn(x_v)P_L} \tag{4}$$

Then, assumed that servo valve that controls a motion of spool valve, x_v as approximately a first-order linear system with a time constant, τ [9], as described in (5),

$$\dot{x}_v = \frac{1}{\tau}(u - x_v) \tag{5}$$

2.2 Suspension System with Hydraulic Actuator

The dynamics of the system with hydraulic actuator can be further re-arranged into a state space form. The state variables are defined as follows;

$$\dot{x}_1 = x_1 - x_2 = x_2 - x_4; \quad \dot{x}_2 = \ddot{x}_1; \quad \dot{x}_3 = \dot{x}_2 - \dot{w}; \quad \dot{x}_4 = \ddot{x}_2; \quad \dot{x}_5 = \dot{P}_L; \quad \dot{x}_6 = \dot{x}_v$$

The dynamics equation of motion for a nonlinear quarter car model can be obtained as;

$$\dot{x}_1 = x_2 - x_4$$

$$\dot{x}_2 = -\frac{1}{m_s}\left[\begin{array}{l} k_{sl}(x_1 - x_2) + k_{snl}(x_1 - x_2)^3 + b_{sl}\left(\dot{x}_1 - \dot{x}_2\right) - b_{ssym}\left(\dot{x}_1 - \dot{x}_2\right)^2 \\ + b_{snl}\sqrt{\left(\dot{x}_1 - \dot{x}_2\right)}sgn\left(\dot{x}_1 - \dot{x}_2\right) + Ax_5 \end{array}\right]$$

$$\dot{x}_3 = x_2 - \dot{w}$$

$$\dot{x}_4 = \frac{1}{m_u}\left[\begin{array}{l} k_{sl}(x_1 - x_2) + k_{snl}(x_1 - x_2)^3 + b_{sl}\left(\dot{x}_1 - \dot{x}_2\right) - b_{ssym}\left(\dot{x}_1 - \dot{x}_2\right)^2 \\ + b_{snl}\sqrt{\left(\dot{x}_1 - \dot{x}_2\right)}sgn\left(\dot{x}_1 - \dot{x}_2\right) - K_t(x_2 - w) - Ax_5 \end{array}\right]$$

$$\dot{x}_5 = -\beta x_5 - \alpha A\left(\dot{x}_1 - \dot{x}_2\right) + \gamma x_6 \sqrt{P_s - sgn(x_6)x_5}$$

$$\dot{x}_6 = \frac{1}{\tau}(u - x_6) \qquad (6)$$

The values of parameters system applied for the simulation in this nonlinear quarter car model can be referred to the previous literature research in [17], as defined in Appendix.

2.3 Controller Design

a. Feedback Linearization

This process basically involves dynamic inversion by means to invert the dynamic of an original systems. In general, a linearization for Input-Output such as SISO class can be defined in the form below,

$$\dot{x} = f(x) + g(x) \qquad (7)$$

$$y = x(t) \qquad (8)$$

which the detail works can be seen in [18]. The linearization of the system is done where the relative degree of the system become one that same goes to the order of the system, and the control input, u will be produced by taking one time differentiation on the output [8]. The linearizing feedback control can illustrate as,

$$u = \frac{1}{g(x)}(-f(x) + v) \tag{9}$$

Therefore, $\dot{x}$ in Eq. (7) now is,

$$\dot{x} = v \tag{10}$$

where v can be designed with any method that gives to a good tracking performance for the actuator output forces to be supplied to the system.

b. Sliding Mode Control

In the early 50's, sliding mode control (SMC) with variable structure control (VSC) was proposed by [19, 20] in the Soviet Union, Russia. Until now, sliding control approaches are applied in a wide variety of engineering system by considering an actuator dynamic as in related previous works [21–24]. Here, the design of sliding control Can be separated in two stages. First to determine the necessary spool valve position in order to generate the force desired by actuator. Second, to generate the control input, u to the servo valve in order to obtain the desired spool valve position. In addition, the particle swarm optimisation (PSO) algorithm also will be used to provide the best values of proportional gain k in a way to meet a necessary sliding condition, as given in [9].

To begin with, sliding surfaces is defined as an error between the state variable and the desired value needs for the system. Based on the linearizing feedback control in Eq. (9), a special case of this controller yields as below,

$$v = -k_i s_i + \dot{x}_{desired} \tag{11}$$

The pressure generated in the dynamic system by electro-hydraulic can classify in the linearized form as in Eq. (7),

$$\dot{x}_5 = -\beta x_5 - \alpha A\left(\dot{x}_1 - \dot{x}_2\right) + \gamma x_6 \sqrt{P_s - sgn(x_6)x_5} \quad \text{with}$$

$$f(x) = -\beta x_5 - \alpha A\left(\dot{x}_1 - \dot{x}_2\right) \quad \text{and} \quad g(x) = \gamma x_6 \sqrt{P_s - sgn(x_6)x_5}$$

Thus, the necessary spool valve position that will guarantee the actual output force by actuator to approach the desired force can be given as,

$$x_{6desired} = \frac{1}{\gamma\sqrt{P_s - sgn(x_6)x_5}}\left(\beta x_5 + \alpha A\left(\dot{x}_1 - \dot{x}_2\right) - k_1 s_1 + \dot{x}_{5desired}\right) \tag{12}$$

The desired actuator force which generated by the skyhook damping dynamics [9], can be obtained as,

$$x_{5desired} = \frac{-Cx_2}{A} \tag{13}$$

Next, the second stage of sliding control is to induced the control input, u to the servo valve in a way to obtain the needed spool valve position (X_{6d}). After satisfying the same sliding condition through a proper chosen the gain k_2 by PSO algorithm, the control input of the second sliding surfaces can be obtained as follows,

$$u = x_6 + \tau \dot{x_6} = x_6 + \tau \left(\dot{x_{6d}} - k_2 s_2 \right) = (1 - \tau k_2)x_6 + \tau k_2 x_{6d} + \tau \dot{x_{6d}} \tag{14}$$

3 Simulation Results

The simulation design of the nonlinear active suspension systems is carried out using MATLAB and Simulink. For the assessment of the controller response, a double bump road input profile was implemented in this system as a road disturbance, referred from previous research [5]. The characteristic equation of the road input is described as

$$r(t) = \begin{cases} \frac{a}{2}(-\cos 8\pi t) & \text{if } 0.50 \leq t \geq 0.75 \text{ and } 3.00 \leq t \geq 3.25 \\ 0 & \text{Otherwise} \end{cases} \tag{15}$$

where a is the amplitude of bump input. In detailed, amplitude of first and second bump were equally set to 0.11 m and 0.5 m respectively as illustrated in Fig. 3.

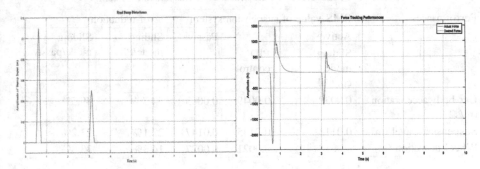

Fig. 3. Double bump road input   **Fig. 4.** Performance of force tracking of actuator

The implementation of PSO fed to the algorithm in sliding control includes the number of particles in each population that is 30, the maximum number of iterations is 15, and the dimension of problems is 2. Integral Absolute Error (IAE) was utilised as an objective function that used to calculate the minimum error produced in searching the best values. The car body acceleration (sprung mass) was considered as the fitness function, described as

$$J = \int_0^T |\ddot{X}_s| d(t) \tag{16}$$

In order to meet the satisfying sliding trajectory, the optimal values of proportional gain, k_1 and k_2 obtained from particle swarm activity at the end of searching process up to its maximum iterations are 1 and 12.9930 respectively.

In the simulation, Proportional Integral Derivative (PID) control is utilised as comparative method to evaluate the performances of proposed controller that has been presented in this paper for nonlinear active suspension system in terms of vertical car body acceleration, suspension travel, and wheel deflection. The transient response for both active suspension controls and passive system are determined in time domain analysis under double bump input road profile. It is important to check is the controllability of the force tracking controller [16]. The force tracking error of the hydraulic actuator model is measured using sliding control for the particular road profile as function of target force is shown in Fig. 4 which shows that the output force generated by electro-hydraulic actuator able to track the desired force well.

The results of comparative performances of active suspension systems over passive regarding the root mean square (RMS) values are given in Table 1. From this. the overall result is significantly improved as compared to PID control technique. In addition, the proposed method has simpler controller design where it only requires one control loop to achive the trade-off performances despite of using two control loops in the PID controller design.

Table 1. RMS values of Performances of Suspension System

Performances	RMS value of suspension system			% of reduction	
	Active		Passive	Sliding mode/PID	Sliding mode/passive
	Sliding mode control	PID control			
Car body acceleration (m/s2)	0.0032	0.0049	0.0063	34.7%	49.5%
Suspension travel (m)	0.0113	0.0145	0.0147	22.1%	23.2%
Wheel deflection (m)	0.0018	0.0021	0.0027	14.3%	33.3%

Figure 5 described a vertical car body acceleration of active and passive suspension system. It clearly shown that the vibration of the vertical acceleration can be effectively track reference system as well as suppressed by the proposed sliding mode control. The RMS value of car body acceleration are strictly related to the ride passenger comfort by means to specify the amount of acceleration transferred to the car body. It shows as much as 34.7% of percentage reduction in sliding control compared to PID control for active suspension which means the proposed method was successfully minimised in terms of less noticeable effect on vibration felt by passenger that guarantee the stability of vertical motion of car body.

The suspension travel for both active and passive suspension system are also analysed as shown in Fig. 6, clearly demonstrates that the suspension travel will travel between ±8 cm range. The performance of active suspension with sliding mode control has improved the rattle-space dynamics from passive suspension system by 23.2% and PID control by 22.1% of percentage reduction, which extent improved the passenger ride comfort.

For road handling ability, considering tire or wheel deflection that determines how well the car wheel make a contact with road surfaces in which in this case the output signals produced closed to zero. Figure 7 prove that sliding mode control has better contact between the tire to road surface with the improvement of 14.3% and 33.3% reduction over the PID control and passive system, respectively as shown in Table 1. The reduction in vibration of wheel deflection in proposed active suspension had ensured a good road handling ability.

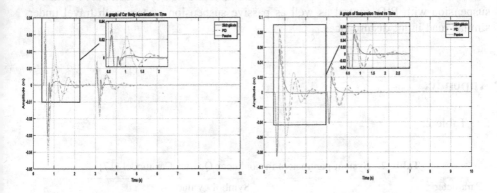

Fig. 5. Car body Acceleration   **Fig. 6.** Suspension Travel

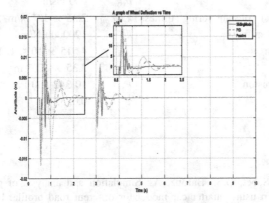

Fig. 7. Wheel Deflection

4 Conclusion

In this work, the approach control technique for non-linear active suspension system with electro-hydraulic actuator dynamic consideration using sliding control through an optimally controlled Sky-hook as reference model was presented. PSO algorithm is adopted to serve an optimal value of switching gain in sliding control for a smooth version of tracking performance. The control system focused on tracking the desired force of nonlinear system which the major nonlinearity was caused by an actuator dynamic and some with nonlinear spring stiffness and damping coefficient in the quarter car model itself. This adaptation to obtain the real effects and results of model used in practical manners. In overall, the performances of the proposed sliding mode control method for active suspension system in terms of vertical car body acceleration, suspension travel and wheel deflection offering a good improvement in ride passenger comfort with a minimum rattle-space and road handling ability as compared to active suspension with PID control as well as passive suspension system with travel under similar road input disturbances.

Appendix

See Table 2.

Table 2. System parameters in nonlinear Quarter Car model [17]

Parameter	Symbol	Value
Sprung mass	m_s	290 kg
Unsprung mass	m_u	40 kg
Linear and non-linear damping coefficient	b_{sl}, b_{snl}	980 Ns/m, 400 Ns/m
Damping symmetry	b_{ssym}	400 Ns/m
Linear and non-linear constant spring stiffness	k_{sl}, k_{snl}	2.35×10^4 N/m, 2.35×10^6 N/m
Constant tire spring stiffness	k_t	1900000 N/m
Actuator parameters	α, β, γ	4.515×10^{13}, 1, 1.545×10^9
Area of piston	A	3.35×10^{-4} m^2
Pressure supply to piston	P_s	10 342 500 Pa
Time constant	τ	0.0333 s

References

1. Agharkakli, A., Sabet, G.S., Barouz, A.: Simulation and analysis of passive and active suspension system using quarter car model for different road profile. Int. J. Eng. Trends Technol. 3(5), 636–644 (2012)
2. Kuber, C.: Modelling simulation and control of an active suspension system. J. Impact Factor Int. J. Mech. Eng. Technol. 5(11), 66–75 (2014)

3. Akbari, E., Farsadi, M.: Observer design for active suspension system using sliding mode control. In: 2010 IEEE SCOReD, pp. 13–14 (2010)
4. Wen, S., Chen, M.Z.Q., Zeng, Z., Yu, X., Huang, T.: Fuzzy control for uncertain vehicle active suspension systems via dynamic sliding-mode approach. IEEE Trans. Syst. Man Cybern. Syst. **47**(1), 24–32 (2017)
5. Sam, Y., Osman, J.H.S., Ghani, M.R.Abd.: Sliding mode control of active suspension system. J. Teknol. **37**(1), 1–10 (2002)
6. Ismail, M.F., Peng, K., Hamzah, N., Sam, Y.M., Aripin, M.K., Che Hasan, M.H.: A linear model of quarter car active suspension system using composite nonlinear feedback control. In: 2012 IEEE Student Conference on Research and Development (SCOReD), pp. 98–103 (2012)
7. Das, M.: Designing optimal controller for linear multi-input multi-output uncertain systems via second order sliding mode. Int. J. Electr. Electron. Comput. Syst. **7**(3), 290–298 (2018)
8. Alleyne, A., Hedrick, J.K.: Nonlinear adaptive control of active suspensions. IEEE Trans. Control Syst. Technol. **3**(1), 94–101 (1995)
9. Alleyne, A., Neuhaus, P.D., Hedrick, J.K.: Application of nonlinear control theory to electronically controlled suspensions. Veh. Syst. Dyn. **22**(5–6), 309–320 (1993)
10. Chen, P., Huang, A.: Adaptive sliding control of active suspension systems with uncertain hydraulic actuator dynamics. Veh. Syst. Dyn. **44**(5), 357–368 (2006)
11. Sam, Y.M., Hudha, K.: Modelling and force tracking control of hydraulic actuator for an active suspension system. In: 2006 1ST IEEE Conference on Industrial Electronics and Applications, pp. 1–6 (2006)
12. Hashemipour, H., Model, A.N.: Nonlinear optimal control of vehicle active suspension considering actuator dynamics. Int. J. Mach. Learn. Comput. **2**(4), 355–359 (2012)
13. Li, X., Zhu, Z.-C., Rui, G.-C., Cheng, D., Shen, G., Tang, Y.: Force loading tracking control of an electro-hydraulic actuator based on a nonlinear adaptive fuzzy backstepping control scheme. Symmetry (Basel) **10**, 155 (2018)
14. Pedro, J.O., Dangor, M., Dahunsi, O.A., Ali, M.M.: Intelligent feedback linearization control of nonlinear electrohydraulic suspension systems using particle swarm optimization. Appl. Soft Comput. J. **24**, 50–62 (2014)
15. Dahunsi, A.: Neural network-based model predictive control of a servo-hydraulic vehicle suspension system. In: IEEE AFRICON, pp. 5–10, September 2009
16. Shafie, A.A.: Active vehicle suspension control using electro hydraulic actuator on rough road terrain. J. Adv. Res. Appl. Mech. **9**(1), 15–30 (2015)
17. Ghazali, R., Paharudin, M., Sam, Y.: Intelligent controller design for a nonlinear quarter car active suspension with electro-hydraulic actuator. J. Eng. Sci. Technol. **12**, 39–51 (2017)
18. Gholamreza Vossoughi, M., Donath, M.: Dynamic feedback linearization for electrohy-draulically actuated control systems. J. Dyn. Syst. Meas. Control **117**, 468–477 (1995)
19. Lin, J., Wang, X.: Advanced Sliding Mode Control for Mechanical Systems: Design, Analysis and MATLAB Simulation, 1st edn. Springer, Heidelberg (2011). https://doi.org/10.1007/978-3-642-20907-9
20. Hung, J.Y., Gao, W., Hung, J.C.: Variable structure control: a survey. IEEE Trans. Ind. Electron. **40**(1), 2–22 (1993)
21. Chamseddine, A., Raharijaona, T., Noura, H.: Sliding mode control applied to active suspension using nonlinear full vehicle and actuator dynamics. In: Proceedings of the 45th IEEE Conference on Decision and Control Manchester Grand Hyatt Hotel, pp. 3597–3602 (2006)

22. Xiao, L., Zhu, Y.: Sliding-mode output feedback control for active suspension with nonlinear actuator dynamics. J. Vib. Control **21**(14), 2721–2738 (2015)

23. Bai, R., Guo, D.: Sliding-mode control of the active suspension system with the dynamics of a hydraulic actuator. Complexity **2018**, 6 pages (2018). Article ID 5907208

24. Sam, Y.M., Suaib, N.M.: Modeling and control of active suspension. J. Mek. **26**, 119–128 (2008)

Interval Estimation of Range of Motion after Total Hip Arthroplasty Applying Monte-Carlo Simulation

Gisun Jung[1], Young Kim[1], Jongyou Choi[1], Younghan Song[1],
Sunwoo Jang[1], Yun Bae Kim[1(✉)], and Jinsoo Park[2]

[1] Sungkyunkwan University, 2066 Seobu-ro, Jangan-gu, Suwon, South Korea
kimyb@skku.edu
[2] Yongin University, 134, Yongindaehak-ro, Cheoin-gu, Yongin, South Korea

Abstract. Total Hip Arthroplasty (THA) is a reconstructive surgery to treat the hip diseases in the field of orthopedics. Quality of total THA is usually evaluated by the range of motion (ROM) a patient can achieve after the transplant. If the required ROM for activities of daily livings is not obtained, dislocation problem should come up to the patient. Before operating the surgery to replace the joint to implant, it is difficult to estimate the ROM of joints of human. In this paper, we propose an interval estimation method of ROM after THA by using Monte-Carlo simulation to reflect uncertainty of surgical operation. Some experiment with a real implant is conducted. Through experiments, the performance of proposed method is fine. Especially, the almost estimated interval covers the measured (actual) value of ROMs.

Keywords: Total Hip Arthroplasty · Range of motion · Monte-Carlo · Interval estimation

1 Introduction

Total Hip Arthroplasty (THA) is a reconstructive surgery to treat the hip diseases which did not respond adequately to conventional medical therapy in the field of orthopedics (Siopack and Jergesen 1995). Related studies such as Rajaee et al. (2018) explain that revision rate of THA in US increased by 30% (2013–2017) for the patients age group of 45 to 64 years. The rate of surgically, however, treated THA dislocations decreased by 14.3% for the same span of time. Those researches mean that advanced techniques and implants for hip joint have been leading to the stability improvement. Researchers in the related fields are working on how to reduce the revision rate of THA. Therefore, emergence of technologies such as 3D printing has also supported to the ease of the practice of THA (Arabnejad et al. 2017).

Patients who have Total Hip Arthroplasty (THA) wish to obtain enough range of motion (ROM) to do activities of daily livings. Thus, quality of total THA is usually evaluated by the range of motion (ROM) a patient can achieve after the transplant, because the ROM plays an important role to perform different activities of daily livings (Yoshimine and Ginbayashi 2012) Before operating THA, medical team and patient

© Springer Nature Singapore Pte Ltd. 2019
G. Tan et al. (Eds.): AsiaSim 2019, CCIS 1094, pp. 103–111, 2019.
https://doi.org/10.1007/978-981-15-1078-6_9

consider and analyze the operation plans (pre-operation plans). If the required ROM for activities of daily livings is not obtained, dislocation problem should come up to the patient. Some studies, however, prove that experimenting different parameters of implant of hip joint may reduce the risk of dislocations (Garbuz et al. 2012 and Langlais et al. 2008). There are other factors causing dislocations, for example, muscle paralysis caused by spinal anesthesia, severe trauma resulting from accidents, and poor surgical techniques (Burroughs et al. 2005). However, these factors are hard to control and plan, but the post-operation achievement of ROM is dependent on pre-operation plans. Surgeons plan and perform operations based on their previous experiences because of the unavailability of authentic quantitative criteria due to several limitations.

In general, the ROMs of joints are influenced by the size of joint and soft tissues such as muscles. Thus, before operating the surgery to replace the joint to implant, it is difficult to estimate the ROM of joints of human. For instance, the ROM of shoulder joint cannot be estimated accurately by mathematical approach and rigid body analysis. The ROM of hip joint, however, can be estimated more accurately than other joints since the hip joint is relatively less influenced by soft tissue. Especially, the range of front motion (i.e. flexion and extension) which is the most important ROM for hip joint has little effect from soft tissue. In this paper, we propose the procedure of estimating ROM after THA which can reflect the uncertainty of operating THA and evaluate the performance of estimation.

This paper is further organized as follows; Sect. 2 contains types of ROM, factors influencing post-operation ROM, and reviews of some related literatures. Section 3 presents the methodology and experiment carried out. Section 4 discusses the results of experiments and evaluates the performance of estimating process. Section 5 is the final section which concludes this study and considers future aspects of the study.

2 Theoretical Background

2.1 Types of ROM of Hip Joint

According to several studies related to ROM, six types of ROM of human being are defined based on the directional and angular movement of legs as shown in Fig. 1. Flexion and Extension, which affect the walking of a person, indicate forward and backward movement of the leg, respectively. Abduction is defined as the movement of the right leg of a standing human to the right direction, whereas Adduction is to the left direction. The last two types of ROM are determined by the direction of the angular motion of the leg; internal rotation (clockwise movement) and external rotation (counterclockwise movement).

2.2 Factors Influencing Post-Operation ROM

According to Yoshimine and Ginbayashi (2012) and Ellison (2012), the patient's ROM after THA is affected by the following five factors related to the implant: (1) cross section of the neck at the impingement point, (2) cup radius at the impingement point which means maximum angle of the acetabular cup or liner, (3) angle of cup inclination also known as angle of cup abduction and denoted as α, (4) angle of cup anteversion or cup anterior opening denoted as β, and, (5) angle of the femoral neck from the transverse plane and the neck anteversion (a and b) where a indicates the angle between the neck position and horizontal plane and b is the angle of the neck anteversion around the vertical axis from coronal plane. a and b depend on α and β. Figure 1 shows the different parts of artificial hip joint and parameters associated with ROM.

The factors (1) and (2) are case-specific. That is, they are determined by the design of implant model. Since the type of implant model is dependent on the characteristics of the patient, these two factors cannot be pre-planned, generally. On the other hand, the 3rd and 4th factors, α and β can be pre-planned before operation to achieve the desired ROM after THA, because the last factors, a and b entirely depend on α and β. Therefore, α and β can be described as the main factors in terms of ROM after THA.

2.3   Literature Review

There have been several studies related to calculating the range of motion while few of them are deserve mention. Jaramaz et al. (1997) applied analytical modeling to predict implant impingement and dislocation through experimental verification to obtain safe ROM. Widmer and Zurfluh (2004) described the factors that should be considered to achieve the intended ROM by developing a mathematical model of THA. This model was developed with the purpose of obtaining a set of parameters to maximize ROM and minimize risk. Matsushita et al. (2009) and Lavigne et al. (2011) proposed that femoral offset and implant's head size can be quite effective in obtaining safe ROM and Yoshimine and Ginbayashi (2012) and Ellison (2012) suggested that the post-operation ROM of the patient is affected by five different factors and also provided the detailed mathematical solutions to calculate ROM based on these five factors. However, recent advanced studies, such as the research of Murphy et al. (2018), used CT to provide a safe zone for ROM. Therefore, there is a gap with previous studies related to authentic mathematical modeling like Yoshimine and Ginbayashi (2012) and Ellison (2012), especially in terms of pre-operation ROM.

3   Methodology and Experiment

3.1   Estimating Process of ROM After THA

To estimate ROM after THA, several values of characteristics are needed; angle of implant (acetabular cup and femoral neck), physical parameter of implant (size of acetabular cup, width of femoral neck, and so on). If medical team selects an implant which is appropriate for a patient, the physical parameter is fixed. It is because the physical parameters are directly connected to the design of the implant. In THA, the femoral neck is inserted to the femur of the patient with proper angle to the patient. Thus, the angle of the femoral neck of the implant is fixed when the patient to be operated is specified and the type of implant is determined.

However, the angle of acetabular cup is considered in the step of pre-operation planning because it can be planned and applied as needed. Medical team and the patient discuss at which angle to insert the implant considering the required ROM for the patient. Medical team set up a target angle of implant, but there should be tolerance. In other words, after operating THA, there must be some error in the angle of implant. Thus, the proposed estimating process in this study includes the stochastic factor of angle of acetabular cup and utilizes the Monte-Carlo technique.

Figure 1 shows the framework for estimating ROM after THA. Estimating ROM after THA, several input parameters are needed; (1) inner radius of acetabular cup (or liner), type of neck, cross-section of the neck on the impingement, angle of femoral neck, and the inserting angle of acetabular cup when operating. How they can be defined and obtained is presented in Subsect. 3.2. The geometrical approach to find the value of ROM was introduced by some papers such as (Yoshimine and Ginbayashi 2012) and Ellison (2012). Whereas they find the values of ROM just solving and calculating mathematically, we perform all the process such as generating points, rotation, and so on.

To explain the estimating process, assume that all the values of parameters be determined. First, we generate the coordinates of acetabular cup and cross-section of femoral neck. All the points with coordinates are latent impingement points. Before we generate the coordinates, the coordinate system should be defined. For estimating ROM after THA, three dimensional cartesian coordinates system of which origin is the center of rotation of hip joint in acetabular cup. Z-axis is extension of the spine of the patient. X-axis is orthogonal to Z-axis; it points to the body front. Naturally, Y-axis is defined as the line orthogonal to both X-axis and Z-axis.

After generating the coordinates of the points, they should be rotated by the angle of acetabular cup and femoral neck to place them as the position after THA operation. The rotational transform matrix is used to rotate the points by the angle of α, β, a, and b. When the rotation is completed, each coordinate represents position in post THA operation.

To enhance content understanding, consider just a type of motion, flexion and extension. Flexion and extension are the type of motion which is parallel to XZ-plane (i.e. orthogonal to Y-axis). Thus, the impingement points on the neck and cup have same Y-coordinate value. Therefore, selecting a point (named as **N**) on the neck, we can find two points (named as **A, B**) on the cup which has same (or most similar) Y-coordinate value. Considering the point **N** on the neck is rotating forward or backward, it will meet the two points **A** and **B** on the cup. Checking the sign of X-coordinate values of **A** and **B**, which point is the impingement point of flexion or extension; the point which has positive X-coordinate value is of flexion, and the other is of extension. Also, as flexion and extension are rotational motion, **A**, **B**, and **N** must be on a circle with the center on Y-axis; let the center be the point **C**. Then, we can calculate flexion and extension as $\angle$**ACN** and $\angle$**BCN** using inner product of vectors. For all the points on the neck, this process can be applied. Finally, estimated flexion (or extension) is the minimum among all the estimated values.

For the other types of ROM (adduction, abduction, internal rotation, external rotation) same process can be applied. Applying the process to six types of ROM, a set of estimated ROMs can be obtained. To reflect the uncertainty of surgical operation, repeat this process as many times with Monte-Carlo technique.

3.2   Experiment

Monte-Carlo simulation technique is a broad class of computational algorithms that rely on repeated random sampling to obtain numerical results. Similarly, we applied to the geometrical estimating process with 500 replications by generating random numbers of α and β. Other parameters are kept constant (see Table 1). α and β follow a normal probability distribution with mean and standard deviation for the probability distribution also presented in Table 1. For the assumption, we refer a surgical case study about the distribution of α and β (Petrella et al. 2009).

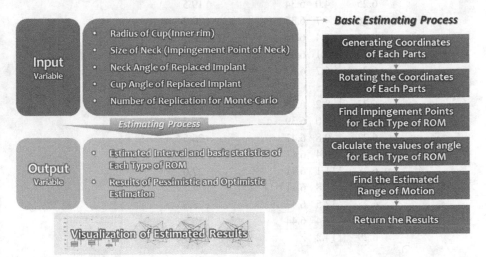

Fig. 1. Framework for estimating ROM after THA

Table 1. Parameter setting of experiments

Input parameter	Scenario 1	Scenario 2	Scenario 3	Scenario 4
Inner radius of cup (R)	19.66 mm			
Cup inclination angle (α)	40°	40°	50°	50°
Cup anteversion angle (β)	20°	10°	20°	10°
Neck angle from transverse plane (a)	54°			
Neck anteversion angle (b)	12°			

To set up some experiments, consider an example of an implant which consists of a cup with radius 19.66 and a femoral neck with free-from (non-circle type). Whereas just the radius on the impingement is needed for the circular neck, polar coordinates on the cross section of the neck where the impingement is predicted (as many as possible points with polar coordinates are needed). The polar coordinates of the example are shown in Table 2. The experiment with four scenarios which is suggested by orthopedic surgeon is set up in this study. Applying the proposed estimating process to these scenarios, the results will be described by interval estimation with boxplot and radar plot of optimistic/pessimistic estimation.

Table 2. Polar coordinates of the cross section of the femoral neck.

r (mm)	θ (°)	r (mm) (continued)	θ (°) (continued)
6.24	0.1	6.30	15.1
6.24	0.8	6.31	16.0
6.24	1.5	6.31	16.7
6.24	2.2	6.32	17.4
6.24	2.7	6.33	18.0
6.25	3.3	6.33	18.9
6.25	4.0	6.34	19.5
6.26	4.7	6.35	20.2
6.25	5.4	6.36	20.9
6.25	6.1	6.36	21.8
6.26	6.7	6.37	22.5
6.25	7.5	6.37	23.2
6.27	8.2	6.38	23.9
6.26	9.0	6.39	24.7
6.27	9.8	6.41	25.5
6.27	10.4	6.41	26.3
6.28	11.1	6.41	27.0
6.28	11.8	6.41	27.7
6.28	12.5	6.43	28.5
6.28	13.4	6.44	29.3
6.29	14.2	⋮	⋮

To evaluate the estimating performance of suggested process, the measured (actual) values of ROMs are needed. For the case used in this study, the measured (actual) values of ROMs are obtained as Table 3. They are measured in 3D software 'Autodesk Invertor 2019'.

Table 3. Measured (actual) values of ROM for each scenario.

ROM	Scenario 1	Scenario 2	Scenario 3	Scenario 4
Flexion	127.3°	116.3°	138.2°	126.7°
Extension	60.5°	74.6°	63.5°	80.3°
Internal rotation	171.1°	165.5°	149.3°	140.5°
External rotation	87.5°	111.0°	74.5°	90.4°
Adduction	63.0°	65.0°	53.0°	55.2°
Abduction	72.1°	74.5°	82.0°	84.5°

4   Results and Discussion

The results of ROM estimation after THA are shown as Tables 4, 5, 6 and 7. The tables consist of measured values (v), mean estimated value of 500 replications (m), difference between measured value and mean estimated value ($d = m - v$), standard deviation of 500 replications (s), lower limit of interval estimation ($l = m - s$), and upper limit ($u = m + s$).

Table 4. Results of estimation for Scenario 1.

ROM	Flexion	Extension	Internal rotation	External rotation	Adduction	Abduction
Measured (v)	127.3°	60.5°	171.1°	87.5°	63.0°	72.1°
Mean (m)	125.6°	65.7°	163.0°	93.7°	62.8°	75.1°
Difference (d)	−1.7°	5.2°	−8.1°	6.2°	−0.2°	3.0°
Std. deviation (s)	8.4°	3.9°	9.5°	17.0°	6.8°	6.1°
Lower limit (l)	117.2°	61.8°	153.5°	76.7°	56.0°	69.0°
Upper limit (u)	133.9°	69.5°	172.5°	110.7°	69.6°	81.2°

In the result of scenario 1, the values of d are about 5, 8, 6° for extension, internal rotation, external rotation. The other values of d are lower than 3°. However, all the measured values except extension are in the estimated interval $[m - s, m + s]$. The estimating performance for the scenario 1 is not perfect, but it shows relatively fine performance.

Table 5. Results of estimation for Scenario 2.

ROM	Flexion	Extension	Internal rotation	External rotation	Adduction	Abduction
Measured (v)	116.3°	74.6°	165.5°	111.0°	65°	74.5°
Mean (m)	116.5°	74.1°	159.9°	106.8°	65.5°	75.3°
Difference (d)	0.2°	−0.5°	−5.6°	−4.2°	0.5°	0.8°
Std. deviation (s)	7.2°	4.9°	10.4°	15.8°	6.3°	6.1°
Lower limit (l)	109.3°	69.2°	149.5°	91.0°	59.1°	69.2°
Upper limit (u)	123.6°	79.1°	170.3°	122.5°	71.8°	81.3°

Table 6. Results of Estimation for Scenario 3.

ROM	Flexion	Extension	Internal rotation	External rotation	Adduction	Abduction
Measured (v)	138.2°	63.5°	149.3°	74.5°	53.0°	82.0°
Mean (m)	139.9°	65.7°	145.8°	71.5°	51.2°	86.1°
Difference (d)	1.7°	2.2°	−3.5°	−3.0°	−1.8°	4.1°
Std. deviation (s)	9.8°	5.7°	11.9°	13.7°	6.8°	6.4°
Lower limit (l)	130.1°	60.0°	133.9°	57.8°	44.4°	79.7°
Upper limit (u)	149.8°	71.4°	157.7°	85.1°	57.9°	92.4°

Table 7. Results of estimation for Scenario 4.

ROM	Flexion	Extension	Internal rotation	External rotation	Adduction	Abduction
Measured (v)	126.7°	80.3°	140.5°	90.4°	55.2°	84.5°
Mean (m)	128.1°	77.9°	145.3°	88.4°	55.3°	85.0°
Difference (d)	1.4°	−2.4°	4.8°	−2.0°	0.1°	0.5°
Std. deviation (s)	9.7°	6.0°	11.9°	14.4°	6.4°	6.0°
Lower limit (l)	118.4°	71.9°	133.4°	74.1°	48.9°	79.0°
Upper limit (u)	137.8°	83.9°	157.2°	102.8°	61.7°	91.0°

For scenario 2, mean estimated values of extension and internal rotation shows little bit high difference about 5 and 4°. The values of d of the others are less than 1°. Also, All the measured values of ROM come under the estimated interval $[m - s, m + s]$. Thus, the performance of estimation for scenario 2 is greater than scenario 1. For scenario 3 and 4, the performance of estimation is fine overall. Especially, the results of interval estimation show prominent performance since all the measured values of ROM are included to the estimated intervals.

Proposed estimating process almost shows superb estimating performance except little cases. Accurate estimation of ROM is essential in order patient to get enough ROM for activities of daily livings, the proposed process can contribute to the filed of orthopedics (especially hip joint parts). However, there are little cases relatively inaccurate, more experiment and evaluation are needed.

5   Concluding Remarks

In this study, we suggest an interval estimation method for ROM after THA based on Monte-Carlo simulation. Our method utilizes the geometrical approach and Monte-Carlo technique to estimate ROMs. Reflecting stochastic factor of surgical operation to parameter α and β which follows Normal distribution, the tolerance of THA operation can be considered in estimating process. When medical team and patients prepare pre-operation plans, proposed method can be utilized to obtain enough ROM as they need. Since the accuracy of estimation is comparatively fine, they can have confidence in the estimated results.

Because proposed method uses Monte-Carlo methods and utilizes the coordinates of cross section of the neck (not all points), there can be some factors which can cause error. Thus, more case studies including performance evaluation is also needed. Utilizing proposed process for pre-operation planning with risk analysis, it may help many orthopedic surgeons to plan surgery at pre-operation step.

References

Siopack, J.S., Jergesen, H.E.: Total hip arthroplasty. West. J. Med. **162**(3), 243 (1995)

Rajaee, S.S., Campbell, J.C., Mirocha, J., Paiement, G.D.: Increasing burden of total hip arthroplasty revisions in patients between 45 and 64 years of age. JBJS **100**(6), 449–458 (2018)

Arabnejad, S., Johnston, B., Tanzer, M., Pasini, D.: Fully porous 3D printed titanium femoral stem to reduce stress-shielding following total hip arthroplasty. J. Orthop. Res. **35**(8), 1774–1783 (2017)

Yoshimine, F., Ginbayashi, K.: A mathematical formula to calculate the theoretical range of motion for total hip replacement. J. Biomech. **35**(7), 989–993 (2012)

Garbuz, D.S., et al.: The frank stinchfield award: dislocation in revision THA do large heads (36 and 40 mm) result in reduced dislocation rates in a randomized clinical trial. Clin. Orthop. Relat. Res.® **470**(2), 351–356 (2012)

Langlais, F.L., Ropars, M., Gaucher, F., Musset, T., Chaix, O.: Dual mobility cemented cups have low dislocation rates in THA revisions. Clin. Orthop. Relat. Res. **466**(2), 389–395 (2008)

Burroughs, B.R., Hallstrom, B., Golladay, G.J., Hoeffel, D., Harris, W.H.: Range of motion and stability in total hip arthroplasty with 28-, 32-, 38-, and 44-mm femoral head sizes: an in vitro study. J. Arthroplasty **20**(1), 11–19 (2005)

Ellison, P.: Mathematical formulae to calculate the theoretical range of motion of prosthetic hip implants with non-circular neck geometry. Proc. Inst. Mech. Eng., Part H: J. Eng. Med. **226** (10), 804–814 (2012)

Jaramaz, B., Nikou, C., Simon, D.A., DiGioia, A.M.: Range of motion after total hip arthroplasty: Experimental verification of the analytical simulator. In: Troccaz, J., Grimson, E., Mösges, R. (eds.) CVRMed-MRCAS 1997, LNCS, vol. 1205, pp. 573–582. Springer, Berlin, Heidelberg (1997). https://doi.org/10.1007/BFb0029282

Widmer, K.-H., Zurfluh, B.: Compliant positioning of total hip components for optimal range of motion. J. Orthop. Res. **22**(4), 815–821 (2004)

Matsushita, A., Nakashima, Y., Jingushi, S., Yamamoto, T., Kuraoka, A., Iwamoto, Y.: Effects of the femoral offset and the head size on the safe range of motion in total hip arthroplasty. J. Arthroplasty **24**(4), 646–651 (2009)

Lavigne, M., Ganapathi, M., Mottard, S., Girard, J., Vendittoli, P.A.: Range of motion of large head total hip arthroplasty is greater than 28 mm total hip arthroplasty or hip resurfacing. Clin. Biomech. **26**(3), 267–273 (2011)

Murphy, W.S., Yun, H.H., Hayden, B., Kowal, J.H., Murphy, S.B.: The safe zone range for cup anteversion is narrower than for inclination in THA. Clin. Orthop. Relat. Res. **476**(2), 325–335 (2018)

Petrella, A.J., Stowe, J.Q., D'Lima, D.D., Rullkoetter, P.J., Laz, P.J.: Computer-assisted versus manual alignment in THA: a probabilistic approach to range of motion. Clin. Orthop. Relat. Res. **467**(1), 50–55 (2009)

Simulation Applications: Blockchain, Deep Learning and Cloud

Agent-Based Simulation of Blockchains

Edoardo Rosa[1], Gabriele D'Angelo[2]([⊠]), and Stefano Ferretti[2]

[1] Intuity, Padova, Italy
edoardo.rosa@studio.unibo.it
[2] University of Bologna, Bologna, Italy
{g.dangelo,s.ferretti}@unibo.it

Abstract. In this paper, we describe LUNES-Blockchain, an agent-based simulator of blockchains that is able to exploit Parallel and Distributed Simulation (PADS) techniques to offer a high level of scalability. To assess the preliminary implementation of our simulator, we provide a simplified modelling of the Bitcoin protocol and we study the effect of a security attack on the consensus protocol in which a set of malicious nodes implements a filtering denial of service (i.e. Sybil Attack). The results confirm the viability of the agent-based modelling of blockchains implemented by means of PADS.

Keywords: Blockchain · Simulation · Distributed ledger · Bitcoin

1 Introduction

Blockchain technologies are getting more and more hype these days, due to the vast range of possibilities of application in many distributed systems and networks [8,23]. Traceability, auditing, attestation-as-a-service, regulation, cooperation, are just few examples of scenarios, other than the traditional fintech applications that made this technology famous.

The blockchain can be treated as a protocol stack, in which each layer refers to a specific aspect of the blockchain. Figure 1 shows a simplified view of such blockchain protocol stack. At a coarse grained level of description, there are at least three main layers, on top of the Internet layer. The blockchain has an underlying peer-to-peer protocol, in charge of disseminating information on novel blocks being produced, to be added to the blockchain, or novel transactions that might be inserted into novel blocks. A flooding mechanism is often used to disseminate information, while the peer-to-peer overlay is built using some peer discovery mechanism [14]. For instance, a random selection protocol is used in Bitcoin, while Ethereum employs a UDP-based node discovery mechanism inspired by Kademlia [16]. A consensus algorithm is used in order to let all nodes agree on the blockchain evolution. While the famous Bitcoin blockchain exploits a Proof-of-Work consensus scheme, many other possibilities exist, ranging from Proof-of-Stake and its plethora of variants, Proof-of-Authority, up to the Practical Byzantine Fault Tolerance consensus [22]. On top of the consensus layer, we have the transaction ledger, that records transactions and data.

© Springer Nature Singapore Pte Ltd. 2019
G. Tan et al. (Eds.): AsiaSim 2019, CCIS 1094, pp. 115–126, 2019.
https://doi.org/10.1007/978-981-15-1078-6_10

In the so called blockchain 2.0, i.e. since Ethereum, these technologies offer the possibility to develop smart contracts, executed on the blockchain. A smart contract is a program representing an agreement that is automatically executable and enforceable by nodes that participate in the blockchain management. The execution of the program is triggered by transactions generated by an external account (i.e. a user), and the program deterministically executes the terms of a contract, specified as software code [8].

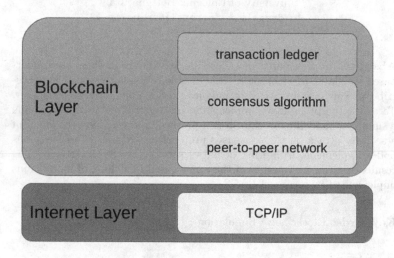

Fig. 1. Blockchain protocol stack.

It is clear that, while this layered organization of a blockchain allows to isolate the very different aspects of this technology and allows obtaining a better understanding of the components' protocols, the functioning of each layer influences the performance of other layers. Thus, it becomes interesting to evaluate all possible alternatives of each component, and how possible modifications affect other aspects of the blockchain. However, the complexity of this technology, and the large scale nature of this distributed system make extremely difficult the evaluation process. In this sense, the simulation of the blockchain becomes an interesting evaluation strategy.

In this work, we present a novel blockchain simulator called LUNES-Blockchain that is able to exploit Parallel And Distributed Simulation (PADS) functionalities. The simulator mimics several functionalities of a blockchain, such as the peer-to-peer overlay management, its message dissemination scheme, the mining process (i.e. the generation of a novel block) based on the generation of transactions. In particular, we show a specific implementation of the Bitcoin blockchain. Using the simulator, we then study a simple Denial-of-Service (DoS) attack (i.e. Sybil Attack [11]) to the Bitcoin blockchain. As concerns the evaluation, in order to show the feasibility of the simulator, we provide some results related to different configurations of the DoS attack when applied to a simulated network composed of a large number of nodes.

The remainder of this paper is organized as follows. Section 2 describes the background related to the paper subject. Section 3 presents the blockchain simulator. The analysis of a DoS attack on the Bitcoin network is described in Sect. 4. Finally, Sect. 5 provides some concluding remarks.

2   Background and Related Work

Blockchain is a technology that was initially proposed in the Bitcoin system, in 2009, by an anonymous author with the pseudo-name of Satoshi Nakamoto [18]. In its first wave, the blockchain allowed parties to transact directly, i.e. without any intermediary, by exchanging crypto money (Bitcoin) with confidence that no double spend was occurring. This was basically achieved using three key technologies: (i) a globally shared ledger managed in a peer-to-peer fashion, (ii) a mechanism for reaching consensus on the state of the ledger, and (iii) immutability of the ledger and transactions (see Fig. 1). All parties exploit pseudonyms, thus while transactions are known in the ledger, it is extremely difficult (even if not impossible, in some cases) to identify the involved parties, i.e. the blockchain is pseudo-anonymous.

While Bitcoin basically allows for money transfers, a second wave of blockchain platforms followed, such as Ethereum, that enable other types of more complex applications. These platforms are based on the use of "smart contracts", that promote the development of decentralized applications, based on a Turing complete scripting language [4]. The execution of the public code composing the smart contract is carried out by the multiple nodes that are part of the system.

2.1   The Peer-to-Peer Overlay and the Distributed Ledger

Blockchains are distributed ledgers. To realize this, the system is organized as a peer-to-peer system, in which each participant has a copy of the shared ledger. This ledger records all the transactions within the blockchain. In Bitcoin, the ledger is a set of records of transactions that have occurred. Transactions are grouped in blocks. Each block contains a hash pointer to a previous block. It is this list of concatenated blocks that creates the blockchain.

Each novel transaction, generated by a node, is disseminated through the peer-to-peer system using a flooding dissemination protocol [6,12]. Such novel transaction will be considered, together with other not yet confirmed transactions, for the creation of a novel block. The generation of a block is based on a specific consensus scheme, which varies depending on the blockchain (see next section). Once a novel block has been generated, this block is disseminated in the overlay, through the same flooding dissemination scheme.

2.2   Consensus Scheme

The consensus scheme is in charge of ensuring that all nodes in the peer-to-peer system maintain the same view of the blockchain. Put in other words, a mechanism is needed to allow all participants with copies of the ledger to come to consensus about the current state of the ledger and the uniqueness of transactions in the ledger. Several consensus schemes have been proposed in the past in the distributed system research area. Some of these schemes are utilized today in blockchain technologies (e.g. Practical Byzantine Fault Tolerance [5]). However, the principle approaches in blockchain are the Proof-of-Work (Pow, used in Bitcoin and the actual Ethereum) and Proof-of-Stake (PoS, used in the novel Ethereum version) [22].

PoW works as follows. Participants submit their transactions to the network. Nodes that participate to the transactions validation are called "miners". Miners verify that the submitted transactions are valid. Miners group these transactions into "blocks". Using this block as an input, the miners solve a computational crypto-puzzle that requires a large amount of computational power. When they solve the puzzle, they propagate the answer to other nodes along with the block of transactions. The other miners will accept the solution along with the block of transactions and add those transactions to the blockchain. As mentioned, a hash of this previous block in the chain is inserted in the novel block. This way, everyone can verify the ledger state in a tamper-proof manner.

The miners work is not for free. A financial reward is assigned to the first node that solves the crypto-puzzle. PoW is often criticized for being a highly inefficient means of transacting, since the crypto-puzzle requires a tremendous waste of computation, hence causing a vast energy waste.

2.3   Simulation of the Blockchain

At the time of writing, literature on blockchain simulators is scarce. Usually, the main focus was on the analysis of the blockchain, the use of smart contracts and security issues. The typical approach is to develop smart contracts and test them using local blockchains. Remix, Metamask, Ganache, Multichain and the Ethereum test networks (e.g. Ropsten, Rinkeby) are examples of environments thought to write, compile and debug smart contracts. In accordance to the multi-layered vision of a blockchain we discussed on the previous section, a common approach is to simulate just few aspects of a blockchain at a time.

In [2], a blockchain network simulator is presented. It is an event-driven simulator, that simulates the neighbor nodes selection of the peer-to-peer overlay. The mining activity is not simulated in detail, but a block generation is mimicked based on the computational capabilities of nodes.

In [15], the mining strategy of Bitcoin is simulated and studied. A network is modeled, but the propagation of transactions is not simulated, since the focal point is to study the impact of the block size, block interval, and the block request management system.

VIBES is a blockchain simulator, thought for large modeling scale peer-to-peer networks [20]. The rationale behind this simulator is to provide a blockchain simulator that is not confined to the Bitcoin protocol, trying to provide support for large-scale simulations with thousands of nodes.

BlockSim is proposed as a Python framework to build discrete-event dynamic system models for blockchain systems [1]. BlockSim is organized in three layers: incentive layer, connector layer and system layer. Particular emphasis is given on the modeling and simulation of block creation through PoW.

In [17] is described a new methodology that enables the direct execution of multi-threaded applications inside of Shadow that is an existing parallel discrete-event network simulation framework. This is used to implement a new Shadow plug-in that directly executes the Bitcoin reference client software (i.e. Shadow-Bitcoin).

At best of our knowledge, LUNES-Blockchain is the first simulator of blockchains that is able to take advantage of the performance speedup and extended scalability provided by PADS.

3   Simulation of the Bitcoin Network

With the aim to make this paper as much self-contained as possible, in this section we introduce some background on Discrete Event Simulation (DES) and Parallel And Distributed Simulation (PADS) techniques. After that, we describe the ARTÌS/GAIA simulation middleware and the LUNES simulation model that have been used for implementing LUNES-Blockchain.

DES is a simulation paradigm much appreciated for its usability and ability to model complex systems [13]. In a DES, a simulation model is represented through a set of state variables and the model evolution is modelled by the processing of events in chronological order. To respect the causality constraint of events in the real-world, each simulated event is timestamped (i.e. occurs at a specific instant in the simulated time) and it represents a change of the state variables. Under the implementation viewpoint, the changes in the simulated system can be seen as the processing of an ordered sequence of timestamped events in the simulated model.

In a monolithic (i.e. sequential) simulation, all the model state variables representing the simulated model are allocated in a single Physical Execution Unit (PEU) that is in charge of generating new events, managing the pending event list and processing the events that are extracted from the ordered list in timestamp order. This kind of simulator is very simple and it can be implemented using a single executing process. On the other hand, the simplicity of this simulator is often paid in terms of performance and scalability. For example, the scalability of the simulator is limited, both in terms of time required to complete the simulation runs and complexity of the system that can be modelled [10].

An alternative approach, that is called PADS, is based on the parallelization/distribution of the simulator load. More specifically, a set of networked PEUs (e.g. CPU cores, processors or hosts [6,13] is in charge of executing the simulator. In this case, the simulation model is partitioned in a set of Logical Processes (LPs) that are executed on top of the PEUs that participate in the parallel/distributed simulation. Under the implementation viewpoint, each LP manages a local pending event list and the events that need to be delivered to parts of the simulation model that are allocated in other PEUs are encapsulated in messages. The main advantage of PADS is that it enables the modelling and the processing of larger and more complex simulation models with respect to DES. On the other hand, the partitioning of the simulated model is not easy [9] and a synchronization algorithm among LPs is needed to guarantee the correct simulation execution [13].

3.1 ARTÌS/GAIA

The *Advanced RTI System* (ARTÌS) is a parallel and distributed simulation middleware in which the simulation model is partitioned in a set of LPs. As previously described the parallel/distributed simulator is composed of interconnected PEUs and each PEU runs one or more LPs. The main service provided by ARTÌS to LPs is time management (i.e. synchronization) that is necessary for obtaining correct simulation results in a parallel/distributed setup.

In a PADS, a relevant amount of execution time is spent in delivering the interactions between the model components. The means that the wall-clock execution time of PADS is highly dependent on the performance of the communication network (i.e. latency, bandwidth and jitter) that connects the PEUs. It is obvious that reducing the communication overhead can speed up the simulator runs.

The *Generic Adaptive Interaction Architecture* (GAIA) is a software layer built on top of ARTÌS [7]. In GAIA, the simulation model is partitioned in a set of Simulated Entities (SEs) that can be seen as small model components. Each LP allocates some SEs and provides to them the basic simulation services (e.g. synchronization and message passing). In other words, the simulated model behavior is obtained through the interactions among the SEs. Under the implementation viewpoint, the interactions are encapsulated by timestamped messages exchanged between the LPs. From the simulation modelling viewpoint, GAIA follows a Multi Agent System (MAS) approach in which each SE represents an agent. In fact, each SE is an autonomous agent that is able to perform some specific actions (i.e. implementing an individual behavior) and to interact with other agents in the simulation (i.e. implementing group behaviors).

GAIA is able to reduce the communication overhead, that is common in PADS, clustering in the same LP the SEs that frequently interact together. In terms of communication overhead, clustering the heavily-interacting entities permits to reduce the amount of costly LAN/WAN/Internet communications that are replaced by efficient shared memory messages. In the current version of GAIA, the clustering of entities is based on a set of high-level heuristics that analyze the communication behavior in the simulation model without any knowledge of the specific simulation domain.

3.2 LUNES

LUNES (Large Unstructured NEtwork Simulator) is a simulator of complex networks implemented on top of ARTÌS/GAIA. The main goal of LUNES is to provide an easy-to-use tool for the modeling and simulation of interaction proto-col on top of large scale unstructured graphs with different network topologies [6]. The tool is implemented following a modular approach (i.e. network creation, dissemination protocols definition, analysis of results) that facilitates its reuse. A main point of LUNES is that it is designed and implemented for PADS using the services provided by ARTÌS (i.e. parallel and distributed processing) and GAIA (i.e. adaptive self-clustering, dynamic computational and communication load-balancing). This permits the efficient simulation of very large scale models even in presence of a high-level of details in the modelled systems. The commu-nication between nodes in the unstructured graphs is modelled in LUNES using a set of dissemination protocols that are based on gossip. The usage of LUNES is quite simple since it provides to the simulation modeller a high-level Appli-cation Programming Interface (API) for the implementation of the protocols to be simulated.

3.3   LUNES-Blockchain

LUNES-Blockchain is a simulation model based on LUNES that implements an agent-based representation of a generic blockchain. In LUNES-Blockchain, each node is represented by means of an agent that implements a local behavior and interacts with other agents. The representation of network nodes by means of agents simplifies the development of the model and, in our view, it adds a high-level of extensibility to the simulation model.

In this preliminary work, we assess if it possible to study, via simulation, some security issues common to blockchains. In particular, we are interested in the behavior of the Bitcoin blockchain. This aspect has influenced some of the design choices that have been taken and that will be discussed in the following of this section. The design of LUNES-Blockchain has been organized in steps: (i) modeling and simulation of a generic blockchain; (ii) modelling of the specific aspects of the Bitcoin blockchain; (iii) modelling of a malicious filtering DoS attack on Bitcoin.

Since the implementation in LUNES of the dissemination mechanism used in Bitcoin (called Dandelion/Dandelion++) is currently under development, LUNES-Blockchain models the dissemination in the Bitcoin network using one of the gossip protocols already provided by LUNES (i.e. the degree dependent dissemination algorithm [6]). The main effect of this choice is the better commu-nication delay (i.e. latency) provided by the degree dependent dissemination with respect to Dandelion (due to the absence of the anonymity phase implemented in Dandelion).

The next version of LUNES-Blockchain will support Dandelion and a more accurate representation of the Bitcoin network topology [19]. These modifica-tions will be useful to study some specific behaviors of the Bitcoin network. For example, when studying scalability aspects that are related to the Bitcoin implementation.

A relevant aspect in the modelling of the Bitcoin blockchain is the network size. Given its dynamic nature, it not possible to identify a specific number of nodes, but estimates assert that the Bitcoin network size is about 10.400 nodes [3]. It is worth noticing that not all active nodes in the network are miners. In fact, it is not mandatory that all nodes participate in the creation of new block to be added to the blockchain. On the other side, all active nodes participate in the reception, validation and broadcast of new blocks, thus maintaining updated their local copy of the blockchain. Due to how PoW has been designed, in Bitcoin the majority of miners are part of mining pools. In this work, we are not interested in modelling each miner that is part of a mining pool. This is due to the fact that the malicious behavior we are interested in, considers each mining pool as a single node. The current implementation of LUNES-Blockchain permits to define the percentage of simulated nodes acting as miners, and for each miner its specific hashrate. The hashrate is defined as the speed at which a processing unit is able to complete the hash operations that are used to solve the cryptopuzzle of the PoW. In LUNES-Blockchain, the simulation of the mining process is modelled to respect the difficulty and behavior of the Bitcoin mining process, but without the computational overhead caused by the real implementation of PoW.

Another relevant issue is the modeling of time in the simulation. The current behavior of the Bitcoin network is to create and publish a new block every 10 min. On the other hand, the simulation implements a time-stepped synchronization algorithm [13] in which the simulated time is dived in a sequence of time-steps. In the current implementation of LUNES-Blockchain, each time-step represents one minute of simulated time. This means that, on the average, every 10 time-steps a new simulated block is created and propagated to the whole network by means of the gossip-based dissemination protocol.

LUNES-Blockchain is available for peer-review and it will be included in the forthcoming release of LUNES that will be available in source code format on the research group website [7].

4   Evaluation of a DoS Attack

In this paper we investigate the modelling and simulation of a well-known type of DoS attack on the Bitcoin network. To foster the reproducibility of our experiments, all the parameters used to setup up LUNES-Blockchain are described in Table 1. The parameters reported in the table mimic the Bitcoin network as it resulted in the fourth quarter of 2018.

The results shown in the following section have been obtained running the simulator on an Intel i7-6700 3.40 GHz with 16 GB of RAM and Arch Linux (x64) as operating system. The execution of a single simulation run of LUNES-Blockchain with the model parameters described in Table 1 and using a single LP (i.e. sequential simulation) requires an average of 60 s. This means that LUNES-Blockchain is quite efficient in the simulation of limited size blockchains even in a sequential (i.e. monolithic) setup. More populated networks, the modelling of more complex attacks and the simulation of blockchains supporting Smart Contracts will benefit of the PADS approach provided by ARTÌS/GAIA.

In future works, the preliminary evaluation reported in this paper, it will be followed by a full-fledged validation and scalability assessment of the simulator.

Table 1. Simulation and model parameters.

Name	Value	Description
TTL	16	Time-To-Live
DISSEMINATION	7	Dissemination protocol
PROBABILITY_FUNCTION	2	Dissem. probability function
FUNC_COEFF_HIGHER	4	Dissem. high-order function coef
FUNC_COEFF_LOWER	74	Dissem. low-order function coef
END_CLOCK	5000	Time-steps in each run
NODES	10000	Number of nodes
MINERS_COUNT	70%	Percentage of miners
DIFFICULTY	6489747252517	Difficulty value
HASHRATE	43983561622000000000	Total hashrate (Hashes per sec.)
Network Topology	Random graph	Topology of the Bitcoin network
Edges per Node	8	Number of edges per node

The attack that has been implemented is a filtering DoS in which a set of malicious nodes silently drop all messages that originated from a given node. This kind of filtering evolves in a Sybil Attack when the attacked node is completely surrounded by attackers. In other words, we simulate the condition in which the attacked node is totally unable to communicate with the rest of the network, with the effect that all its mining outcomes and transactions are discarded by the malicious sybils, and none among honest nodes in the blockchain overlay receive them. This specific experiment has been implemented as a sequence of simulation runs. We varied the number of malicious nodes from 1 up to 9999. With 9999 attackers, the network is all made of malicious nodes, with the exception of the attacked one. For every run, the average number of nodes reached by each message originated from the attacked node has been calculated.

It is worth noticing that this kind of evaluation, under the simulation viewpoint, is quite costly. In fact, many simulator runs have to be executed both for exploring all the different configurations and for obtaining statistically significant results. In other words, the efficiency of the simulator (i.e. execution speed) is of main importance. The results that have been obtained are reported in Figs. 2 and 3. The outcomes reported in the figures are comparable with theoretical results expected for this kind of attack against peer-to-peer botnets [21]. Clearly, this does not represent a validation of the proposed simulation model but it is a positive outcome.

Figure 2 shows that the average number of nodes reached by the messages proportionally decreases with the increase of attackers. When the number of attackers is larger than 7000, there is a sharp decrease in the number of nodes

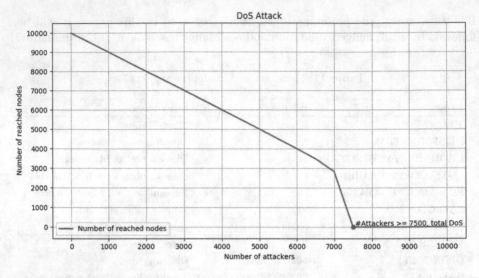

Fig. 2. Average number of reached nodes during a DoS filtering attack.

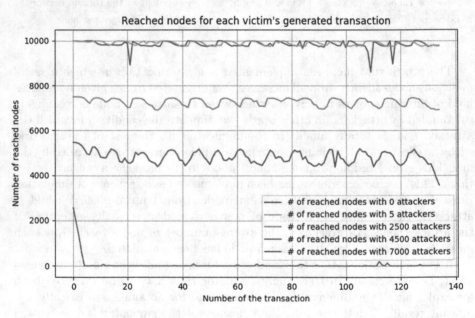

Fig. 3. Number of reached noes for each transaction during a DoS filtering attack. Different setups with an increasing number of attacking nodes.

reached by the messages. With more than 7500 attackers, the Sybil Attack is complete and the attacked node is disconnected from the network.

Figure 3 shows the number of reached nodes when considering up to 140 transactions that are one-by-one disseminated in the network. In the figure, it is possible to see the effect of an increasing number of malicious nodes on each transaction that is delivered in the network. When there are no attackers (or a few of them), almost every transaction obtains a complete broadcast. When we increase the number of malicious nodes, then the filtering effect is evident on the number of reached nodes.

5   Conclusions

In this paper, we have introduced a new agent-based simulator called LUNES-Blockchain for the simulation of large scale and complex blockchains. LUNES-Blockchain has been used for implementing a preliminary model of the Bitcoin network and to study a simple filtering Denial-of-Service that is usually called Sybil Attack. To the best of our knowledge, this is the first blockchain simulator that is able to exploit the performance speedup and improved scalability offered by Parallel and Distributed Simulation (PADS).

As a future work, we plan to perform a more extended validation of LUNES-Blockchain, to improve the accuracy the Bitcoin model implementing the Dandelion/Dandelion++ dissemination protocol and to consider a more accurate topology of the Bitcoin network. On the other hand, LUNES-Blockchain can be extended to model blockchains that are capable of Smart Contracts execution (e.g. Ethereum). Finally, we plan to investigate other common attacks on the network that are based on the presence of malicious nodes.

References

1. Alharby, M., van Moorsel, A.: Blocksim: a simulation framework for blockchain systems. SIGMETRICS Perform. Eval. Rev. **46**(3), 135–138 (2019)
2. Aoki, Y., Otsuki, K., Kaneko, T., Banno, R., Shudo, K.: Simblock: a blockchain network simulator. In: Proceedings of the 2nd Workshop on Cryptocurrencies and Blockchains for Distributed Systems. CryBlock 2019, IEEE (2019)
3. Bitnodes: Global Bitcoin Nodes Distribution (2019). https://bitnodes.earn.com/
4. Buterin, V.: A next-generation smart contract and decentralized application platform. White Paper (2018). https://github.com/ethereum/wiki/wiki/White-Paper, https://github.com/ethereum/wiki/wiki/White-Paper. Last accessed 02 Mar 2018
5. Castro, M., Liskov, B.: Practical byzantine fault tolerance. In: Proceedings of the Third Symposium on Operating Systems Design and Implementation, pp. 173–186. OSDI 1999, USENIX Association, Berkeley, CA, USA (1999)
6. D'Angelo, G., Ferretti, S.: Highly intensive data dissemination in complex networks. J. Parallel Distrib. Comput. **99**, 28–50 (2017)
7. D'Angelo, G., Ferretti, S.: Parallel And Distributed Simulation (PADS) Research Group (2019). http://pads.cs.unibo.it
8. D'Angelo, G., Ferretti, S., Marzolla, M.: A blockchain-based flight data recorder for cloud accountability. In: Proceedings of the 1st Workshop on Cryptocurrencies and Blockchains for Distributed Systems, pp. 93–98. CryBlock 2018, ACM, New York, NY, USA (2018)
9. D'Angelo, G.: The simulation model partitioning problem: an adaptive solution based on self-clustering. Simul. Model. Pract. Theor. (SIMPAT) **70**, 1–20 (2017)

10. Egea-Lopez, E., Vales-Alonso, J., Martinez-Sala, A., Pavon-Mario, P., Garcia-Haro, J.: Simulation scalability issues in wireless sensor networks. Commun. Mag. IEEE **44**(7), 64–73 (2006)
11. Eyal, I., Sirer, E.G.: Majority is not enough: bitcoin mining is vulnerable. Commun. ACM **61**(7), 95–102 (2018)
12. Ferretti, S.: Gossiping for resource discovering: an analysis based on complex network theory. Future Gener. Comput. Syst. **29**(6), 1631–1644 (2013)
13. Fujimoto, R.: Parallel and Distributed Simulation Systems. Wiley & Sons, Hoboken (2000)
14. Gencer, A.E., Basu, S., Eyal, I., van Renesse, R., Sirer, E.G.: Decentralization in bitcoin and ethereum networks (2018). CoRR abs/1801.03998
15. Gervais, A., Karame, G.O., Wüst, K., Glykantzis, V., Ritzdorf, H., Capkun, S.: On the security and performance of proof of work blockchains. In: Proceedings of the 2016 ACM SIGSAC Conference on Computer and Communications Security, pp. 3–16. CCS 2016, ACM, New York, NY, USA (2016)
16. Maymounkov, P., Mazières, D.: Kademlia: a peer-to-peer information system based on the xor metric. In: Druschel, P., Kaashoek, F., Rowstron, A. (eds.) Peer-to-Peer Syst., pp. 53–65. Springer, Berlin (2002). https://doi.org/10.1007/3-540-45748-8_5
17. Miller, A., Jansen, R.: Shadow-bitcoin: scalable simulation via direct execution of multi-threaded applications. In: 8th Workshop on Cyber Security Experimentation and Test (CSET 2015). USENIX Association, Washington, D.C. (August 2015)
18. Nakamoto, S.: Bitcoin: a peer-to-peer electronic cash system (2009). http://bitcoin.org/bitcoin.pdf
19. Neudecker, T., Andelfinger, P., Hartenstein, H.: Timing analysis for inferring the topology of the bitcoin peer-to-peer network. In: 2016 International IEEE Conferences on Ubiquitous Intelligence Computing, Advanced and Trusted Computing, Scalable Computing and Communications, Cloud and Big Data Computing, Internet of People, and Smart World Congress, pp. 358–367 July (2016)
20. Stoykov, L., Zhang, K., Jacobsen, H.A.: Vibes: fast blockchain simulations for large-scale peer-to-peer networks: Demo. In: Proceedings of the 18th ACM/IFIP/USENIX Middleware Conference: Posters and Demos, pp. 19–20. Middleware 2017, ACM, New York, NY, USA (2017)
21. Verigin, A.L.: Evaluating the Effectiveness of Sybil Attacks Against Peer-to-Peer Botnets (2018). http://hdl.handle.net/1828/5095
22. Xiao, Y., Zhang, N., Lou, W., Hou, Y.T.: A survey of distributed consensus protocols for blockchain networks (2019). CoRR abs/1904.04098
23. Zichichi, M., Contu, M., Ferretti, S., D'Angelo, G.: Likestarter: a smart-contract based social dao for crowdfunding. In: Proceedings of the 2nd Workshop on Cryptocurrencies and Blockchains for Distributed Systems. CryBlock 2019, IEEE (2019)

Robot Arm Control Method of Moving Below Object Based on Deep Reinforcement Learning

HeYu Li[1]([⊠]) [iD], LiQin Guo[1,2,3], GuoQiang Shi[1,2,3],
YingYing Xiao[1,2,3], Bi Zeng[1], TingYu Lin[1,2,3], and ZhengXuan Jia[1]

[1] Beijing Complex Product Advanced Manufacturing Engineering Research
Center, Beijing Simulation Center, HaiDian District 100854 Beijing, China
liheyu93@163.com

[2] State Key Laboratory of Intelligent Manufacturing System Technology,
Beijing Institute of Electronic System Engineering, Haidian District,
100854 Beijing, China

[3] Science and Technology on Space System Simulation Laboratory,
Beijing Simulation Center, Haidian District, 100854 Beijing, China

Abstract. The existing robot arm control system has long commissioning time and the control system has poor scope of application. In this paper, the Deep Deterministic Policy Gradient (DDPG) algorithm has been adopted and adapted to control the robot arm to move below the object at any position, thereby enhancing the flexibility of the control algorithm and shortening the adjusting time. In addition, to address the problem that physical production line cannot be utilized directly or provide sufficient data for training deep reinforcement learning agent, this paper constructs a virtual model containing both the robot arm and the object as training environment for the agent. Simulation experiment has been performed with state variables and reward properly designed. As is shown by the results, the control agent trained in this paper show good performance in controlling the robot arm, which in turn confirms the effectiveness of the training algorithm with effective data support of the constructed simulation environment.

Keywords: Deep learning · Modeling · Deep Deterministic Policy Gradient · Robot arm

1 Introduction

With the rapid development of automation technology, the robot arm as an independent machine system is widely used in the industrial field. In order to make the robot arm complete a special task, commissioning is needed before it is put into application. When the task involves some complicated processes which require precise assemblies or subtle operations, it puts higher requirements on the motion performance of the robot arm, as it is expected to have a high absolute positioning accuracy and repeatedly track the previous motion trajectory, thus placing higher demands on the control system.

© Springer Nature Singapore Pte Ltd. 2019
G. Tan et al. (Eds.): AsiaSim 2019, CCIS 1094, pp. 127–136, 2019.
https://doi.org/10.1007/978-981-15-1078-6_11

On the basis of control theory, the control methods are improved to achieve more precise movements of the robot arm. Yin proposes a control algorithm for the bending process, using a state machine and a knowledge base to generate programs which realize the function of avoiding obstacles through heuristic rules [1]. Flacco proposes a model that provides an efficient procedure for the calculation of intra-articular motion, enabling the end effect motion to track a given geometric curve at a specified linear and an angular velocity [2]. Cho uses specific points and vectors as the normal vectors of the control plane to implement an active control method based on matrix enhancement [3]. Li designs a fuzzy output feedback stabilization control method for nonlinear switching systems with non-strict feedback, so that the output of the control system converges to a very small neighborhood near the origin [4]. Yu combines the generalized nonlinear system with the adaptive inversion control method to achieve the control effect of coarse quantization, in which the state converges to the neighborhood near the origin [5]. Li constructs an adaptive updating law using smooth switching functions to implement an adaptive distributed control method for interconnected nonlinear systems, which guarantees asymptotic stability [6]. Wang uses the Lyaounov equation and the fuzzy system to approximate the nonlinear function for discrete switched nonlinear systems, thereby reducing the parameter adjustment pressure of robot arm [7].

Deep reinforcement learning combines deep learning with reinforcement learning. With the development of computer technology and data science, algorithms such as DQN (Deep Q-network), DDPG (Deep Deterministic Policy Gradient), TRPO (Trust Region Policy Optimization), A3C (Asynchronous Advantage Actor-Critic), DPPO (Distributed Proximal Policy Optimization) have been proposed [8–13]. Scholars have applied neural networks to the robot arm for better results. Zhang introduces repeated motion indicators as optimization criteria, in which quadratic optimization and recurrent neural networks are used to solve the redundancy analysis problem [14]. He uses a neural network-based compensation control strategy for the problem of nonlinear frictional dead zone in space manipulators [15]. Xie applies neural network algorithms to adaptive control for the solution of uncertainty in the manipulator model [16]. Ngo proposes a robust control scheme based on neural network, which compensates for the parameter changes such as interferences and frictions to achieve higher control precision [17]. Lee proposes an adaptive control method based on deep learning for unknown environment of the robot arm contact, in which the neural network is used to estimate the location environment model [18].

This paper constructs a 3D simulation model, including a robot arm and an object, which is used to simulate the relative relationship between two parts. The DDPG algorithm is used for training the agent in the virtual environment, where the neural network parameters are adjusted according to the rewards returned by the simulation environment, achieving convergence of parameters and completing specific control requirements. In the process of moving the gripper below the object, factors such as collision, multiple joint cooperation need to be considered. Therefore, the state variables and reward functions in DDPG algorithm must be delicately designed.

2 Robot Arm Control Method Based on Deep Reinforcement Learning

2.1 System Structure

The system consists of two parts: the DDPG agent and the robot arm model. The former is trained for realizing the control of the robot arm to move below the corresponding object. The latter simulates the robot arm and the object, which receives the control variables, and transmits the corresponding environment information mainly including next instant states and reward to the DDPG agent. According to the received information including instant state variables, DDPG agent calculates the control variables and updates the neural network parameters according to the reward values, as shown in Fig. 1.

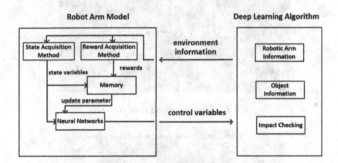

Fig. 1. System structure.

2.2 Robot Arm Model

In this paper, Unity is used to model the simulation environment that simulates the robot arm using the fork-panel gripper to move below the object. The simulation interface and the random initialization position of the object are shown in Fig. 2(a) and (b), respectively.

The robot arm consists of five joints and rods. Each joint has a degree of freedom to realize the rotation operation. It is described by two parameters: the offset of the rod that refers to the distance from one rod to the next along the joint axis and the joint angle, which refers to the angle of the joint rotation relative to the next. The relative position between the coordinate axes of two adjacent joints can be obtained, as the rod is regarded as a rigid body. The size, position, height of the object and other information can be set in Unity. The robot arm is initialized at the certain angle for each axis, and the object is initialized at a specific position directly in front of it.

Collision detection is performed through collision box in Unity, which is added to the parts of the model to capture collision events. During the simulation, if a collision occurs, the collision position and the number of the corresponding rod are sent.

(a) Control interface.

(b) Random initialization of position.

(c) Target position.

Fig. 2. Robot arm model.

By receiving the control variables, the forward motion method is used to calculate the position information of the corresponding joints. The algorithm first establishes the joint coordinates and the Cartesian coordinate, by which the positions and attitudes are determined. The joint coordinate $oxyz$ whose origin is the center of each axis, is used to describe the motion of each independent joint. Assign motion to each rod and move the end of the robot arm to a specific position for the control of each joint. The origin of the

Cartesian coordinate $OXYZ$ is at the center of the base, the axis X is horizontal to the right, and the axis Z is perpendicular to the object in the horizontal plane of the axis X. The axis Y is determined by the right hand rule:

$$
\begin{aligned}
{}_{i-1}{}^{i}T &= Rot(z_{i-1}, \theta_i)Trans(0, 0, d_i)Trans(a_i, 0, 0)Rot(x_i, a_i) \\
&= \begin{bmatrix} c\theta_i & -s\theta_i & 0 & 0 \\ s\theta_i & c\theta_i & 0 & 0 \\ 0 & 0 & 1 & 0 \\ 0 & 0 & 0 & 1 \end{bmatrix} \begin{bmatrix} 1 & 0 & 0 & 0 \\ 0 & 1 & 0 & 0 \\ 0 & 0 & 1 & d_i \\ 0 & 0 & 0 & 1 \end{bmatrix} \begin{bmatrix} 1 & 0 & 0 & a_i \\ 0 & 1 & 0 & 0 \\ 0 & 0 & 1 & 0 \\ 0 & 0 & 0 & 1 \end{bmatrix} \begin{bmatrix} 1 & 0 & 0 & 0 \\ 0 & c\alpha_i & -s\alpha_i & 0 \\ 0 & s\alpha_i & c\alpha_i & 0 \\ 0 & 0 & 0 & 1 \end{bmatrix} \\
&= \begin{bmatrix} c\theta_i & -s\theta_i c\alpha_i & s\theta_i s\alpha_i & a_i c\theta_i \\ s\theta_i & c\theta_i c\alpha_i & -c\theta_i s\alpha_i & a_i s\theta \\ 0 & s\alpha_i & c\alpha_i & d_i \\ 0 & 0 & 0 & 1 \end{bmatrix}
\end{aligned}
$$

$$(1)$$

Where: ${}_{i-1}{}^{i}T$ is the transformation formula between two adjacent rods; a_i is the length of common perpendicular between the joint axes at both ends of the rod i; α_i is the angle between the joint axes at the ends of the rod i in the normal plane of α_i; α_i and a_i respectively intersect the axis of the joint J_i at two points, between which the distance is denoted by d_i; θ_i is the angle between a_{i-1} and a_i in the plane perpendicular to the axis of the joint J_i, called the angle between adjacent rods i and $i - 1$.

2.3   DDPG-Based Robot Arm Control Method

The reinforcement learning algorithm receives the state variables of the current environment, and adopts specific actions through policy π. After the actions are applied, the environment returns rewards to the agent, by which the internal parameters are updated.

The DDPG algorithm uses two sets of neural networks, *eval* and *target*, to represent the actor and the critic. The actor in the *eval* network receives the state variables and outputs the corresponding robot arm control variables, which are fed back to the environment. The critic in the *eval* network gets the expected rewards of the actor's output values according to the state variables and the corresponding actor. The actor in the *target* network receives the state variables and obtains the control variables. The critic in the *target* network gets the expected rewards by the state variables and the outputs of the actor. The algorithm flow is shown in Fig. 3. The parameters of the target network are performed by means of soft update:

$$
soft\ update \begin{cases} \theta^{Q'} \leftarrow \gamma\theta^Q + (1-\gamma)\theta^{Q'} \\ \theta^{\mu'} \leftarrow \gamma\theta^\mu + (1-\gamma)\theta^\mu \end{cases}
$$

$$(2)$$

Where: θ^Q are the parameters of $Q(s, a|\theta^Q)$ in the *eval* network, θ^μ are the parameters of $\mu(s|\theta^\mu)$ in the *eval* network, $\theta^{Q'}$ are the parameters of $Q'\left(s, a|\theta^{Q'}\right)$ in the

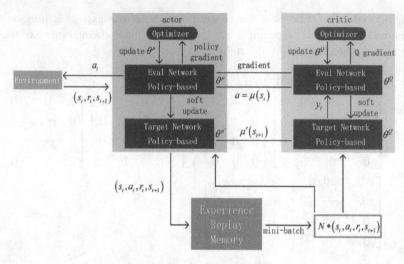

Fig. 3. The structure of DDPG.

target network, and $\theta^{\mu'}$ are the parameters of $\mu'\left(s\middle|\theta^{\mu'}\right)$ in the *target* network. The actor in the *eval* network is optimized using the policy gradient method:

$$\nabla_{\theta^\mu} J \approx \frac{1}{N}\sum_i \nabla_a Q\left(s, a\middle|\theta^Q\right)\big|_{s=s_i, a=\mu(s_i)} \nabla_{\theta^\mu}\mu(s|\theta^\mu)\big|_{s_i} \tag{3}$$

Where: s_i are the state variables of the current time. The critic in the *eval* network uses the root mean square error to define the loss and optimize the network parameters by the gradient descent method:

$$\begin{cases} loss = \frac{1}{N}\sum_i \left(y_i - Q(s_i, a_i|\theta^Q)\right)^2 \\ y_i = r_i + \gamma Q'\left(s_{i+1}, \mu'\left(s_{i+1}\middle|\theta^{\mu'}\right)\middle|\theta^{Q'}\right) \end{cases} \tag{4}$$

In the case of random initialization of the object position, the DDPG algorithm is used to control the robot arm and move the gripper to a specified position below the object, as shown in Fig. 2(c). To this end, the algorithm designs the states and the rewards. The state variables generated by the environment information is a total of 79 dimensions, as shown in the following equation:

$$\begin{cases} dis\_jt_i = (joint_i - tgt_i)/2 \\ dis\_jj_i = (joint_i - joint_0)/2 \\ dis\_th_i = (tpoint_i - hpoint_i)/4 \qquad i = 1, 2, 3, 4 \\ dis\_hj_i = (hpoint_i - joint_i)/4 \\ dis\_col \end{cases} \tag{5}$$

Where: *joint* is the three-dimensional point of each joint, *tgt* is the three-dimensional point of the object, *tpoint* is the three-dimensional point of the point below the object, *hpoint* is the three-dimensional point above the gripper, *dis_col* is the occurrence of collision. The left side of (5) are the state variables.

Guide the robot arm to make the correct action through the rewards, which is divided into two stages. The first stage guides the gripper to the position below the object:

$$\begin{cases} jre_1 = \left(\sum_{i=0}^{3} \|tpoint_i - hpoint_i\|/4 \right) \\ jre_2 = \left(\sum_{i=0}^{3} |hpoint\_x_i|/4 \right) \\ jre_3 = \left(\sum_{i=0}^{3} |hpoint\_y_i|/4 \right) \\ jre_4 = \cos(\textbf{hvect}, \textbf{tvect}) \end{cases} \quad (6)$$

Where: *jre* is the reward, *hpoint_x* is the x coordinate value of *hpoint*, *hpoint_y* is the y coordinate value of the *hpoint*, **hvect** is the normal vector of gripper plane, **tvect** is the normal vector of object-bottom plane.

The second stage guides the gripper to move up horizontally:

$$\begin{cases} part_1 = \left(\sum_{i=0}^{3} \|\textbf{tpoint}_i - \textbf{hpoint}_i\|/4 \right) \\ part_2 = \left(\sum_{i=0}^{3} \cos((\textbf{tpoint}_i - \textbf{hpoint}_i), \textbf{y})/4 \right) \end{cases} \quad (7)$$

3 Experiment

In order to verify the advancement of the algorithm in this paper, the comparisons between the running time, the reward and the relative distance are used to measure the effect of the algorithm on calculation efficiency and accuracy.

Conventional robot arm commissioning depends on proficiency and requires a period between 2 and 5 days where takes the median. The paper statistics the training time of neural network, and the results are shown in Table 1:

Table 1. Time comparsion of different methods.

	Conventional method	Neural network
Required time (h)	84.0	33.2

As can be seen from the data in the table, the traditional commissioning method takes longer time. When using the deep reinforcement learning algorithm to control the robot arm, it takes only 33.2 h for the robot arm to pick up the object by adjusting parameters, where the efficiency is increased by 60.5%.

After finalizing the neural network parameters and reward functions, the learning process from the initial state is recorded, as shown in Fig. 4. The x-axis represents the learning time, and the y-axis represents the reward values obtained in each cycle. It can be seen that after the data accumulation phase, the neural network adjusts its own parameters through back propagation and obtains larger rewards. The neural network reaches a steady state after training for about 34 h.

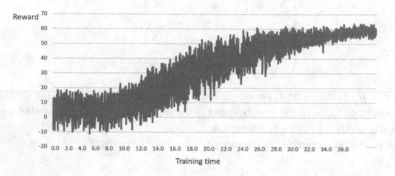

Fig. 4. The relationship between training time and the reward values

The value of the reward in each cycle is counted to verify whether the action neural network selected in each cycle could obtain a larger reward value as the learning progresses, that is, a better control effect is achieved. When the dimension of each layer of neurons is 300, the reward value of the network in each period is shown in Fig. 5. After the data is filled and enters the learning phase, the reward value begins to increase gradually, indicating that the neural network could change its own parameters through training, and the actions are made more and more satisfactory.

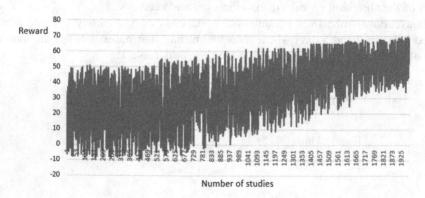

Fig. 5. Reward value for each cycle.

In addition, to intuitively reflect whether the arm can move to the specified position below the object, the paper measures the average distance between the four points above the gripper of the robot arm and the corresponding points below the object. At each initialization, the arm moves to a fixed position with the average distance of 80 cm. When the distance is less than 1 cm, the robot arm is considered to have successfully moved to the specified position below the object. Figure 6 shows the average distance in a cycle after learning. It can be seen that the distance between the arm and the object is continuously reduced, and finally stabilizes at 1 cm, so the converged neural network can perform the task well.

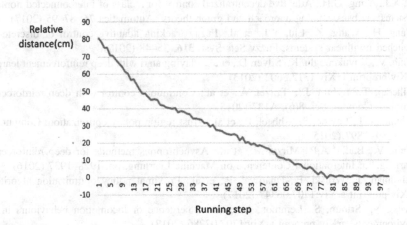

Fig. 6. The average distance between four points above the gripper and corresponding points below the object.

4   Conclusion

This paper applies the deep reinforcement learning algorithm to the robot arm control for specific task. In view of the lack of effective data in the real environment, this paper constructs a deep learning model, including the robot arm and the object, to provide data for the training of the DDPG algorithm that realizes the control of the robot arm to accomplish specific actions. Through verification, the trained DDPG algorithm can control the robot arm to complete specific tasks, and the commissioning time is faster than the traditional algorithm.

Acknowledgment. This work is supported by the National Key R&D Program of China 2008YFB1004005. We are grateful to their financial support.

References

1. Yin, X.G., Wang, H.P., Wu, G.: Path planning algorithm for bending robots. In: 2009 IEEE International Conference on Robotics and Biomimetics (ROBIO), pp. 392–395 (2009)

2. Flacco, F., Luca, A.D., Khatib, O.: Motion control of redundant robots under joint constraints: Saturation in the null space In: 2012 IEEE International Conference on Robotics and Automation, pp. 285–292. IEEE (2012)
3. Cho, H.C., Song, J.B.: Null space motion control of a redundant robot arm using matrix augmentation and saturation method. In: 12th International Conference on Motion and Vibration Control. Japan Society of Mechanical Engineers (2014)
4. Li, Y.M., Tong, S.C.: Adaptive fuzzy output-feedback stabilization control for a class of switched nonstrict-feedback nonlinear systems. IEEE Trans. Cybern. **47**(4), 1007–1016 (2017)
5. Yu, X., Lin, Y.: Adaptive backstepping quantized control for a class of nonlinear systems. IEEE Trans. Autom. Control **62**(2), 981–985 (2017)
6. Li, X.J., Yang, G.H.: Adaptive decentralized control for a class of interconnected nonlinear systems via backstepping approach and graph theory. Automatica **76**, 87–95 (2017)
7. Wang, H., Wang, Z., Liu, Y.J., et al.: Fuzzy tracking adaptive control of discrete-time switched nonlinear systems. Fuzzy Sets Syst. **316**, 35–48 (2017)
8. Mnih, V., Kavukcuoglu, K., Silver, D., et al.: Playing atari with deep reinforcement learning. arXiv preprint arXiv:1312.5602 (2013)
9. Lillicrap, T.P., Hunt, J.J., Pritzel, A., et al.: Continuous control with deep reinforcement learning. Comput. Sci. **8**(6), A187 (2015)
10. Schulman, J., Levine, S., Abbeel, P., et al.: Trust region policy optimization. Comput. Sci. **37**, 1889–1897 (2015)
11. Mnih, V., Badia, A.P., Mirza, M., et al.: Asynchronous methods for deep reinforcement learning. In: International Conference on Machine Learning, pp. 1928–1937 (2016)
12. Schulman, J., Wolski, F., Dhariwal, P., et al.: Proximal policy optimization algorithms. arXiv preprint arXiv:1707.06347 (2017)
13. Heess, N., Sriram, S., Lemmon, J., et al.: Emergence of locomotion behaviours in rich environments. arXiv preprint arXiv:1707.02286 (2017)
14. Zhang, Y., Li, W., Zhang, Z.: Physical-limits-constrained minimum velocity norm coordinating scheme for wheeled mobile redundant manipulators. Robotica **6**, 1325–1350 (2015)
15. He, W., David, A.O., Yin, Z., et al.: Neural network control of a robotic manipulator with input deadzone and output constraint. IEEE Trans. Syst. Man Cybern. Syst. **46**(6), 759–770 (2016)
16. Xie, J., Liu, G.L., Yan, S.Z., et al.: Study on neural network adaptive control method for uncertain space manipulator. Yuhang Xuebao/J. Astronaut. **31**(1), 123–129 (2010)
17. Ngo, T.Q., Wang, Y.N., Mai, T.L., et al.: Robust adaptive neural-fuzzy network tracking control for robot manipulator. Int. J. Comput. Commun. Control **7**(2), 341–352 (2014)
18. Lee, C.H., Wang, W.C.: Robust adaptive position and force controller design of robot manipulator using fuzzy neural networks. Nonlinear Dyn. **85**(1), 343–354 (2016)

Distributed 3D Printing Services in Cloud Manufacturing: A Non-cooperative Game-Theory-Based Selection Method

Sicheng Liu[1,2], Ying Liu[1,2], and Lin Zhang[1,2,3]($\boxtimes$)

[1] School of Automation Science and Electrical Engineering,
Beihang University, Beijing 100191, China
johnlin9999@163.com
[2] Engineering Research Center of Complex Product Advanced
Manufacturing Systems, Ministry of Education, Beijing 100191, China
[3] Beijing Advanced Innovation Center for Big Date-Based Precision Medicine,
Beihang University, Beijing 100083, China

Abstract. 3D printing, as a symbol for the 4th of industrial revolution, is now changing many aspects of our life, ranging from rapid manufacturing, mass customization to health care devices. There is no 3D printer that can produce a 3D object without a digital 3D model. Thus, the construction of the 3D model to achieve mass customization inevitably involves service matching and task scheduling in Cloud manufacturing (CMfg) platform. However, such a complex and dynamic CMfg environment poses a challenge to traditional service matching and selection. In this research, a non-cooperative dynamic game model based selection is presented. To obtain Nash equilibrium point, an evolution solving algorithm is designed to find an optimal solution. Experimental results indicate that the proposed method is practical and valid.

Keywords: Cloud manufacturing · 3D printing service ·
Non-cooperative game · Nash equilibrium

1 Introduction

With the gradual enhancement of computer functions and the further development of computing technology, more and more applications are changing the objective world and the interaction between human and the objective world by information technology. 3D printing, as a symbol for the third wave of industrial revolution, is one such technology that will undoubtedly have a profound impact on our lives. There is no 3D printer that can produce a 3D object without a digital 3D model. Thus, Mai et al. [6] indicate the construction of the 3D model in a cloud platform to achieve mass customization. Li et al. [4] think that cloud manufacturing (CMfg) is emerging as a new service-oriented manufacturing paradigm built on dynamic, flexible and on-demand resource allocation and sharing, supporting and driving revolutionizing manufacturing, reflected the

© Springer Nature Singapore Pte Ltd. 2019
G. Tan et al. (Eds.): AsiaSim 2019, CCIS 1094, pp. 137–145, 2019.
https://doi.org/10.1007/978-981-15-1078-6_12

philosophy of "Design Anywhere, Manufacture Anywhere (DAMA)". Xu [9] consider it provides a mode that large-scale, heterogeneous and distributed physical manufacturing resources (hardware and software) and capabilities are effectively organised and encapsulated into different types of on-demand, configurable and self-contained cloud services available to different consumers through virtualisation and servitisation technologies and managed in an integration way. Given the dynamic nature of 3D printing services in CMfg, ever-changing progress in the execution procedure pose a challenge to traditional method of matching and selection. As a consequence, there is an urgent need to look for a new method aiming to solve this problem. With the economic development and the in-depth understanding of the objective world, game theory has gradually entered into people's horizons. Myerson et al. [7] state that game theory is the study of competition and cooperation among rational decision-makers. Since Von et al. [8] introduced game theory into the economic research field, it provides a vital decision-making analysis tool to solve various problems. This paper presents the method of matching and selection based on non-cooperative game to obtain optimal result. An improved genetic algorithm (IGA) as a solution procedure is designed in search of Nash equilibrium (NE) point.

The remainder of this paper is structured as follows. The next section reviews the works related to service scheduling in CMfg. Section 3 describes the proposed non-cooperative game model. Section 4 presents the proposed scheduling method of 3D printing service. Section 5 gives a case study to illustrate the feasibility of this method. Section 6 presents concludes and future works.

2   Related Works

Since cloud computing as a today's IT paradigm has widely applied to provide a driving force for manufacturing industry how to provision manufacturing resources and capabilities with complexity and variety, another new manufacturing paradigm is generated. With the introduction of the term 'Cloud Manufacturing' coined in 2010, Li et al. [4] are often credited with introducing the first conceptual description of the relationship between manufacturing resource service and customer demand task. Since that time, many scholars have begun to concern with service matching and task scheduling within CMfg. 3D printing is one of the most successful application demonstrations in the area of CMfg. Besides its unique feature, 3D printing is inevitably characterized by a very strong colour of task scheduling, which is a typical NP-hard problem. By far the usual practice to seek the solution to the practical problem is to formulate mathematical modelling. Therefore such a problem can be transformed as the multi-objective optimization problem. Then an improved algorithm is proposed to find an optimal solution to the problem. The typical method based on heuristic algorithm makes remarkable progress in multi-objective optimization problem of task scheduling in CMfg. Laili et al. [3] introduced a new comprehensive model to solve the optimal allocation of computing resources in consideration of main computation, communication, and reliability constraints. Cao et al. [2] presented a service selection and scheduling model for a single task in consideration of criteria TQCS and then proposed an improved ant colony optimization algorithm

(IACO) to search overall optimal solution. In particular, the weight coefficient was calculated according to the analytic hierarchical process (AHP) in order to combine linearly into a single objective optimization. Mai et al. [6] developed a specific cloud platform to address how to intelligently and effectively manage and schedule distributed 3D printing services in CMfg. Zhou et al. [10] presented a service transaction model of distributed 3D printing services in CMfg and then designed an improve GA (IGA) to solve the multi-task scheduling problem. In this model, service attributes, task attributes and logistics were considered. Game theory is born for dealing with how to choose competition and cooperation among rational decision-makers. Game theory has been cut a striking figure as one of the most competitive strategy selection methods for task scheduling problem in the manufacturing industry. Liu et al. [5] investigated an underlying mechanism that can promote the development and implementation of CMfg. The evolutionary game theory was introduced to set up the model of CMfg system as a scale-free network, where nodes represent enterprises while links stand for a certain kind of relationship between two enterprises, and to analyze the saturation degree of manufacturing task which affects on CMfg platform. Bai et al. [1] analyzed the task scheduling problem and introduced a Public Goods Game (PGG) model realized in the BA scale-free network of to CMfg system. In this model, each manufacturing basic attribute was mapped to three elements of the game.

3   Problem and Model

3.1   3D Printing Service Matching in CMfg

Based on the 3D printing service matching process shown in Fig. 1, the critical attributes of the 3D printing service is as follow:

(1) Dimension

The dimension of 3D printing service can be described from length, width and height:

$$min(l_{i,j}, w_{i,j}, h_{i,j}) <= min(L_k, W_k, H_k) \tag{1}$$

$$max(l_{i,j}, w_{i,j}, h_{i,j}) <= max(L_k, W_k, H_k) \tag{2}$$

Equations (1) and (2) define allowable variation range of the dimension of 3D printing service.

(2) Materials

The materials of 3D printing service can be expressed:

$$m_{i,j} = M_k \tag{3}$$

Equation (3) ensures the same types of materials of 3D printing service.

(3) Precision

The precision of 3D printing service can be expressed:

$$p_{i,j} => P_k \tag{4}$$

Equation (4) enforces that the preciseness of 3D printing service is not low than that of 3D printing task.

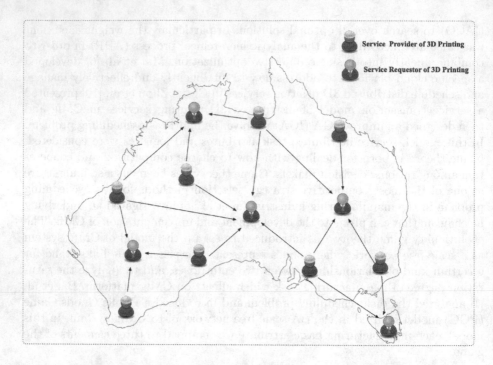

Fig. 1. The 3D printing service matching process in CMfg.

3.2　3D Printing Task Scheduling Model in CMfg

To simplify the 3D printing task scheduling model, the makespan of all tasks is considered.

$$Min \quad f_i = makespan = Max \quad C_{ijk} \quad i \in [1, n], \quad j \in [1, n_i], \quad k \in [1, m] \quad (5)$$

3.3　Non-cooperative Game Model

A n-person non-cooperative game model can be composed as a tuple:

$$G = (P, S, u_i(s)) \tag{6}$$

Where $P = \{p_1, p_2, \cdots, p_n\}$ is the set of n players. $S = S_1 \times S_2 \cdots S_n$ represents the strategy profile space. $s = (s_1, s_2, \cdots, s_n) \in S$ is the strategy vector. $u_i(s) : S \rightarrow R$ represents the utility function of player i.

A Nash equilibrium (NE) is an ordered set of strategy choices, one for each player who can not reduce other payoff by unilaterally changing his strategy. So the strategy profile of NE $(s_i^*, s_{-i}^*) \in S$ can be denoted:

$$u_i(s_i^*, s_{-i}^*) >= u_i(s_i, s_{-i}^*) \tag{7}$$

Where $s_{-i}^* = (s_1^*, \cdots, s_{i-1}^*, s_{i+1}^*, \cdots, s_n^*)$ is the strategy profile except strategy of player $i(i = 1, 2, \cdots, n)$.

The non-cooperative game in this study can be described:

- Players $\{p_1, p_2, p_3\}$: the CMfg service provider
- Strategies S: the set of available tasks and services from the CMfg service provider
- Utility functions $\{u_1(s), u_2(s), u_3(s)\}$: the makespan.

4   3D Printing Service Scheduling

4.1   Scheduling Method

The n-person non-cooperative dynamic game based matching selection of 3D printing service is described as follows.

(Step 1) Service allocation. Available services of 3D printing are allocated to three objectives sequentially until completed.

(Step 2) Objective mapping. Each objective corresponds to each player who can make decisions, independent of another player.

(Step 3) Strategy formation. The unallocated subtasks of each task are put into cloud service pool in which available services can match the corresponding subtasks according to the allocated rules.

(Step 4) Utility calculation. The three players from each feasible strategy profile are calculated their utility functions $u_1(s)$, $u_2(s)$ and $u_3(s)$.

(Step 5) NE solving. The NE of the non-cooperative dynamic game is solved by IGA.

Figure 2 shows the non-cooperative dynamic game structure of 3D printing task scheduling in CMfg.

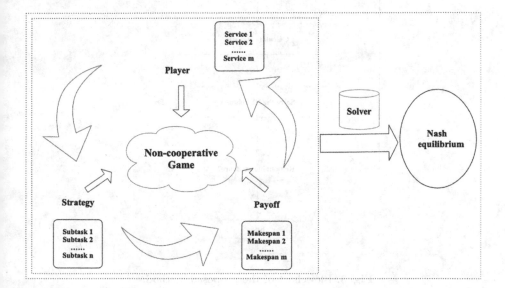

Fig. 2. The non-cooperative dynamic game structure of 3D printing task scheduling.

4.2   Solving Method of NE

Nash equilibrium is the most essential and the most core concept of game theory, which no player has any propensity to unilaterally deviate from the equilibrium. As mentioned above, how to search the NE of the non-cooperative dynamic game is urgent. Therefore, in this paper, we apply an improved genetic algorithm (IGA) to do this. The flowchart of the proposed method is illustrated in Fig. 3.

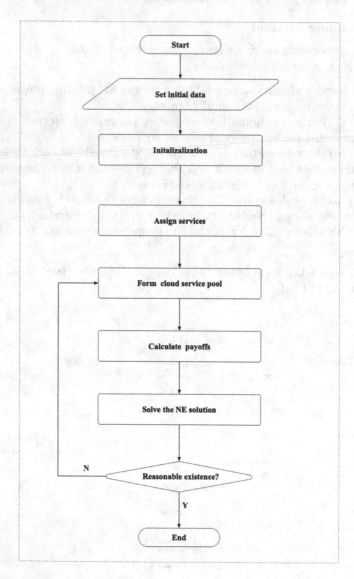

Fig. 3. Flowchart of the proposed method.

5 Case Study

5.1 Experimental Setting

We view the problem of 50 tasks × 100 services in the CMfg environment. The parameters of the experiment are given in Table 1.

Table 1. The parameter setting of the experiment.

Parameter	Range	Unit	Definition
M	50	/	Sum of 3D printing tasks
N	100	/	Sum of 3D printing services
$l_{i,j}$	(0.1,0.9)	km	Length of each task
$w_{i,j}$	(0.1,0.9)	km	Width of each task
$h_{i,j}$	(0.1,0.9)	km	Height of each task
L_k	(0.3,1.2)	km	Maximum length of services
W_k	(0.3,1.2)	km	Maximum width of services
H_k	(0.3,1.2)	km	Maximum height of services
$m_{i,j}$	1,2,3	/	Required printing material type of each task
M_k	1,2,3	/	Printing material type of services
$p_{i,j}$	(0.03,0.06)	mm	Printing accuracy requirements of each task
P_k	(0.01,0.18)	mm	Printing accuracy range of services
$Lt_{i,k}$	(1,6)	h	Processing time of each task
$Lc_{i,k}$	(1,10)	$	Processing cost of each task
α	0.7	/	Selection rate
β	0.8	/	Crossover rate
γ	0.7	/	Mutation rate

5.2 Results and Analyses

Compared with non-cooperative games based scheduling method (NDG), 3DPSS method [10] is selected as the reference. The convergence curves of the service selection solution is shown in Fig. 4.

For both 3DPSS and NDG, two methods shown in Fig. 4 can converge to the optimal solution. But the difference is that NDG can achieve smaller fitness value than 3DPSS with the increase of generation. Because 3D printing among services compete for tasks. However, game theory is the study of competition and cooperation among rational decision-makers, which gives 3D printing services to tend to choose cooperation for maximizing their own benefit. This indicates that the NDG has more efficiency and better probability to obtain the best results.

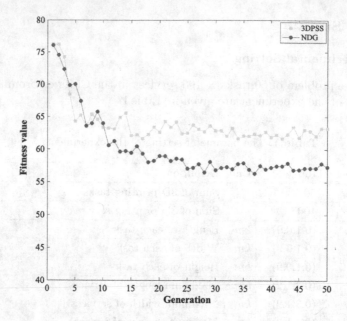

Fig. 4. The convergence curves of the service selection solution.

6   Conclusion

Service matching and task scheduling are one of the research hotspots of 3D printing services. However, existing scheduling methods have difficulty in adjusting given decision-making for ever-changing progress in the dynamic CMfg environment. In this research, we proposed a non-cooperative dynamic game-theory-based scheduling method for distributed 3D printing services in CMfg to generate optimal task solutions. Experimental results of this case study demonstrate the validity and practicality of the proposed method as well as illustrate why they are efficient. This contribution provides managers with new insight into blurring the lines between manufacturing and services.

In addition to the insights mentioned above, research directions for future work include: (1) investigating a comprehensive service matching and task scheduling policy for 3D printing including capacities of logistics services and multiple subtask sequences; (2) study uncertain events that affect the 3D printing service scheduling.

Acknowledgement. This work is supported by the National Natural Science Foundation of China under Grant No. 61873014.

References

1. Bai, T., Liu, S., Zhang, L.: A manufacturing task scheduling method based on public goods game on cloud manufacturing model, pp. 1–6 (2018)

2. Cao, Y., Wang, S., Kang, L., Gao, Y.: A TQCS-based service selection and scheduling strategy in cloud manufacturing. Int. J. Adv. Manuf. Technol. **82**(1–4), 235–251 (2016)
3. Laili, Y., Tao, F., Zhang, L., Sarker, B.R.: A study of optimal allocation of computing resources in cloud manufacturing systems. Int. J. Adv. Manuf. Technol. **63**(5–8), 671–690 (2012)
4. Li, B.H., et al.: Cloud manufacturing: a new service-oriented networked manufacturing model. Comput. Integr. Manuf. Syst. **16**(1), 1–7 (2010)
5. Liu, Y., Zhang, L., Tao, F., Wang, L.: Development and implementation of cloud manufacturing: an evolutionary perspective. In: ASME 2013 International Manufacturing Science and Engineering Conference collocated with the 41st North American Manufacturing Research Conference, pp. V002T02A007–V002T02A007. American Society of Mechanical Engineers (2013)
6. Mai, J., Zhang, L., Tao, F., Ren, L.: Customized production based on distributed 3d printing services in cloud manufacturing. Int. J. Adv. Manuf. Technol. **84**(1–4), 71–83 (2016)
7. Myerson, R.B.: Game Theory. Harvard University Press, Cambridge (2013)
8. Von Neumann, J., Morgenstern, O.: Theory of Games and Economic Behavior (Commemorative edition). Princeton University Press, Princeton (2007)
9. Xu, X.: From cloud computing to cloud manufacturing. Robot. Comput. Integr. Manuf. **28**(1), 75–86 (2012)
10. Zhou, L., Zhang, L., Laili, Y., Zhao, C., Xiao, Y.: Multi-task scheduling of distributed 3d printing services in cloud manufacturing. Int. J. Adv. Manuf. Technol. **96**(9–12), 3003–3017 (2018)

Simulation and Visualization

Visual Guide to Improving Depth Perception in See-Through Visualization of Laser-Scanned 3D Point Clouds

Kyouma Nishimura[1(✉)], Liang Li[2], Kyoko Hasegawa[2], Atsushi Okamoto[3], Yuichi Sakano[4,5], and Satoshi Tanaka[2]

[1] Graduate School of Information Science and Engineering,
Ritsumeikan University, Kyoto, Japan
is0272ss@ed.ritsumei.ac.jp
[2] College of Information Science and Engineering,
Ritsumeikan University, Kyoto, Japan
[3] Faculty of Cultural and Historical Studies, Otemae University, Nishinomiya, Japan
[4] Center for Information and Neural Networks (CiNet),
National Institute of Information and Communication Technology, Koganei, Japan
[5] CiNet and Graduate School of Frontier Biosciences, Osaka University, Suita, Japan

Abstract. The activity of saving and utilizing cultual heritage items as digital data by three-dimensional (3D) measurement is called digital archive. Digital archiving requires visualization that is accurate and easy for the observer to understand the structure. Therefore, visualization combining see-through visualization and stereoscopic presentation is considered effective. In previous studies, it has been reported that the depth is perceptually underestimated in see-through stereoscopic vision of 3D point clouds. In this research, in order to solve the problem, we propose an edge highlighting method for the 3D structure of data and show its effectiveness by an evaluation experiment. Moreover, in this research, new depth information is added by applying the method of dashed lines to the extracted edge. We conduct another evaluation experiment and show that these dashed lines have influences on perceived depth.

Keywords: See-through visualization · 3D point cloud · Stereoscopic vision · Feature region extraction

1 Introduction

Digital archiving describes an activity that is intended to scan cultural heritage items, store them as digital data, and use them for inheritance and analysis [1,2]. In recent years, it has become possible to acquire complex 3D-shaped cultural heritage items as point cloud data by scanning using a laser or photography. To make use of point clouds in digital archives, it is necessary to accurately visualize the digital data obtained by scanning, with which the observer can easily grasp the structure. See-through visualization is one of the visualization methods that

© Springer Nature Singapore Pte Ltd. 2019
G. Tan et al. (Eds.): AsiaSim 2019, CCIS 1094, pp. 149–160, 2019.
https://doi.org/10.1007/978-981-15-1078-6_13

can support structural understanding. The advantage of see-through visualization is that internal structures can be visualized even in structures with complex shapes. As a general method for visualizing the internal structure of a building, there is a method of creating a cross section using CAD, etc, but simultaneous visualization with external structures cannot be realized with this method. On the other hand, see-through visualization allows simultaneous visualization of internal and external structures. Stochastic point-based rendering (SPBR) [3,4] has been developed as one of the see-through visualization methods. The method is good at visualization of large-scale 3D point clouds because of its advantage of low calculation cost. In addition, using a stochastic algorithm makes it unnecessary to sort point clouds, and this method is suitable for digital archives in that depth information can be accurately visualized. As a visualization method to support structural understanding of digital data, use of stereoscopic 3D images is also effective. In previous studies, for the purpose of developing a new representation method of 3D digital data, contents for digital archives using a 3D display and VR have been produced [5]. However, all studies have used opaque images and objects instead of see-through images. In this research, we propose a visualization method that combines see-through visualization and stereoscopic vision for the 3D point cloud of tangible cultural heritage items. By using stereoscopic vision, the observer can recognize the shape more accurately because the observer can be given a depth cue that is not given in the 2D image. However, while see-through visualization makes it possible to visualize the internal structure, the visualization results become complicated because multiple objects appear to overlap. As a result, the effects of "occlusion" and "motion parallax", which are depth cues obtained by stereoscopic vision, are lost, and the accuracy of depth perception is considered to be reduced. The "motion parallax" is an important cue for recognizing the direction and the distance of the depth, and is an effect that is caused when the observer's head actively moves [6]. "Occlusion" is an important cue to recognize the direction of depth, and it is an effect that is caused when the object in front is hiding the object in back [6]. In previous studies, it is reported that depth is underestimated in see-through stereoscopic vision using SPBR [7]. In digital archives, it is necessary to present the visualization results of digital data correctly to the observer, and misleading representation methods are not suitable. Therefore, it can be noted that there is room for improvement in the current visualization methods in which the depth is underestimated. As a method for improvement, it seems easy to draw a scale on the side of the object to be visualized. However, this method ultimately has no effect because the observer cannot identify the object the drawn scale points to if the relationship of the front and back positions of the object that is drawn as see-through is unknown. In other words, in order to improve the accuracy of depth perception, it is necessary to increase the visibility of the object itself to be visualized as see-through. In this research, we propose two visualization methods of visual guides to improve underestimation of depth due to loss of depth cues. The first is a method to extract high curvature portions of a 3D structure using the eigenvalues obtained by principal component analysis, and to highlight only those portions. This method is confirmed to be effective in suppressing the decrease in the visibility of shapes that occur as the opacity decreases in 2D images [8]. In the see-through stereoscopic vision, it is possible to obtain the effects of "occlusion" and "motion parallax" without losing the see-through effect by drawing only those parts as opaque that are particularly necessary for grasping the shape. The second is a method to make the edges obtained by feature extraction of dashed lines. It is possible to obtain the effect of "texture gradient" which is a depth cue, by making the edges dashed lines. "Texture gradient" is proven to be obtained from the change of a uniform pattern given to an object [9]. In general, it is considered that changes in size, density, and aspect ratio of the texture produce a sense of depth. It is difficult to identify line segments because the 3D point cloud obtained by scanning does not have connection information between points. In this approach, we propose a method to identify line segments in a pseudo manner by focusing on the first principal component vector.

2   Conventional Methods Used in This Research

2.1   Feature Region Extraction Method

We describe the feature region extraction method used in this research. The feature region refers to the high curvature part, such as the vertex or the boundary between the surface and the surface (ridgeline) of a 3D structure. In this method, only the parts have high curvature in the 3D structure are extracted. First, principal component analysis is performed on the coordinate values of the point cloud that exists inside the sphere, centering on the point to be processed, and the feature value is defined by the combination of the obtained covariance matrix eigenvalues. Next, the feature values are calculated for all points, and only points with feature values larger than an arbitrarily set threshold are extracted. The Change of curvature [10] is effective as a feature value to extract only vertices and ridgelines. The feature value Change of curvature C_λ is defined by formula (1):

$$C_\lambda = \frac{\lambda_3}{\lambda_1 + \lambda_2 + \lambda_3}. \tag{1}$$

In formula (1), λ_1, λ_2 and λ_3 are the eigenvalues of the covariance matrix, and $\lambda_1 > \lambda_2 > \lambda_3$. Since the ratio of the minimum eigenvalue λ_3 tends to be larger at the vertices or ridgelines of the 3D structure, the value of C_λ is larger than that of the surface. An extraction example is shown in Fig. 1. Figure 1(a) is a result of the see-through visualization of surface data of a cuboid, and Fig. 1(b) is a visualization of only the feature region of the data in Fig. 1(a). The radius of the search sphere for principal component analysis is 1/150 of the diagonal length of the bounding box, and the threshold for feature extraction is 0.03. By changing the color of the feature region to red and rendering it opaque as shown in Fig. 1(b), it becomes a "visual guide" that supports shape recognition. The result of fusion visualization of the surface data and feature region highlighting is shown in Fig. 1(c). Compared to Fig. 1(a), it can be confirmed that the visibility of the vertices and the ridgelines are enhanced by the change of color and the increase of the opacity. This effect is predicted to enhance the effects of "motion parallax" and "occlusion" in stereoscopic vision.

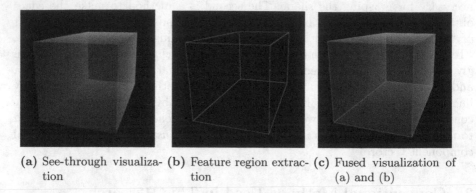

(a) See-through visualiza- (b) Feature region extrac- (c) Fused visualization of
tion   tion   (a) and (b)

Fig. 1. An example of feature region extraction using a cuboid (Color figure online)

2.2 Dashed Line Method

In this research, the edge is used as a texture by changing the edge visualized as solid lines to dashed lines. The dashed lines make it possible to identify the relationship of front and back positions of the object, and it can be a cue to recognize the depth magnitude by changing the "element size" and "density" of the texture in the viewing direction. The procedure for creating the dashed line is as follows.

First, feature regions (edges) are extracted by the method described in Sect. 2.1. In this method, solid lines are changed to dashed lines by "cutting out" edges once extracted. Next, the feature values given to the points are zeroed at regular intervals in parallel to a plane vertical to the axis. Points with a zero feature value are not extracted because their values are smaller than the threshold. In this method, it is possible to change the size and density of the dashed lines toward the gaze direction by changing a parameter called "interval value" that determines the interval of "cutting out" the edges. The "interval value" is calculated from the diagonal length of the bounding box.

An example of visualization is shown in Fig. 2. The data we are using is "Hachiman-yama", one of a "Yamahoko" used at the Gion Festival. Figure 2(a) and (b) show the result of visualization of Hachiman-yama using opaque point rendering and the result of visualization with SPBR applied. The result of visualizing only the feature region using the feature value linearity [10] is shown in Fig. 2(c). The threshold is 0.35. Further, a result of uniformly changing the whole feature region to dashed lines using the dashed line method is shown in Fig. 2(d). The interval value is 1/150. In addition, the ratio of the length of one line segment constituting a dashed line to the length of the interval between the line segments is 1:1. Finally, Fig. 2(e) shows the visualization results in which the length and the interval of the dashed lines are changed toward the gaze direction. The interval value is 1/300. The ratio of the length of one line segment constituting the dashed line to the length of the interval between the line segments changes sequentially from 10:1 to 1:1 from the area closest to the viewpoint. Comparing Fig. 2(c) and (d), it is possible to confirm that the edges change to dashed lines while leaving the edges necessary for shape recognition. Moreover, Fig. 2(e) makes it easier to distinguish between the edges present in the front and the edges present in the back compared with Fig. 2(c) and (d). In addition, it can be confirmed that the size and density of the dashed lines are changed toward the gaze direction.

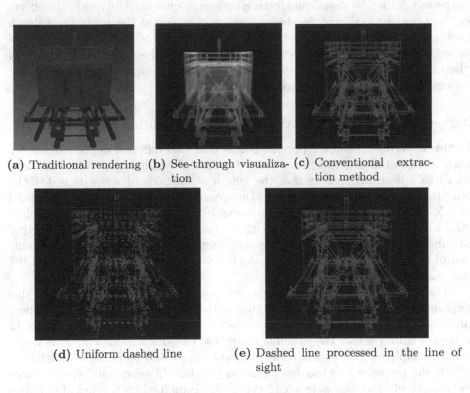

(a) Traditional rendering (b) See-through visualiza- (c) Conventional   extrac-
                                      tion   tion method

(d) Uniform dashed line   (e) Dashed line processed in the line of
                                      sight

Fig. 2. Visualization results of Hachiman-yama

3   Evaluation Experiment on See-Through Stereoscopic Vision

3.1   Depth Cues in See-Through Stereoscopic Vision

In this chapter, we describe the experiment to verify the effects of feature region highlighting and dashed lines in see-through stereoscopic vision. In this experiment, we used a multiview autostereoscopic display MV-4200 manufactured by TRIDELITY for presenting stereoscopic images. This display uses a lenticular lens system, which can give the observer motion parallax (5 parallaxes) in the horizontal direction. It is designed to obtain the maximum stereoscopic effect when the distance between the display and the observer is 3.0 m.

The effects of "motion parallax" and "occlusion", which are depth cues, are as described in Sect. 1. However, the effect of "occlusion" is lost in see-through visualization because the number of objects to be visualized increases with the uniform reduction of the inside and outside opacity. In addition, previous research shows that depth is underestimated in see-through stereoscopic vision using SPBR, and it is reported that accuracy decreases with decreasing opacity [7]. This research provides a "visual guide" that serves as a cue for shape recognition by visualizing feature regions as opaque. As a result, the effects of "motion parallax" and "occlusion" are enhanced and the accuracy of depth perception is improved without losing the advantage of the see-through characteristic. Furthermore, as described in Sect. 2.2, in this research, the effect of "texture gradient", which is one of the depth cues, is incorporated by performing processing to make the extracted edges dashed lines.

3.2 Conditions of the Feature Region Highlighting Experiment

In this experiment, three types of cuboids that had different depth lengths are used as an initial experiment to verify the effect. In addition, these cuboid data had two squares. Assuming that the length of one side of a square is 1.0, the length of each side in the z-axis direction representing the depth of each cuboid is 0.5, 1.0, and 2.0. Hereafter, each cuboid used for the experiment is called "0.5× cuboid", "1.0× cuboid", and "2.0× cuboid". Figure 3 shows three types of cuboid polygon data. Poisson disc sampling [11] is used for each of the point-sampled data. SPBR is applied to make it a see-through image. The color of the point cloud is cyan.

The experimental conditions are as follows. The stimulus images used in this experiment are of six types that combine the conditions of cuboids (3 types) and the condition of the presence or absence of feature region highlighting (2 types). Figure 4 shows the stimulus image used in this experiment. This figure is an example of 2.0× cuboid. The subjects were asked to perform 24 trials in which the presence or absence of motion parallax (2 types) and the presence or absence of binocular parallax (2 types) are combined for 6 types of stimulus images. This experiment is performed with all the conditions in random order. At the time of image switching, a black image is presented so that no afterimage is left on the retina. The subjects are twenty men and women in their 20s and 30s. Prior to the experiment, the Titmus stereo fly test [12] is performed on all subjects to confirm a healthy stereoscopic vision function. The subject answers the question regarding the length of the side of the cuboid extending in the z-axis direction, assuming that the length of one side of the square is 1.0. For example, if the stimulus image is a cube, the correct value is 1.0. When the condition is "monocular", the subject hides one eye with an occluder and observes with only the dominant eye. In addition, when the condition is "no motion parallax", the subject's head is positioned on the chin rest and remains fixed so that there is no movement. The height of the seat is adjusted for each subject so that the height of the head matches the height of the display.

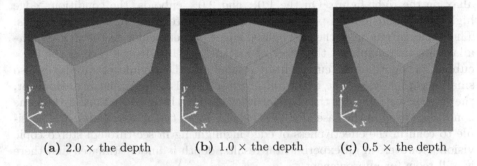

(a) 2.0 × the depth   (b) 1.0 × the depth   (c) 0.5 × the depth

Fig. 3. Polygon data of three types of cuboids (Color figure online)

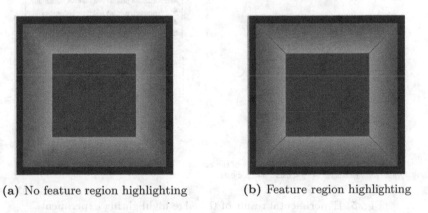

(a) No feature region highlighting   (b) Feature region highlighting

Fig. 4. Visual stimuli (cuboid with H:W:D = 1.0:1.0:2.0) used in the experiment

3.3 Experimental Result of Feature Region Highlighting

We use ANOVA and Tukey's HSD test for analysis. The experimental results are shown in Fig. 5. The left and right figures show the effect of edge highlighting and the interaction between edge highlighting and motion parallax, respectively. The vertical axis in the figure is the error of the perceived depth, and the formula is (2) as follows:

$$\varepsilon = \frac{\text{Measured value} - \text{Correct value}}{\text{Correct value}}. \tag{2}$$

Error bars represent standard errors of the mean. As shown in the left figure of Fig. 5, in all cuboids, the condition "edge highlighting" improves the accuracy of depth perception and its effectiveness is obvious. The highlighted edges extending toward the gaze direction may have played an important role in this improvement as a linear perspective cue because the visibility of these edges were more enhanced than those of the front and back squares. This result suggests that the shape recognition can be enhanced by edge highlighting.

Next, we describe the interaction effect of edge highlighting and motion parallax on the right figure. On the 1.0× and 2.0× cuboids, the condition "edge highlighting and motion parallax" is more accurate than all other conditions. The apparent reason is the highlighted edges perpendicular to the motion parallax direction amplified the effect of motion parallax. In the case of the 0.5× cuboid, the depth of the cuboid itself is small and the amount of parallax is also small accordingly, so, the effect did not reach statistical significance. However, the same figure indicates that the accuracy tends to be improved under the same conditions, even in the case of a 0.5× cuboid. From the above results, it is possible to confirm the effectiveness of edge highlighting in see-through stereoscopic vision. However, in all experimental results, depth is underestimated and there is still room for improvement.

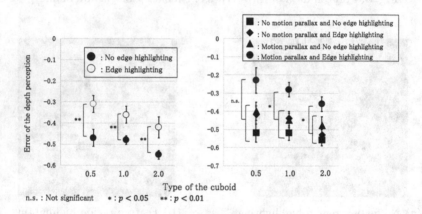

Fig. 5. Experimental result of the edge highlighting experiment

3.4 Conditions of the Dashed Edge Experiment

In this experiment, three types of cuboid created by the same procedure as the experiment in Sect. 3.2 are used. The length of the side in the z-axis direction of each cuboid is 0.6 times, 1.2 times, and 1.8 times.

The experimental conditions are as follows. The stimulus images used in this experiment are of 12 types, combining the conditions of cuboids (3 types) and feature region highlighting methods using dashed edges (4 methods). Four methods of feature region highlighting are shown in Fig. 6. The figure is an example of a 1.8× cuboid. The feature region is extracted using the Change of curvature, and the threshold is 0.03. Figure 6(a) shows the conventional feature region highlighting, and Fig. 6(b) shows the edge extracted in Fig. 6(a) changed to dashed edges that were uniform in the simulated 3D scene rather than in the 2D image presented on the display. In addition, in Fig. 6(c) and (d), the length of the line segment and the length of the interval are changed toward the gaze direction. The ratio of the length of one line segment composed the dashed line to the distance between the line segments is 1:1 in the whole region. In Fig. 6(c), the length modulation of the line segment in the 2D image due to perspective was exaggerated by a factor of two. In Fig. 6(d), the length modulation of the line segment due to perspective was reversed and exaggerated by a factor of two. The interval values in Fig. 6(b)(c)(d) are all 1/150. Hereafter, the enhancing methods in Fig. 6(a)(b)(c)(d) are called "solid line" "dashed line" "(texture gradient) enhanced dashed line" and "(texture gradient) reverse enhanced dashed line". A total of 48 trials are conducted with the subject, combining the presence or absence of motion parallax (2 types) and the presence or absence of binocular parallax (2 types) on 12 types of stimulus images. The other experimental conditions are the same as those in Sect. 3.2.

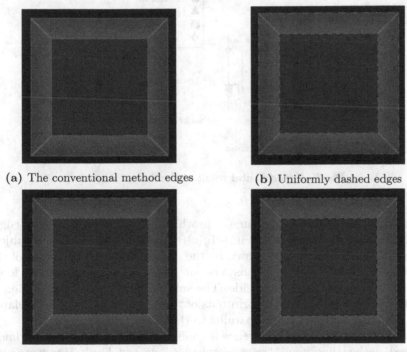

(a) The conventional method edges

(b) Uniformly dashed edges

(c) Dashed edges that become finer depending on the distance from the view point

(d) Dashed edges that become rougher depending on the distance from the view point

Fig. 6. Visual stimuli (cuboid with H:W:D = 1.0:1.0:1.8) used in the dashed edges experiment

3.5   Experimental Result of Dashed Edge Experiment

Again, we use ANOVA and Tukey's HSD test for analysis. The experimental results are shown in Fig. 7. The vertical axis in the figure is the error of the depth perception, determined by the formula (2). In each figure, the horizontal axis is the type of cuboid, and the plotted values are the average values for each condition. Error bars represent standard errors of the mean. In the 1.8× cuboid, the condition "reverse enhanced dashed line" is more accurate than the other conditions. As a factor, monocular static information was likely to influence the depth perception because the interaction effect of the "reverse enhanced dashed line", "motion parallax" and "binocular parallax" is not confirmed. From the result obtained this time, we hypothesized that since the length of one side looks longer by increasing the number of elements of the dashed line near the viewpoint, the depth looks more deeper. We test this hypothesis below.

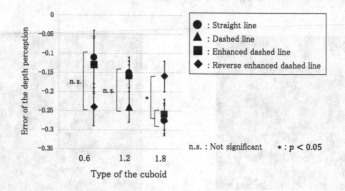

Fig. 7. Experimental result of the dashed edge

Figure 8(a)(b)(c) are stimulus images in which only the front and back edges of the bottom of the cuboids in Fig. 6(b)(c)(d) are drawn. Then, the subject compares the length of the line drawn on the upper side with the length of the line drawn on the lower side, and answers how many times the upper side looks similar to the length of the lower side. The subjects are 10 men and women in their 20s. In this experiment, the printouts of the stimulus images are displayed 80 cm away from the subject and parallel to the subject's forehead.

As a result, no significant difference is confirmed between the "dashed line", "enhanced dashed line" and "reverse enhanced dashed line". However, each answer's average value is 0.74, 0.76, 0.71, and the ratio of the two dashed lines is the smallest in the "enhanced dashed line" and the largest in the "reverse enhanced dashed line". This result indicates, according our hypothesis, that the observer tends to perceive the length of the dashed line as longer when observing the dashed line that has many elements.

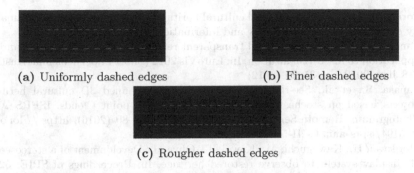

(a) Uniformly dashed edges   (b) Finer dashed edges

(c) Rougher dashed edges

Fig. 8. Auxiliary experimental result of the dashed edge

4   Conclusion

In this study, we proposed see-through stereoscopic vision as a visualization method to support an accurate understanding of the structure of data used in digital archives. Although there is a problem that the observer underestimates the depth in see-through stereoscopic vision, we proposed a visual guide that highlights and visualizes the feature region of the 3D structure as a solution. In addition, we proposed a method to make the extracted edges dashed lines. In the visualization experiment about the dashed line, it is confirmed that proposed method can make the dashed line correctly and it is possible to distinguish the positional relationship of the edges. Next, from the evaluation experiments about edge highlighting, it became clear that edge highlighting has the effect of improving the underestimation of depth. Moreover, the effect of edge highlighting was significant especially when the motion parallax was available. However, the depth remained underestimated even after the improvement. Finally, from the evaluation experiment about the dashed line, a result that differs from our expectation of the effect of "texture gradient" is obtained. Before the experiment, we expected that the "dashed line" and "enhanced dashed line", which incorporate the effect of "texture gradient", among the 4 proposed enhancing methods, have improvement effects. However, as a result, the improvement effect is confirmed in the "reverse enhanced dashed line" scenario in which the effect of "texture gradient" is not incorporated. In auxiliary experiments to test hypotheses considered from these results, we obtain results tending to support the hypotheses. In the future, it is necessary to experiment with data similar to the shape of tangible cultural heritage items or with tangible cultural heritage item data.

Acknowledgement. We thank the Hachiman-Yama Preservation Society for its cooperation in our laser-scanning activities.

References

1. Parry, R.: Digital heritage and the rise of theory in museum computing. Mus. Manag. Curatorship **20**(4), 333–348 (2005)

2. Zorich, D.M.: A survey of digital cultural heritage initiatives and their sustainability concerns. Council on Library and information Resources (2003)
3. Tanaka, S., et al.: Particle-based transparent rendering of implicit surfaces and its application to fused visualization. In: EuroVis 2012 (Short Paper), Vienna, Austria, 5–8 June 2012, pp. 35–29 (2012)
4. Tanaka, S., et al.: See-through imaging of laser-scanned 3D cultural heritage objects based on stochastic rendering of large-scale point Clouds. ISPRS Ann. Photogramm. Remote Sens. Spat. Inf. Sci. **III-5**, 73–80 (2016). https://doi.org/10.5194/isprs-annals-III-5-73-2016
5. Morikawa, H., Kawaguchi, M., Kawai, T., Ohya, J.: Development of a stereoscopic 3D display system to observe restored heritage. In: Proceedings of SPIE, 5291, Stereoscopic Displays and Virtual Reality Systems XI, pp. 415–422 (2004)
6. Heine, L.: Uber Wahrnehmung und Vorstellung von Entfernungsunterschieden. Experimentelle Ophthalmologie, vol. 61, pp. 484–498 (1905)
7. Kitaura, Y., et al.: Effects of depth cues on the recognition of the spatial position of a 3D object in transparent stereoscopic visualization. In: The 5th International KES Conference on Innovation in Medicine and Healthcare (KES-InMed 2017), Vilamoura, Portugal, 21–23 June 2017, pp. 277–282 (2017)
8. Okamoto, N., Hasegawa, K., Li, L., Okamoto, A., Tanaka, S.: Highlighting feature regions combined with see-through visualization of laser-scanned cultural heritage. In: Proceedings of 2017 International Conference on Culture and Computing, 10 September 2017, pp. 7–12 (2017)
9. Cumming, B.G., Johnston, E.B., Parker, A.J.: Effects of different texture cues on curved surfaces viewed stereoscopically. Vis. Res. **33**(5/6), 827–838 (1993)
10. Weinmann, M., Jutzi, B., Mallet, C.: Feature relevance assessment for the semantic interpretation of 3D point cloud data. ISPRS Ann. Photogramm. Remote. Sens. Spat. Inf. Sci. **II–5/W2**, 313–318 (2013)
11. Ebeida, M.S., Patney, A., Mitchell, S.A.: Efficient maximal poisson-disk sampling. The definitive version appears in ACM Transactions on Graphics, vol. 30, no. 4 (2011)
12. Vancleef, K., Read, J.C.A.: Which stereotest do you use? A survey research study in the British isles, the United States and Canada. Br. Ir. Orthopt. J. **15**(1), 15–24 (2019)

Realizing Uniformity of 3D Point Clouds Based on Improved Poisson-Disk Sampling

Yuto Sakae[1(✉)], Yukihiro Noda[1], Liang Li[2], Kyoko Hasegawa[2],
Satoshi Nakada[3], and Satoshi Tanaka[2]

[1] Graduate School of Information Science and Engineering,
Ritsumeikan University, Kyoto, Japan
is0259rv@ed.ritsumei.ac.jp
[2] College of Information Science and Engineering,
Ritsumeikan University, Kyoto, Japan
[3] National Institute for Environmental Studies, Tsukuba, Japan

Abstract. With the development of digital technology, large-scale three-dimensional point cloud data are formed from data obtained by output from three-dimensional (3D) laser measurements and numerical fluid simulations. The complex shape described by 3D laser measurements is utilized in the project of digital archiving, which is an effort to leave cultural property to future generations. The data obtained by numerical fluid simulation is also useful for analyzing the dynamic behavior of the ocean. For utilization and analysis of these point clouds, visualization is important as visual support. The quality of visualization depends on the uniformity of the point distribution. However, in the case of a 3D point cloud obtained by measurement or fluid simulation, bias of point density may occur in the point distribution due to the measurement environment or the process of converting to a point cloud. This will impair the visualization quality. In previous studies, we used Poisson disk sampling (PDS) to eliminate point distribution bias and improve visualization quality. However, in point reduction by the naive PDS, since point selection is randomly performed in processing, the uniformity of the inter-point distance between points is insufficient. In this paper, we propose "dual-shell PDS" as a method to improve PDS and generate point clouds with constant distance between points and improved visualization quality.

Keywords: Large-scale three-dimensional point cloud · Visualization · The uniformity of the point distribution · Poisson disk sampling · Dual-shell PDS

1 Introduction

3D point clouds are used in many fields such as cultural assets, measurement, manufacturing, and medical care. Improvements in digital technology [1–3] have

© Springer Nature Singapore Pte Ltd. 2019
G. Tan et al. (Eds.): AsiaSim 2019, CCIS 1094, pp. 161–173, 2019.
https://doi.org/10.1007/978-981-15-1078-6_14

made it possible to easily acquire point clouds of large-scale and complex structures. In our research, we render 3D point clouds obtained by measurement and fluid simulation as they are and perform semitransparent visualization. Translucent visualization is useful for understanding 3D structure because it can simultaneously reveal the inside and outside structures of a point cloud.

We have been studying digital archiving of cultural assets and also utilization of the archived data [4–6]. Recently, digital archiving by using 3D measurement, which produces large-scale point cloud data, is becoming popular [7]. Since the point cloud obtained by 3D measurement has accurate 3D coordinates and color information, visualization can be useful not only for understanding the structure but also for supporting viewing and restoration. Additionally, as support for ocean analysis, we are visualizing ocean behavior related to the Nankai Trough massive earthquake [8]. The tsunami caused as a secondary disaster also caused great damage to Japan, an earthquake-prone country. To reduce the damage, it is necessary to analyze the behavior of the tsunami. To analyze the behavior of the tsunami, visual support is provided by converting numerical data obtained by fluid simulation such as particle method and finite volume method to a point cloud for visualization.

We use stochastic point-based rendering (SPBR) developed in our laboratory for transparent visualization of 3D point clouds [9,10]. Since this can express the depth of points without the need for sorting, even large-scale point clouds can undergo translucent rendering quickly and accurately. The opacity of the point cloud rendering is proportional to the point density. However, in the 3D measurement point cloud, the point distribution may be biased depending on the weather, location condition, and surveying technology at the time of measurement. Additionally, in the fluid simulation, when converting from the unstructured grid model representation to the point cloud, the point distribution may be biased. If there is a bias in point density, the point rendering will be inaccurate. To address this problem, it is necessary to improve the point cloud quality by appropriately thinning points of the original 3D point cloud data. A high-quality point cloud needs to satisfy three conditions: (1) high point density, (2) local uniformity of point density, and (3) uniformity of distance between adjacent points. Recent 3D point cloud are large-scale datasets, so the first condition may be satisfied but (2) and (3) may not be. Therefore, in previous research, the quality of the point cloud was improved by using Poisson-disk sampling (PDS) [11]. PDS can eliminate the bias of point density without moving the point cloud or modifying the data such as generating a new point. Therefore, it can be said that a high-quality point cloud is realized that improves he quality of the transparent visualization by probabilistic point rendering. However, while PDS can meet condition (2), it is insufficient to satisfy condition (3).

Therefore, in this study, we propose a modified PDS method that supports higher-quality transparent visualization by extending the PDS to ensure the above (2) and (3). The proposed method is called "dual-shell PDS", and aims to distribute 3D point cloud at maximum and uniform distance. In the conventional PDS, the point cloud is made more uniform by thinning out the points using a

3D sphere so that there is only one point in each sphere. Dual-shell PDS uses double 3D spheres. In the process of performing point reduction, the positions of points that exist on the shell of the double 3D sphere are recorded, and then the next search point is selected from the recorded points. This makes it possible to improve the quality of the point cloud maintaining a constant distance between points. By using this proposed method to generate a high-quality point cloud, we improve the transparent visualization quality of the point cloud by SPBR.

2 Method of Transparent Visualization

Transparent visualization helps to support analysis by visualizing not only the surface of the point cloud but also the internal structure at the same time. However, in the case of a general transparent visualization method with a large-scale point cloud, it is necessary to sort them in the direction of the line of sight, and the amount of computation becomes enormous. Therefore, in this research, SPBR is used as a transparent visualization method. SPBR can render at high speed without the need to sort the point cloud. SPBR performs rendering in three steps: (1) point generation, (2) point projection, and (3) pixel luminance value determination. The first step of this task is to generate points in the volume space in proportion to the transfer function based on the data to be visualized. In the visualization of 3D measurement data, the measurement point cloud itself is the point generation. The second step is to project and store the nearest point from the line of sight at each pixel in the image plane. At this time, the generated points are projected into an arbitrary number of groups. In the third step, luminance values are determined by applying an ensemble average to the image group created in step 2. The determination of the luminance value by the ensemble average is expressed by the following Eq. (1) [12].

$$B = \frac{1}{L_R} \sum_{i=0}^{L_R-1} B^{[i]} \tag{1}$$

where B is the luminance value of the image to be drawn, B_i is the luminance value of the i th image generated in step 2, and L_R is the number of groups. In SPBR, the number of points generated in step 1 are controlled by opacity. The opacity control is calculated based on the binomial distribution. The determination of the number of generated points by the opacity is expressed by the following Eq. (2).

$$n = \frac{\ln(1-\alpha)}{\ln(1-\frac{s}{S})} L_R \tag{2}$$

where n is the number of generation points, α is the opacity, S is the local area of the point cloud on the planar image, and s is the cross-sectional area of the point.

Formula (2) indicates that we can control opacity by tuning point density in visualization with SPBR. However, Formula (2) holds under the assumption that point density is locally uniform. Therefore, we propose to thin out the original points appropriately such that the local uniformity is realized as much as possible.

3   Dual-Shell PDS

In the measurement point cloud data, measurement noise may sometimes occur at the point depending on the measurement situation. When converting unstructured grid data created by fluid simulation to point data, since the points are generated in space using the Monte Carlo method, the uniformity of the points—in particular, the uniformity of the distance between points—is not guaranteed. This non-uniformity of point density and inter-point distances impairs image quality of SPBR. In order to make the point density and the distance between points uniform, down sampling by PDS is effective.

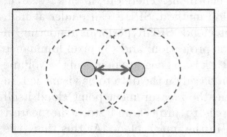 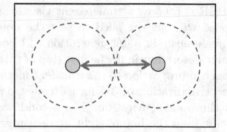

Fig. 1. The two extreme cases of the interpoint distances made by PDS. The left figure shows the case that the distance takes the minimum value r, whereas the right figure shows the case that the distance takes the maximum value R

PDS is originally used for point drawing in the field of image processing [13]. The sampling criteria for PDS by a two-dimensional image were determined by a circle for the attention point. By extending this criterion to a sphere, it is applied to a 3D point cloud. However, in the downsampling by conventional PDS, the selection of the attention point is performed at random. Therefore, the distance between points is guaranteed more than the radius r of the sphere, but depending on the distribution state of the point cloud, there are cases where points separated by more than r become adjacent points. An image of the change in the distance between points is shown in Fig. 1. As shown in Fig. 1, the distance between adjacent points changes between r and $2r$ according to the degree of overlap of the spheres. This problem is particularly noticeable for volume data, and the points are reduced more than necessary. Thus, in conventional PDS, the uniformity of the point distance is insufficient. To solve this problem, in our study, we propose a "dual-shell PDS" with improved PDS and uniform distance between points.

3.1 Distance Equalization Between Points by Dual-Shell PDS

To realize highly-uniform inter-point distances, we use double concentric spheres (dual shell) in executing PDS, whereas the conventional PDS uses a single sphere. In addition, Point selection is controlled by assigning a priority weight to the point (attention point) selected as the center of the sphere for point reduction by PDS. Processing in a dual-shell PDS is shown in the Fig. 2. A dual shell consists of two spheres, an inner sphere of small radius r and an outer sphere of large radius R. After discarding all other points in the inner sphere centered at the attention point, the priority of the points remaining in the outer sphere is made higher. Either a point on the dual shell spherical shell centered at the attention point or an existing attention point is then selected as the next attention point. The distance between points on the spherical shell and the attention point takes values from r to R. The value of R is a user parameter. By changing the value in the range from r to $2r$, variation (r to $2r$) in the distance between adjacent points can be reduced compared to the point cloud to which the conventional PDS is applied. The concrete algorithm of dual-shell PDS is as follows.

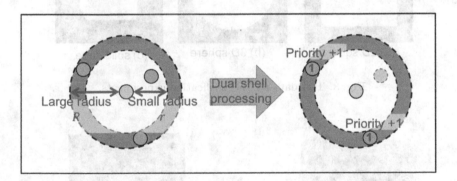

Fig. 2. Schematic illustration of the process of dual-shell PDS

Step 1. Assign an initial value 0 to the priority for all points in the input point cloud data of n points.

Step 2. Set the small radius r and the large radius R of the dual shell, and randomly select the first attention point from the input point cloud. (The small radius r is the same size as the conventional PDS radius, and it is assumed that $r < R$.)

Step 3. Accept the attention point and reject the existence of any other point within the small radius r centered at the attention point.

Step 4. Increment the priorities of all points remaining in the large radius R other than the attention point.

Step 5. The next attention point is randomly selected from the point cloud having the highest priority among the point cloud, and the process returns to Step 3. If you cannot select the next attention point from the point cloud, then exit.

3.2   High-Quality Verification of Point Cloud by Dual Shell PDS

We conduct a verification experiment on high-quality of point cloud using our dual-shell PDS. As a verification method, polygon meshes are generated for surface data, and side lengths and aspect ratios of triangular polygons are calculated. The sides of the polygon represent the distance between adjacent points. Therefore, the closer the aspect ratio is to 1, the smaller the difference between the longest side and the shortest side, and the more uniform the distance between adjacent points. On the other hand, since volume data cannot form a polygon mesh, the distance between adjacent points and number of generation points are verified. Verification by number of points is compared with the number of points when points are arranged at intervals of radius r set by PDS.

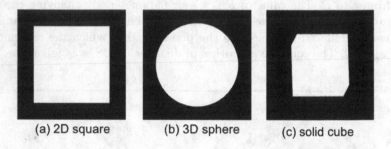

(a) 2D square   (b) 3D sphere   (c) solid cube

Fig. 3. Test data for the verification experiments

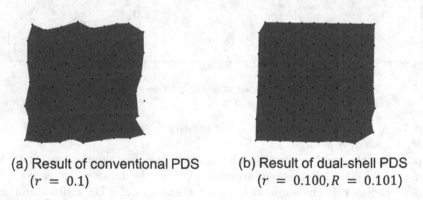

(a) Result of conventional PDS   (b) Result of dual-shell PDS
($r = 0.1$)   ($r = 0.100, R = 0.101$)

Fig. 4. Polygon meshes created based on the square-shaped point clouds refined by (a) the conventional PDS and (b) our dual-shell PDS

The data used for verification experiments are 2D squares and 3D spheres of surface data and solid cube of volume data. Assuming application to a large-scale point cloud, 10 million points are randomly generated. The visualization image of verification data is shown in Fig. 3. Figures 4 and 5 show the results of meshing the point cloud where the conventional PDS and dual-shell PDS are applied, respectively to the two surface data with verification data.

The radius r of both PDSs was set to 0.1 for 2D square and 0.15 for 3D sphere. Additionally, the large radius R of the dual-shell PDS is arbitrarily set to be as small as possible in the range from r to $2r$. The verification results are shown in Table 1. From the Table 1, for the average side length of the conventional PDS, the square has an average side length of 0.137 for the setting radius $r = 0.1$ of PDS, and the sphere has an average side length of 0.200 for the setting radius $r = 0.15$ of PDS. On the other hand, in the dual-shell PDS, square has an average side length of 0.104, and sphere has an average side length of 0.166. From this, it can be seen that the average side length of the point cloud after applying the dual-shell PDS is closer to the value of radius r. Next, the average aspect ratio is compared. According to the Table 1, the average aspect ratio is closer to 1 using the dual shell PDS than in the random order PDS in both datasets. From this, it can be seen that polygons having a shape close to an equilateral triangle are

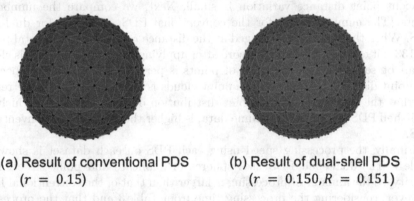

(a) Result of conventional PDS   (b) Result of dual-shell PDS
($r = 0.15$)   ($r = 0.150, R = 0.151$)

Fig. 5. Polygon meshes created based on the sphere-shaped point clouds refined by (a) the conventional PDS and (b) our dual-shell PDS

Table 1. Verification result for surface data

Method		PDS	Dual-shell PDS
2D square	Number of points	73	117
	Average side length	0.137	0.104
	Average aspect ratio (95% confidence interval (CI))	1.404 (±0.037)	1.104 (±0.032)
	Standard deviation (SD) of average aspect ratio	0.204	0.238
3D sphere	Number of points	387	539
	Average side length	0.200	0.166
	Average aspect ratio (95% CI)	1.380 (±0.014)	1.207 (±0.013)
	SD of average aspect ratio	0.195	0.209

formed in the point cloud to which the dual-shell PDS is applied. Comparing the standard deviation of the aspect ratio and the 95% confidence interval, it is almost the same, so you can see that there is no difference in the variation from the average value. From the above results, it can be demonstrated that the uniformity of point cloud distributions where dual-shell PDS is applied to surface data is higher than that achieved by the previous PDS.

Next, Table 2 shows the results of a point cloud where conventional PDS and dual-shell PDS were applied to volume data for verification. The radius r of both PDSs was set to 0.1. The average adjacent point distance in Table 2 is 0.102 in the conventional PDS and 0.100 in the dual-shell PDS. In addition, comparing the maximum distances between points, it can be seen that the dual-shell PDS is shorter. Furthermore, in the standard deviation of the average distance between adjacent points and the 95% confidence interval, both values after applying dual-shell PDS are lower, so it is considered that the uniformization effect is higher. From this, it can be seen that the average adjacent point distance of the point cloud applying the dual shell PDS is closer to the value of radius r, and the adjacent point distance variation is small. Next, we compare the number of points. The number is 856 for the conventional PDS, and 1021 for dual-shell PDS. When the points are arranged at the distance r, the number of total points are 1331, it can be seen that the score after applying the dual-shell PDS is closer. It can be seen that the existence of points is permitted more densely because the point distance between all the point clouds is shortened. The above results tell that the uniformity of the point distribution of point clouds, to which the dual-shell PDS is applied to volume data, is higher than that of the conventional PDS.

Finally, the processing speed using each PDS on each dataset is shown in Table 3. The dual-shell PDS uses spheres in duplicate and point selection by priority, so the amount of processing is larger than that of the conventional PDS. However, considering the processing time from Table 3 and that the processing time when dual-shell PDS is applied when the 3D sphere contains 100 million points under the same conditions is 114,330 ms, it is sufficiently applicable.

Table 2. Verification result for volume data

Method		PDS	Dual-shell PDS
Solid cube	Number of points	856	1021
	Average point distance (95% CI)	0.102 ($\pm 2.198 \times 10^{-4}$)	0.100 ($\pm 0.120 \times 10^{-4}$)
	Maximum distance between points	0.126	0.101
	Minimum distance between points	0.100	0.1
	SD of average point distance	3.281×10^{-3}	0.196×10^{-3}

Table 3. Processing speed for each PDS

Method		PDS	Dual-shell PDS
2D square	Processing speed	1885.04 ms	3741.99 ms
3D sphere	Processing speed	2811.25 ms	5680.34 ms
Solid cube	Processing speed	4303.44 ms	8801.75 ms

4   Application to Large-Scale Point Clouds

We improve the quality of the point cloud using point cloud data actually generated by 3D measurement and point cloud generated from fluid simulation. The data used the Stanford Bunny and data simulating the tsunami in Nankai Trough massive earthquakes predicted in Japan. The original number of points of the bunny are 35,947. Here, we randomly sampled points on the triangulated surface, and the points are increased to 9,965,248. The simulation data of the tsunami was conducted by the unstructured grid triangular column model generated by FVCOM (Finite Volume Coastal Ocean Mode)[14]. The analysis area includes Osaka Bay, Harima Nada and Kii Channel. The number of triangular polygons is 4,648,536. Monte Carlo method is executed in this triangular prism model to generate points. Here, the total points are 7,310,742. The Stanford bunny has a radius of $r = 0.002$ and a large radius of $R = 0.0025$. For the Stanford bunny surface data, an image obtained by meshing the point cloud to which each PDS is applied is shown in Fig. 7 and the verification result is shown in Table 4. A visualized image of the object data is shown in Fig. 6. The Stanford bunny has a complex shape with much surface unevenness. Our dual-shell PDS is more suitable for such a surface than the conventional PDS: the dual-shell PDS realizes better inter-point-distance uniformity and better aspect ratio when polygonized. This feature of the dual-shell PDS leads to better rendering quality whether the

(a)Point cloud of Stanford bunny
(9,965,248 points)

(b) Point cloud that describes tsunami simulation
of the Nankai Trough massive earthquake
(7,310,742 points)

Fig. 6. Point cloud used for the verification experiments

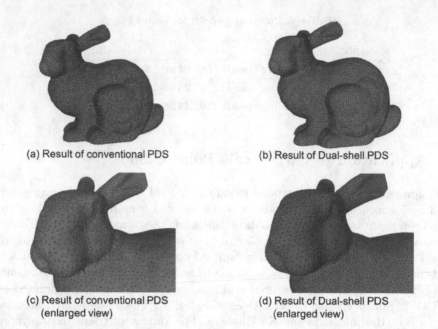

(a) Result of conventional PDS

(b) Result of Dual-shell PDS

(c) Result of conventional PDS
(enlarged view)

(d) Result of Dual-shell PDS
(enlarged view)

Fig. 7. Comparison of polygon meshes created based on the point cloud of Stanford Bunny (see Fig. 6(a)) refined by the conventional PDS and our dual-shell PDS

Table 4. Verification result for Stanford bunny

Method		PDS	Dual-shell PDS
Stanford Bunny	Number of points	9712	13448
	Average side length	0.00268	0.00226
	Average aspect ratio (95% CI)	1.399 ($\pm 0.284 \times 10^{-2}$)	1.206 ($\pm 0.271 \times 10^{-2}$)
	SD of average aspect ratio	0.206	0.226

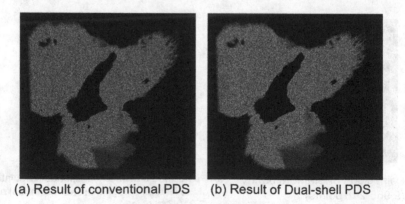

(a) Result of conventional PDS

(b) Result of Dual-shell PDS

Fig. 8. Transparent visualization based on the point cloud of the tsumami simulation data (see Fig. 6(b)) refined by (a) the conventional PDS and (b) our dual-shell PDS

adopted rendering algorithm is SPBR or the conventional polygon rendering. We can also see that our dual-shell PDS more original points, which is beneficial in the sense that we can keep the original surface shape as much as possible.

Next, for the simulation volume data, an image of the point cloud to which each type of PDS is applied is shown in Fig. 8 and the verification result is shown in Table 5. The simulation data has a radius of $r = 0.06$ and a large radius of $R = 0.064$. From the results summarized in the table, we can see that the average inter-point distance is more uniform than in the result of the dual-shell PDS compared with the conventional PDS. In fact, the range width of the inter-point distances is 0.487 for the dual-shell PDS and 0.951 for the conventional PDS.

Let us investigate the variation of points in the tsunami simulation data applying dual-shell PDS (see Fig. 8(b)). Figure 9 shows the frequency distribution and cumulative frequency distribution of the distance between points by application of dual-shell PDS. As seen from Fig. 9, the ratio of distances between points is the largest at 0.6 to 0.62, and the distance between points of at least 90% takes values up to the large radius $R = 0.64$. The dual-shell PDS is considered to be sufficiently applicable because the distance between points equalization effect can be seen at most points although there is variation due to the size of the maximum value. In the frequency distribution of the tsunami simulation

Table 5. Verification result for tsunami simulation data

Method		PDS	Dual-shell PDS
Simulation data	Number of points	119668	132185
	Average point distance (95% CI)	0.640 ($\pm 2.100 \times 10^{-4}$)	0.614 ($\pm 1.029 \times 10^{-4}$)
	Maximum distance between points	1.551	1.087
	Minimum distance between points	0.6	0.6
	SD of average aspect ratio	3.707×10^{-2}	2.227×10^{-2}

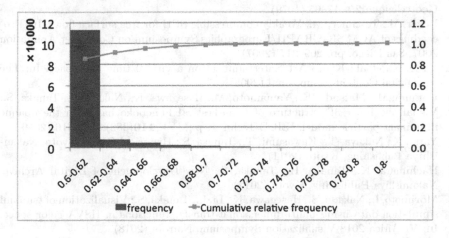

Fig. 9. Frequency distribution and cumulative frequency distribution of the distance between points of simulation data applying dual-shell PDS

data (see Fig. 8(a)) to which the conventional PDS is applied, The proportion of point cloud having the distance between points of up to 0.64 is about 60%. Also, the range of values for the distance between points taken by the 90% point clouds is 0.6 to 0.7. From this, it can be understood that the dual-shell PDS has a higher distance between points equalization effect than the conventional PDS. From the above, it can be seen that dual-shell PDS has useful effects on data with complex shapes.

5   Conclusion

In this paper, we have proposed the dual-shell PDS, which is an improved Poisson-disk sampling (PDS) aiming at improving the uniformity of inter-point distances. The key idea is to prepare double concentric Poisson disks (3D spheres) and adopt points existing in the region between the large and small spheres with higher priority. We evaluated the proposed method by applying to large-scale point clouds describing surface and volume with complex shapes, and successfully proved the superiority of our method compared with the conventional PDS. The high-level uniformity realized by our dual-shell PDS works well for transparent visualization of surface and volumes, which are described as large-scale point clouds. Therefore, our method is useful for realizing comprehensible 3D transparent visualization of, for example, laser-scanned data and results of large-scale particle simulation of fluids.

References

1. Lucy, L.B.: A numerical approach to the testing of the fission hypothesis. Astron. J. **82**, 1013–1024 (1977)
2. Cundall, P.A., Strack, O.D.L.: A discrete numerical model for granular assemblies. Geotechnique **29**, 47–65 (1979)
3. Bcker, M., Teschner, M.: Weakly compressible SPH for free surface flows. In: Proceedings of ACM SIGGRAPH/Eurographics Symposium on Computer Animation 2007, San Diego, pp. 209–217 (2007)
4. Yano, K., et al.: Kyoto Art Entertainment on a virtual time and space. In: The 1st Digital Content Symposium (2005)
5. Uemura, M., Matsuda, K., Yamamoto, M., Hasegawa, K., Nakata, S., Tanaka, S.: Visualizing inner 3D structure of Gion-Festival Funeboko based on the opaque illuminant particle model. IEICE Techn. Rep. MVE **110**(382), 311–316 (2010)
6. Yano, K., Nakaya, T., Kawasumi, T., Tanaka, S.: Historical GIS of Kyoto. Nakanishiya Publishing, Kyoto (2011)
7. Hachimura, K., Tanaka, H., Tanaka, S.: New Development of Digital Archive. Nakanishiya Publishing, Kyoto (2012)
8. Morimoto, I., Nakada, S., Hasegawa, K., Li, L., Tanaka, S.: Visualization of tsunami simulation data using multi-dimensional transfer functions in HSVA color space. In: VizAfrica 2018 Visualization Symposium, Nairobi (2018)
9. Tanaka, S., et al.: Particle-based transparent rendering of implicit surfaces and its application to fused visualization. In: EuroVis 2012, Vienna, pp. 25–29 (2012)

10. Tanaka, S., et al.: See-through imaging of laser-scanned 3D cultural heritage objects based on stochastic rendering of large-scale point clouds. ISPRS Ann. Photogramm. Remote Sens. Spat. Inf. Sci. III-5, 73–80 (2016). https://doi.org/10.5194/isprs-annals-III-5-73-2016
11. Yanai, S., Umegaki, R., Hasegawa, K., Li, L., Yamaguchi, H., Tanaka, S.: Improving transparent visualization of large-scale laser-scanned point clouds by using Poisson disk sampling. In: 2017 International Conference on Culture and Computing, Kyoto, pp. 13–19 (2017)
12. Sakamoto, N., Nonaka, J., Koyamada, K., Tanaka, S.: Particle-based volume rendering. In: Asia-Pacific Symposium on Visualization 2007, Sydney, pp 129–132 (2007)
13. Bridson, R.: Fast Poisson disk sampling in arbitary dimensions. In: ACM SIGGRAPH 2007 Sketches, Article No. 22, San Diego (2007)
14. Nakada, S., Hayashi, M., Koshimura, S., Taniguchi, Y., Kobayashi, E.: Salinization by Tsunami in a semi-enclosed bay: Tsunami-Ocean 3D simulation based on the great earthquake scenario along the Nankai Trough. J. Adv. Simul. Sci. Eng. 3(2), 206–214 (2016)

Effect of Multiple Iso-surfaces in Depth Perception in Transparent Stereoscopic Visualizations

Daimon Aoi[1]([✉]), Kyoko Hasegawa[2], Liang Li[2], Yuichi Sakano[3,4], and Satoshi Tanaka[2]

[1] Graduate School of Information Science and Engineering, Ritsumeikan University,
1-1-1 Noji-higashi, Kusatsu, Shiga, Japan
`is0291fe@ed.ritsumei.ac.jp`
[2] College of Information Science and Engineering, Ritsumeikan University,
1-1-1 Noji-higashi, Kusatsu, Shiga, Japan
[3] Center for Information and Neural Networks (CiNet)
National Institute of Information and Communications Technology,
Osaka University, 1-4 Yamadaoka, Suita, Osaka, Japan
[4] Graduate School of Frontier Biosciences, Osaka University,
1-4 Yamadaoka, Suita, Osaka, Japan

Abstract. With the development of imaging technologies, it has become easier to obtain three-dimensional data of the internal human body by Computed Tomography and Magnetic Resonance Imaging. Visualizing these data helps us to understand the complicated internal structure of the human body. Transparent stereoscopic visualization is a good way to visualize the internal body structure with depth information. However, the position and depth information often become unclear when three-dimensional data are rendered transparently. In this study, we examined how depth perception changes by overlaying multiple iso-surfaces on transparently rendered images for structural understanding and correct depth perception in transparent stereoscopic visualization. We tested two types of figures: rectangular and medical data. The experimental results showed that multiple iso-surfaces improved the accuracy of perceived depth. For both figures, it was effective when the opacity of the inner iso-surface was high and the distance between the inner iso-surface and the outer iso-surface was large. In addition, the effect was particularly high when the distance between the inner and the outer iso-surface was large and the size of the inner iso-surface was small.

Keywords: Transparent stereoscopic visualization · Multiple iso-surfaces · Depth perception · Medical volumetric data

1 Introduction

The analysis of three-dimensional data is performed in the field of science and medicine. Visualization is one such analytical method. It is possible to obtain

© Springer Nature Singapore Pte Ltd. 2019
G. Tan et al. (Eds.): AsiaSim 2019, CCIS 1094, pp. 174–186, 2019.
https://doi.org/10.1007/978-981-15-1078-6_15

scanning images of the body by imaging with Computed Tomography (CT) and Magnetic Resonance Imaging (MRI). The ray casting method, the marching cube method, cross-section visualization, etc., are used to visualize these data. The human body is very complicated because it has irregular shapes, such as bones, blood vessels and organs. In the case of visualization, it needs to be transparent to visualize lesions inside the body. Typical purposes for visualizing three-dimensional medical data include diagnosis and informed consent. The purpose of viewing these visualizations is not limited to doctors. It is necessary to make accessible visualizations for patients who do not have medical knowledge. However, previous studies have shown that it is very difficult to perceive the correct position and depth.

In the case of perceiving 3D images, depth is perceived by much information. For example, binocular parallax due to differences in the images seen both eyes, motion parallax due to differences in the images due to a change in the position of the object due to motion of the observer, and relative sizes [1]. In other words, many hints needed to perceive depth correctly. Overlapped faces are another type of hint information. Overlapping faces increases the information of a hint, and hiding the background faces makes it easier to perceive the relationship between the foreground and background. These factors make it easier to correctly perceive depth. Research on transparent visualization has been conducted on human anatomical data that should be transparently visualized because of such complex shapes [2]. Furthermore, research combining transparent visualization with stereoscopic visualization has been conducted, and it has been found that opacity and texture gradients are effective in depth perception [3, 4].

In this research, we improve depth perception by using multiple iso-surfaces for transparent stereoscopic visualization. In the case of rendering transparent stereoscopic images, we use stochastic point-based rendering (SPBR) [5–8] that was developed in our laboratory.

2   Visualization of Multiple Transparent Iso-surfaces

To convert volume data that are 3D field data iso-surfaces to transparent stereoscopic images, we use the volume stochastic sampling method (VSSM [9]). In the case of converting volume data to surface data, we make points on the iso-surfaces that were generated by the VSSM to be a transparent stereoscopic visualization.

2.1   Generation of the Data by the VSSM

The VSSM is a sampling method that applies the SSM to iso-surfaces extracted from volume data. From the volume data, the VSSM generates a uniform point cloud on the iso-surfaces and makes point cloud data. In this research, the iso-value is specified and applied to the medical volume data. The iso-surface is output as point data on the surface. The SSM makes a point cloud with the moving point based on Brownian motion performed by a gaseous molecule such as the sampling point. First, we define a three-dimensional Euclidean space $\mathbb{R}^3$ consisting of coordinate variables $\mathbf{q} = (q_1, q_2, q_3)$. Consider an iso-surface of Eq. (1) generated from volume data.

$$F(\mathbf{q}) = 0 . \tag{1}$$

Here, $F(\mathbf{q})$ is defined as the scalar field of the volume data. We denote the Brownian particle's position vector as q and consider an appropriate scalar function of $\mathbf{q}$ as $F(\mathbf{q})$. The Brownian motion I_F is expressed by the stochastic differential equation as

$$dq_i^{(T)} \equiv \sum_{j=1}^{d} P_{ij} dw_j, \tag{2}$$

$$dq_i^{(S)} \equiv -\frac{\alpha}{|\nabla F|^2}\left(\frac{\partial F}{\partial q_i}\right)\mathrm{Tr}\{(\partial^2 F) \cdot P\}dt, \tag{3}$$

$$dq_i(t) = dq_i^{(T)}(t) + dq_i^{(S)}(t), \tag{4}$$

where dw_j and P are the Gaussian random variable with statistical properties and the projection operator extracting the movement on tangent plane, respectively.

2.2 Stochastic Point-Based Rendering

SPBR is a visualization method based on a stochastic algorithm using opaque luminescent particles. For this projection, it is necessary to project the opaque transparent particle group onto the image plane and perform ensemble averaging on the transparent image. Therefore, transparent visualization can provide correct depth information because it is necessary to sort the particles. SPBR has four major steps [8]. In SPBR, the opacity is controlled by the point density, and the image quality is controlled by the number of averaged images. In this experiment, the visualization shape is a surface. The steps for transparent visualization by SPBR are as follows.

Step 1: Generation of points
There are different methods for generating points depending on the data type to be visualized. The size of a point is the same as that of one pixel of the projected image.
Step 2: Division of point clouds
The point cloud generated in step 1 is randomly divided into multiple point groups. We call the number of point clouds the "repeat level (L_R)".
Step 3: Projection of the points with hidden point processing
Hidden points are removed from each point group and create an intermediate image projected onto the image plane.
Step 4: Averaging the image
Luminance value of each intermediate image that is created in step 3 is averaged for each pixel to generate an average image. Here, each pixel value is the expected value of each color and background color of many points.

We denote the opacity by α, the number of points that were projected is denoted by n, the cross-sectional area of the point is denoted by s_p, and the surface area of the iso-surface is denoted by s_A. In addition, if all the generated points are uniformly divided into L_R groups, the opacity is defined by

$$\alpha = 1 - \left(1 - \frac{s_A}{s_p}\right)^{\frac{n}{L_R}}. \tag{5}$$

3 Depth Cues

Humans perceive three-dimensional objects using various depth cues, such as binocular parallax, motion parallax, and luminance contrast. In this section, we describe depth cues controlled in the experiment: motion parallax, binocular disparity, luminance contrast, and luminance gradient.

3.1 Luminance Contrast

It is known that perceived depth order depends on luminance contrast between the objects or the contrast against the background [10–12]. In general, an object with higher contrast against the background tends to appear closer to the observer. This perceptual effect of luminance contrast corresponds to that of aerial perspective [12]. Figure 1 shows surfaces extracted from the volume data of hydrogen molecules visualized by SPBR. We denote the iso-value by v and the opacity by α. Figure 1(a) shows the outer iso-surface visualized with $v = 50$, RGB values (0, 255, 0), and $\alpha = 0.03$. Figure 1(b) shows the inner iso-surface visualized with $v = 200$, RGB values (255, 0, 0), and $\alpha = 0.03$. Figure 2(a) shows the result of overlapping Fig. 1(a) and (b) and visualizing both with $\alpha = 0.01$.

(a) $v = 50$ (b) $v = 200$

Fig. 1. Iso-surfaces of molecular hydrogen.

We denote luminance value by Y and the RGB values as R, G and B. Y is calculated by the following formula:

$$Y = 0.299R + 0.587G + 0.114B. \tag{6}$$

The luminance values in Fig. 1(a) are denoted Y_a, and the luminance values in Fig. 1(b) are denoted Y_b. $Y_a = 149.685$, $Y_b = 76.245$, and luminance values are different. Therefore, the inner part in Fig. 2(a) has higher luminance contrast against the background than the outer part, thereby appearing to be closer to the observer. To reduce the effect of luminance contrast, we will equalize luminance of the inner and outer part by adjusting the green component value of the inner part to 125. Figure 2(b) shows that the effect of luminance contrast is reduced; the inner part now appears to be farther than that in Fig. 2(a).

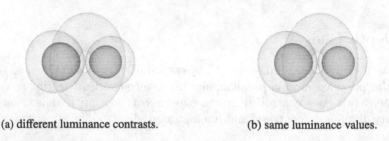

(a) different luminance contrasts.   (b) same luminance values.

Fig. 2. Multiple iso-surfaces for molecular hydrogen.

3.2 Luminance Gradient

We stated in Sect. 2.2 that SPBR calculates the opacity by the point density. When the surface is inclined from the viewing direction, the apparent area of the plane is smaller than when it is perpendicular to the viewing direction. Although the area looks small, the points are generated uniformly, so the point density increases. Therefore, the opacity and the luminance value is increased and emphasized. This phenomenon is called luminance gradient, which is a cue unique to SPBR.

4 Experiment

4.1 Experimental Conditions

The device to present stimulus images in this experiment was the MV4200 autostereoscopic display manufactured by TRIDELITY Display Solutions LLC (New Jersey, United States). An autostereoscopic display can provide stereo effects with the naked eye without requiring other devices and limiting the observation position and range. The display used in this experiment is a parallax barrier, multiview stereoscopic display, and it is possible to project motion parallax images for five viewpoints. The display size is 42 in., and the image resolution is 1920 × 1080.

The experimental conditions were the following four types: Put on the chin and Monocular, Put on the chin and Both eyes, Move the head and Monocular, Move the head and Both eyes. In the case of no motion parallax, the subject placed his or her chin on the chin table and looked without moving his or her head. In the case of no binocular parallax, the non-dominant eye was hidden by a blinder and the stimulus seen with a single eye.

The subjects included 18 men and women in their 20s. The subjects could use their naked eyes or glasses and contacts. In addition, the subject sat at a distance of 3.5 m from the display. It has been explained that an autostereoscopic display could be viewed with multiple viewpoints in advance. We also prepared a test image and confirmed that the subjects could be seen in 3D with multiple viewpoints when the head was moved sideways. The stimulus images were presented in a random order for each subject.

4.2   Determination of Color Considering Luminance Contrast

The color of the inner iso-surfaces was determined considering luminance contrast described in Sect. 3.2. In this experiment, the RGB values were adjusted to an equal luminance so that the perception was not influenced by luminance contrast. Therefore, the color of the outer surface was (0, 255, 0), and the color of the inner surface was (255, 125, 0).

4.3   Experiments on Rectangular Images

The sizes of the image were a 100 mm cube, a 100 mm square in the front and a depth of 150 mm as a rectangular solid (100 mm × 100 mm × 150 mm), and a 100 mm square in the front and a depth of 200 mm as a rectangular solid (100 mm × 100 mm × 200 mm) (see Fig. 3).

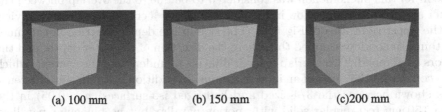

(a) 100 mm   (b) 150 mm   (c)200 mm

Fig. 3. Outline of the experimental images.

From each figure, two kinds of one iso-surface and multiple iso-surfaces are prepared. In the case of the multiple iso-surfaces, the inner size and the opacity were different. For the inner size, the lengths of the inner sides were half and 3/4 of the length of the outer side. There were two types of opacity: one with a larger (dark) inner iso-surface and one with a smaller (light) inner iso-surface, compared to the opacity of the outer iso-surface. We defined the outside opacity as $\alpha = 0.2$. The inside was $\alpha = 0.3$ when the opacity was higher than that of the outside and $\alpha = 0.1$ when the opacity was lower than that of the outside. Figure 4 was an image in which a half-sized iso-surface was placed on the 150-mm rectangular iso-surface with two types of opacity. Figure 5 was an image in which a 3/4-sized iso-surface was placed on the 150-mm rectangular iso-surface with two types of opacity. For each of the above 15 types of images, a total of

60 stimulus images were presented, taking into account the presence of motion parallax and binocular parallax.

The subjects were asked to report the depth length of the figure outside the stimulus image, by giving a number based on the assumption that the length of one side of the front of the figure outside the stimulus image was 1. The answer was 1, 1.5 and 2 respectively. All 60 conditions were presented randomly. The number of subjects was 18.

Figure 6 shows the results for each rectangular parallelepiped size under each condition of binocular parallax depth perceived and motion parallax. The vertical axis was the normalized value of the depth perceived by the subject, and 0.00 was the correct value. The error bars indicated the standard error. The green bar was the result when the stimulus image was the single iso-surface (not the multiple iso-surface). The red bar was the result of multiple iso-surfaces with a half-sized iso-surface overlapping inside. The blue bar was the result of multiple iso-surfaces with 3/4-sized iso-surface overlapping inside. There were two types of red and blue graphs: dark and light. A dark bar showed the result when the inner iso-surface was darker than the outer iso-surface, and a lighter bar showed the result when the inner iso-surface was lighter than the outer iso-surface.

We compared the green bars and the red and blue bars to determine the effect of multiple iso-surfaces. The red and blue graphs were closer to the correct values than the green graph, which showed that the results were closer to the correct values by means of multiple iso-surfaces. Furthermore, focusing on the inner size, the half-sized iso-surface tended to be better than 3/4-sized iso-surface. The reason for this phenomenon was considered to be due to the overlap between the inner and outer sides, as show in Fig. 7. Figure 7 was a cropped and enlarged view of the upper right area of Fig. 5(b). The side in the depth direction of the inner rectangular solid overlapped the side in the direction of the outer depth, and the colors overlapped. This overlap made it difficult to understand the context, which was considered the cause of an incorrect value. In addition, a significant difference was shown between the 3/4-sized and half-sized iso-surfaces ($p < 0.05$) in the thin 150 mm rectangular solid with motion parallax but no binocular parallax. In addition, although any figure was underestimated in the previous research, it

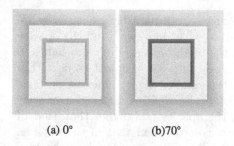

(a) 0°   (b)70°

Fig. 4. Inside opacity patterns of one second of a 150 mm experimental image.

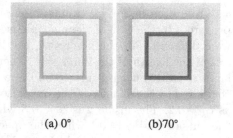

(a) 0°   (b)70°

Fig. 5. Inside opacity patterns of three-quarters of a 150 mm experimental image.

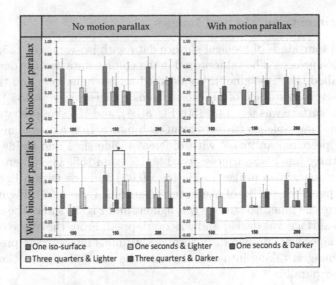

Fig. 6. Results of the cuboid experiment. (Color figure online)

was overestimate in the 100 mm cube in this study. If there was motion parallax, it would be easier to detect the parallax due to foreground and background perception due to occlusion, and it would approach the correct value. If there was motion parallax, the darker one tended to be better when the inner size was halved. In the half-sized iso-surface, the inner and outer sides were uncovered, and the intensity gradient described in Sect. 3.2 gives a clear outline. Therefore, it seemed that the cause was because the distinction between foreground and background was more clearly defined. On the other hand, it tended to be better to draw lighter when the inside is a 3/4-sized iso-surface because the inner and outer sides were covered, so it was thought that the context was difficult to understand if it was too dark.

Fig. 7. Enlarged view of the upper right area of Fig. 5(b).

4.4 Experiments on Medical Images

We prepared four kinds of medical surface data with iso-values of 135, 145, 150, and 155 as iso-surfaces. The value stored in the volume data was the density value (hereafter called the "iso-value"). We denoted an iso-value by v and the opacity by α. The outer iso-surface of all the stimulus images was $v = 135$ (Fig. 8(a)). The inner iso-surface was $v = 145, 150$ (Fig. 8(b)), and 155. We prepared a single iso-surface and multiple iso-surfaces from each figure. In the case of multiple iso-surfaces, we prepared an image with different inside sizes and inside opacities. There were three inner iso-surfaces: $v = 145, 150$, and 155. There were two types of opacity α: one with a darker inside ($\alpha = 0.09$) and one with a lighter inside ($\alpha = 0.03$) than the opacity of the outer iso-surface ($\alpha = 0.06$). Figure 9 shows the case where the inner iso-surface was lighter, and Fig. 10 shows the case where the inner iso-surface was darker and was overlapped. From the above conditions, 7 types of images were prepared. In total, 28 stimulus images were presented for each of the images, taking into consideration the conditions of motion parallax and binocular parallax.

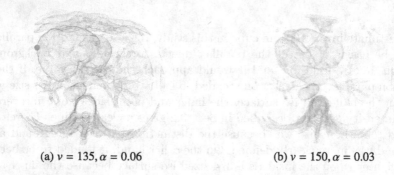

(a) $v = 135, \alpha = 0.06$ (b) $v = 150, \alpha = 0.03$

Fig. 8. Transparent visualization of the iso-surfaces. (Color figure online)

Fig. 9. Multiple iso-surfaces with Fig. 8(a) outside and Fig. 8(b) inside.

Fig. 10. Multiple iso-surfaces with Fig. 8(a) outside and Fig. 8(b) inside. Here, the opacity of the inside surface is 0.09.

The subjects were asked to report the distance in the depth direction from the diameter of the spine cross section (the middle lower cylinder) to a point on the outer edge of the heart (the orange circle of Fig. 8(a)), by giving a number based on the assumption that the radius of the red circle was 1. The correct answer was 2.45. All 28 conditions were presented randomly. The number of subjects was 18.

Figure 11 shows the results for each inner iso-surface for each condition of binocular parallax depth perceived and motion parallax. The vertical axis was the normalized value of the depth perceived by the subject, and 0.00 was the correct value. The error bars indicated the standard error. The green bar was the result of a single non-overlapping iso-surface. The inner multiple iso-surfaces $v = 145$, 150, and 155 were red, blue, and pink bar graphs, respectively. Among the red, blue, and pink bar graphs, when the opacity was lighter than that on the outside, the colors were lighter. When the opacity was darker, the inside was a darker bar.

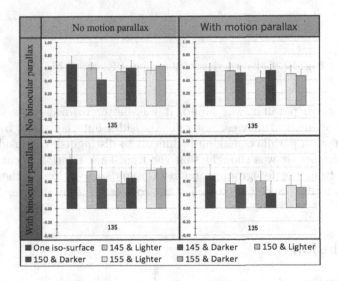

Fig. 11. Results of the experiment using medical images. (Color figure online)

Considering the graph at the bottom right of Fig. 11, the result of the conventional method using a single iso-surface (the green bar) is 0.48. On the other hand, the result of the proposed method using multiple iso-surfaces(the darker blue bar) is 0.21, which is closer to the correct value. An inner v of 150 had the best tendency, but in medical images, there was no significant difference in the inner size cues. This finding was considered to be the cause of the complicated shape of the medical image. In the rectangular solid experiment, the inside was a reduction of the outside and was similar. If it was similar, it could be deduced that if you multiplied the inside, it would become the outside figure. However, in the case of medical data, the surfaces of iso-values near the outside were inside, and although they had shapes near the outside, they were not similar figures. Therefore, it could not be a hint, such as how many times inside. Figure 12 was an enlarged view of the upper left area of Fig. 10. Additionally, as shown in Fig. 12, the distance between the inside and the outside of the medical image was too short compared to that of the rectangular solid, so it was difficult to measure the relative size, and it seemed that the effect was not noticeable.

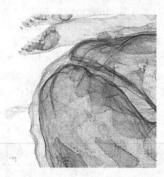

Fig. 12. Enlarged view of the upper left area of Fig. 10.

When motion parallax was found, it was better to draw a denser image. In the case of medical images, not only the sides but the whole overlap was subject to motion parallax, making it difficult to distinguish the inside and the outside. Therefore, it was thought that the front-back relation became easy to understand from the foreground and background perception of the occlusion by motion parallax, and it approached the correct value by drawing the inside clearly.

5   Conclusion

In this research, the depth perception was improved by multiple iso-surfaces. In the rectangular images, the improvement of depth perception was seen largely when the inner iso-surface was farther away from the outer iso-surface. The reason was that if the distance between the inside and the outside was large, each side of the iso-surface did not overlap, and it was easy to distinguish between the inside and the outside. In addition, when the side faced such a rectangular solid with an overlapping 3/4-sized iso-surface, the effect of motion parallax was sufficiently obtained, so it was found that drawing a lower opacity tended to be better. Also in medical images, the improvement by the opacity was observed, especially when the opacity was high. Therefore, it could be concluded that the opacity in multiple iso-surfaces was effective in improving the depth perception related to both images. In addition, the size of the inner iso-surface might have remarkable effects, but there were differences in these effects depending on the shape and the amount of overlap.

As a future perspective, further verification was needed on the size of the inner iso-surface. In this experiment, two types, half-sized and 3/4-sized images in the case of the rectangular images, and 145, 150, and 155 in the case of medical image, were performed inside the iso-surface. We found that using multiple iso-surfaces as a cue to correctly perceive depth depended on the size of the inner iso-surface. Especially in the case of a rectangular image, the influence of perception due to the size of the inner iso-surface was remarkable. We found that the inner size was effective, but it was necessary to research how large the inner size should be. On the other hand, in the case of medical images, the influence of perception due to the iso-value (the inner size) was not seen as much because medical images were complicated and were not known shapes. In medical images, the iso-surface of the iso-value whose value was close to the outer iso-value, but was not similar, was taken as the inner surface. Therefore, the shape of the inner iso-surface was unlikely to be a hint because it was not known to the observer. Therefore, by using a known, simple artificial geometric shape, such as a cube, for the inner iso-surface of the medical image, it was hypothesized that visual hints could be obtained and better depth perception could be achieved. Therefore, in the case of medical images, it was also necessary to research the effect when the inner iso-surface was set to a known and regular figure.

References

1. Sekuler, R., Blake, R.: Perception, 2nd edn. McGraw-Hill, New York (1990)
2. Miyawaki, M., Hasegawa, K., Li, L., Tanaka, S.: Transparent fused visualization of surface and volume based on iso-surface highlighting. In: The 6th International KES Conference on Innovation in Medicine and Healthcare (KES-InMed-18), (Smart Innovation, Systems and Technologies (Short Papers)), GoldCoast, Australia, 19–22 June (June 21) 2018, vol. 71, pp. 267–276 (2018)
3. Kitaura, Y., et al.: Effects of depth cues on the recognition of the spatial position of a 3D object in transparent stereoscopic visualization. In: The 5th International KES Conference on Innovation in Medicine and Healthcare (KES-InMed-17), (Smart Innovation, Systems and Technologies (Short Papers)), Vilamoura, Portugal, 21–23 June (June 23), 2017, vol. 71, pp. 277–282 (2017)
4. Sakano, Y., et al.: Quantitative evaluation of perceived depth of transparently-visualized medical 3D data presented with a multi-view 3D display. Int. J. Model. Simul. Sci. Comput. 9(3), 1840009 (16 pages) (2018)
5. Sakamoto, N., Koyamada, K., Saito, A., Kimura, A., Tanaka, S.: Multi-volume rendering using particle fusion. Poster Proceedings of IEEE Pacific Visualization Symposium 2008 (PacificVis 2008), pp. 33–34, Kyoto, Japan, March 2008 (2008)
6. Sakamoto, N., Kawamura, T., Koyamada, K.: Improvement of particle-based volume rendering for visualizing irregular volume data sets. Comput. Graph. 34(1), 34–42 (2010)
7. Tanaka, S., et al.: Particle-based transparent rendering of implicit surfaces and its application to fused visualization. In: EuroVis 2012 (short paper), Vienna, Austria, June 2012, pp. 25–29 (2012)

8. Hasegawa, K., Ojima, O., Shimokubo, Y., Nakata, S., Hachimura, K., Tanaka, S.: Particle-based transparent fused visualization applied to medical volume data. Int. J. Model. Simul. Sci. Comput. **4**, 1341003[11 pages] (2013)
9. Tanaka, S., Fukuda, Y., Yamamoto, H.: Stochastic algorithm for detecting intersection of implicit surfaces. Comput. Graph. **24**(4), 523–528 (2000)
10. Farne, M.: Brightness as an indicator to distance: relative brightness per se or contrast with the background? Perception **6**(3), 287–293 (1977)
11. Egusa, H.: Effect of brightness on perceived distance as a figure-ground phenomenon. Perception **11**(6), 671–676 (1982)
12. O'Shea, R.P., Blackburn, S.G., Ono, H.: Contrast as a depth cue. Vis. Res. **34**(12), 1595–1604 (1994)

3D Transparent Visualization of Relief-Type Cultural Heritage Assets Based on Depth Reconstruction of Old Monocular Photos

Jiao Pan[1(✉)], Liang Li[2], Hiroshi Yamaguchi[3], Kyoko Hasegawa[2], Fadjar I. Thufail[4], Bramantara[5], and Satoshi Tanaka[2]

[1] Graduate School of Information Science and Engineering,
Ritsumeikan University, Kyoto, Japan
gr0342ir@ed.ritsumei.ac.jp
[2] College of Information Science and Engineering,
Ritsumeikan University, Kyoto, Japan
[3] Nara National Research Institute for Cultural Properties, Nara, Japan
[4] Research Center for Area Studies (P2W), Indonesian Institute of Sciences (LIPI),
Jakarta, Indonesia
[5] Borobudur Conservation Office, Magelang, Indonesia

Abstract. We propose an efficient method to achieve 3D visualization directly from a single monocular 2D image for relief-type cultural heritages. To achieve a proper depth feel of 3D visualization, we first reconstruct the 3D point clouds by estimating the depth from the monocular image using a depth estimation network. We then apply our stochastic point-based rendering mechanism to achieve a 3D transparent visualization of the reconstructed point clouds. Herein, we apply our method to the Buddhist temple heritage of Borobudur Temple, in Indonesia, a UNESCO World Heritage Site with the most complete collection of Buddhist reliefs. The proposed method achieved 90% accuracy of the reconstructed point cloud on average and a promising visualization result with an intuitive understanding.

Keywords: Digital archives · Visualization · Neural networks

1 Introduction

The visualization of digital archives is increasingly important in the preservation and analysis of cultural heritage. In addition to the visualization of digital archives, many meaningful applications can be implemented, such as walkthrough displays, computer-aided design, geographic information systems, and virtual reality applications. Such applications rely on an efficient and accurate digitizing method. With 3D scanning and technologies and 3D modeling tools, it is possible to efficiently acquire and preserve digital data of extant cultural heritages. For cultural heritages that no longer exist, multiple image-based methods

© Springer Nature Singapore Pte Ltd. 2019
G. Tan et al. (Eds.): AsiaSim 2019, CCIS 1094, pp. 187–198, 2019.
https://doi.org/10.1007/978-981-15-1078-6_16

can be used to reconstruct 3D models. However, only a single monocular photo per object remains prevalent in many cases. Hence, a reconstruction method from a single image is urgently required. In this paper, we propose a three-dimensional (3D) visualization method to efficiently reconstruct and visualize cultural heritage from a single monocular photo. The proposed method is successfully applied to an Indonesian cultural heritage, Borobudur temple, and provides a promising result.

Fig. 1. Extant Borobudur reliefs

Fig. 2. The hidden parts of the Borobudur reliefs

Borobudur is a UNESCO World Heritage Site and the largest Buddhist temple in the world. Borobudur comprises approximately 2,672 individual bas-reliefs (1,460 narrative and 1,212 decorative panels), distributed at the hidden foot and the five square platforms as shown in Fig. 1. These reliefs can be divided into five sections based on the different independent stories they tell. The temple, which has high cultural value, has been restored and its foot encasement was re-installed owing to safety concerns. During the restoration, the reliefs of the hidden foot were covered by stones as shown in Fig. 2. Today, only the southeast corner of the hidden foot is revealed and visible to visitors. For the hidden parts, only gray-scale photos taken in 1890 remain and are displayed in the Borobudur Museum. For each relief panel, only one old photo remains.

We first reconstruct the hidden reliefs into point clouds from their monocular gray-scale photos. Our reconstruction method is based on a depth prediction neural network that maps intensity or color measurements to depth values. The monocular images and corresponding depth maps of the visible parts of the Borobudur reliefs are used to train the deep neural network. In our previous work [10], we used only three panels as training data and one panel as test data, which is considered an extremely small data set to train a neural network. In this paper, we apply six new panels to our training dataset as a comparative experiment with our data-driven model. As a result, the accuracy of the reconstructed model is increased by two percentage points. We also measure our reconstructed point cloud by the cloud-to-cloud distance [1] for comparison with the scanning data of real reliefs. Then, 3D point clouds are reconstructed from the remaining photos, and the depth map is predicted by the deep neural network model. Furthermore, due to the Borobudur temple's complex internal structure, we apply our stochastic point-based rendering mechanism to implement transparent visualizations of the reconstructed point clouds.

2   Related Work

With laser-scanned data of intact or defective cultural heritage objects, it is possible to efficiently and flexibly obtain or reconstruct digital data of cultural heritage [3,4,9,11]. However, many cultural heritage objects, like the Borobudur reliefs, are no longer available to acquire 3D information due to irreversible damage. For image-based reconstruction, many available methods use multiple images to reconstruct 3D models [5–7]. However, only a single monocular photo per object remains prevalent in many cases. Hence, a reconstruction method from a single image is urgently required.

Depth estimation from a single image is an ill-posed problem, as it is inherently ambiguous to map intensity or color measurement to a depth value. Handcrafted features and probabilistic graphical models are mainly used to tackle the monocular depth estimation problems in classic methods [12]. Recently, many studies using deep learning have achieved remarkable advances in depth estimation. Most of them were working on indoor or outdoor scenes in which the depth is in meters [2]. We applied such depth prediction network to relief-type data and proved its estimation possibility in centimeters.

For the transparent visualization method for large-scale point clouds, the pioneering approach suffers from a large computational cost due to the depth-sorting process involved. In our previous work, we proposed stochastic point-based rendering, which enables precise and interactive rapid transparent rendering [13]. This method achieves accurate depth feel by employing a stochastic algorithm without depth sorting. We have successfully applied this method to several types of large-scale laser-scanned point clouds of 3D cultural objects and proved its wide applicability [14].

3   Method

To achieve 3D visualization from a single monocular image, we consider 3D reconstruction as the first step. In our case, the only information we can use to reconstruct a 3D model of the Borobudur reliefs is completely within the grayscale photos. We apply a depth estimation neural network to map the intensity in the grayscale photos into a depth value that represents the distance between the point and camera. The scanning data of four panels on the first floor and six panels on the second floor is used as a training dataset to train the supervised model. The proposed method can be divided into three steps: (1) producing a data set from the scanning data of extant reliefs, (2) depth estimation by the neural network, and (3) reconstruction and transparent visualization.

3.1   Relief Dataset

Our training data and the corresponding depth-labeled map are calculated from the large photogrammetric-scanned point clouds. While the training data contain the intensity transformed by the RGB value of the 3D point clouds, the depth map contains the depth information of the point clouds, which is mapped into the range of the gray image. As the point clouds contain only 10 panels in total, we chose 9 panels as training data and 1 panel as our test data for quantitative analysis. The previous work used only 3 panels as training data, and we performed a comparison experiment by using a larger data set. In our case, the Borobudur reliefs contain hundreds of human figures and many decorative objects. Ten panels is considered an extremely small training data set to the deep network so we augment the training data with the following transformations:

- **Rotation:** The input image and the corresponding depth map are rotated by r[−10, 10] degrees.
- **Flips:** The input image and the corresponding depth map are horizontally and vertically flipped.
- **Noise:** 1,000 pixels of input image are randomly chosen to change the intensity to 0, which is a pepper noise.
- **Blurry:** The input images are filtered by two different degrees of Gaussian Blurring.

3.2   Network Structure

The network we employed consists of the global coarse-scale network and the local fine-scale network. The global coarse-scale network can be divided into seven parts and the local fine-scale network can be divided into four parts as shown in Fig. 3.

The Global Coarse-Scale Network. The global coarse-scale network contains five convolutional layers and two max-pooling layers to extract features from the input image. Then, the feature maps are converted to two fully connected layers that contain the entire image in their field of view. The size of each layer is shown in Fig. 3. As the input image is down-sampled by two max-pooling layers by a factor of 2, the output size is at 1/4 resolution compared to the input. The activation of all hidden layers uses rectified linear units except the output layer, coarse 7, using linear activation. After the fully-connected hidden layer 6, we apply a dropout layer to avoid over-fitting.

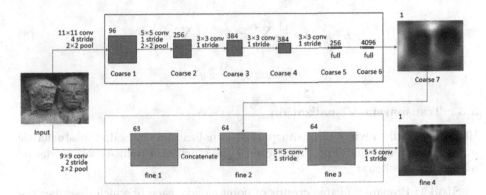

Fig. 3. Network Structure of the proposed method: the orange part on the top represents the global coarse-scale network and the blue part on the bottom represents the local-fine scale network. (Color figure online)

The Local Fine-Scale Network. The local fine-scale network consists of four convolutional layers and one max-pooling layer without any fully connected layer. After the first convolutional layer and a pooling stage, the output of the global coarse-scale network is imported as a feature map and fused with the original feature maps. Note that the size of the feature maps after the fine1 part is the same as the output of the coarse network by design. This size is maintained by zero-padded convolutions of all layers in the local-refine network. All hidden layers use the rectified linear activation except the last layer, which uses linear activation to predict the final depth map.

Loss Function. As demonstrated by Eigen et al. [2], much of the error accrued using current element-wise metrics may be explained simply by how well the mean depth is predicted. A large fraction of the total error is caused by finding the average scale of the scene. Thus, in the case of depth estimation work, how to measure the relationships between points in the scene without considering the absolute global scale is the most important consideration. Here, we apply a scale-invariant error as the loss function following Eigen's work. For a predicted depth map y and ground truth y^*, each with n pixels indexed by i, the scale-invariant mean squared error is defined as

$$D\left(y, y^*\right) = \frac{1}{2n} \sum_{i=1}^{n} \left(\log y_i - \log y_i^* + \alpha\left(y, y^*\right)\right)^2 \tag{1}$$

$$\alpha\left(y, y^*\right) = \frac{1}{n} \sum_i \left(\log y_i^* - \log y_i\right) \tag{2}$$

Inspired by this scale of the scene error, for a predicted depth map y and ground truth y^*, the per-sample training loss is set to

$$L\left(y, y^*\right) = \frac{1}{n} \sum_i d_i^2 - \frac{\lambda}{n^2} \left(\sum_i d_i\right)^2 \tag{3}$$

$$d_i = \log y_i - \log y_i^* \tag{4}$$

3.3   Transparent Visualization

Here, we briefly review our transparent visualization method, the stochastic point-based rendering. The procedure of the stochastic point-based rendering method is as follows:

- **Step 1:** Prepare multiple groups of point clouds, each of which describes the surface equivalently but is statistically independent. The point density of each group should be the same. Here, we denote the number of subgroups by L.
- **Step 2:** For each group in STEP 1, project its constituent 3D points onto the image plane to create an intermediate image. In the projection process, we consider the point occlusion per pixel. A total of L intermediate images are obtained.
- **Step 3:** Average the L intermediate images created in STEP 2 to make the final transparent image.

For the number of points n, the area of the local surface segment S, and the point sectional area s surface opacity in each local surface segment takes the following value:

$$\alpha = 1 - \left(1 - \frac{s}{S}\right)^n \tag{5}$$

Note that there is no depth sorting process along the line of sight in the proposed method. In this method, parameter L controls the image quality because the number of the averaged intermediate images is L. Below, L is denoted as an image-quality parameter.

In addition, according to Eq. 5, the local number of points, n, controls the local surface opacity α. The set of points can be uniformly eliminated to a small one in case of an unexpected large n. On the other hand, in case of a small n, the number of points can be increased by created a proper number of copies of randomly selected points, which means there is no need to add new points to the raw point cloud data.

4   Experiments

In our previous work, the data set we used contains three panels as training data and one panel as test data. As the training data is limited, efforts are needed to avoid over-fitting of the deep neural network. In this paper, a larger training data set is used, and an improvement in accuracy brought by more samples is expected. We perform comparison experiments with the previous work by comparing depth maps using several two-dimensional error metrics. Moreover, we also compare our reconstructed point clouds to the ground-truth using the cloud-to-cloud distance to measure the 3D error in centimeters. Our implementation details of the comparison experiments and the error metrics we used will be presented as follows:

4.1   Implementation Details

As the scanning data we obtained is scanned individually, it is necessary to reduce the effects of light condition and noise. Otherwise, the difference between the old data we used in previous work and the new data we obtained will affect the comparison result. Before our data set is fed to the depth estimation network, batch normalization is applied to the data set to reduce the effect of different light conditions. After the augmentation we explained above, our new data set contains 90k image pairs, an increase of threefold compared to our previous work. For the network of our implementation, all experiments are performed on an NVIDIA GTX 1080Ti GPU with 12 GB memory, and the program is based on TensorFlow. The probability of dropout layers we add after coarse 6 and fine 3 was set to 0.5. The model is trained using an Adam optimizer with the following learning rates: 0.001 for the global coarse-scale network and 0.01 for the local fine-scale network. We train our model on our relief data set with a batch size of 50 for approximately 20 epochs.

4.2   Error Metrics

To measure the accuracy of the proposed method, we apply several error metrics. As the reconstructed point clouds are based on the depth map predicted by the depth estimation network, we first apply error metrics identical to those in related works to the predicted depth maps. These error metrics calculate the difference between the intensity in the predicted depth map and the labels. Note that the intensity of the 2D depth map is in range of 0 to 255, and this value is not the real distance. While the accuracy of predicted depth maps is measured by error metrics, we also measure the difference between the point clouds reconstructed by the proposed method and the ground truth. We calculate the cloud-to-cloud distance between each corresponding point and visualize them in a heat map. The cloud-to-cloud distance represents the real error because the point clouds are reconstructed into the real size of the Borobudur reliefs.

5   Results

The experimental results will be summarized in 3 sections: Depth estimation results, reconstruction results and transparent visualization results. As we mentioned before, we performed a comparison experiment between two data sets with different quantities. The experiment that uses the smaller data set is called Exp1, while the experiment that uses the larger one is called Exp2.

Table 1. Table captions should be placed above the tables.

Experiment	Depth estimation results					Reconstruction results
	Higher is better			Lower is better		Mean distance (meter)
	$\alpha1$	$\alpha2$	$\alpha3$	RMSE	RMSELOG	
Exp1	0.22837	0.43051	0.59197	10.31572	0.42837	0.0156 m
Exp2	0.25047	0.45433	0.60945	10.24803	0.41194	0.0150 m

5.1   Depth Estimation Results

The depth estimation result as shown in Table 1 proves that our method provides promising results in general for the depth prediction task. The error metrics we used are identical to those in previous works [8]. The accuracy of the predicted depth map is slightly improved by including new training samples in the depth estimation network. The most meaningful results are shown in Fig. 4. Because of the limited training samples, Exp1 suffers from background inconsistency and poor performance for decorative objects. In Exp2, the improvement in both background and decorative objects is clear, as shown in the second row and the

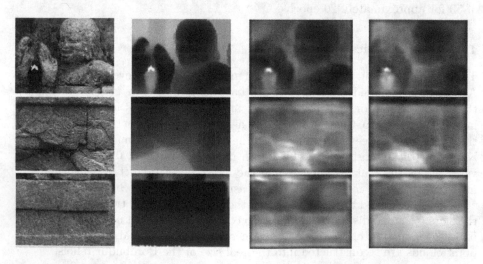

Fig. 4. Depth Estimation Results (from left to right): old photo, ground truth, result of Exp1, and result of Exp2.

third row of Fig. 4. Moreover, There are more than 1,000 panels of reliefs can be scanned and used as training data. Although the improvement by including 3 more reliefs is not very impressive, we believe the accuracy can be improved more by using a much larger dataset in the future.

5.2   Reconstruction Results

Our reconstruction result is measured by the cloud-to-cloud distance [1] after the reconstructed data is zoomed into the real relief size. The distances of each

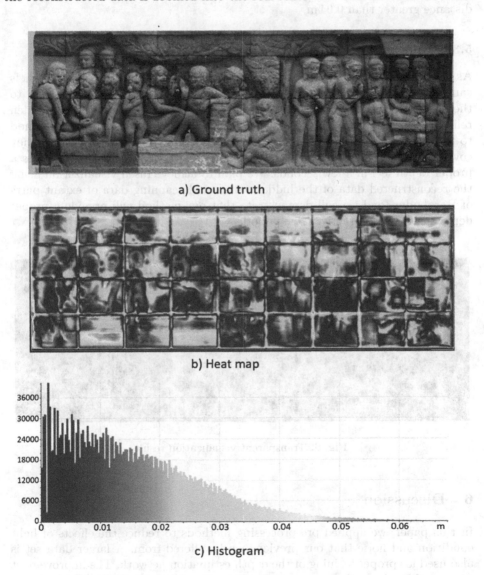

a) Ground truth

b) Heat map

c) Histogram

Fig. 5. Reconstruction result (Color figure online)

of its points relative to the ground truth are computed in meters. The mean distance between the reconstructed point cloud and the ground truth point cloud is approximately 0.015 m, as shown in Table 1. As the real Borobudur relief is 2.7 m in length, 0.92 m in width and 0.15 m in height, the accuracy of our method is 90%. The error distance of each point is visualized in the heat map shown in Fig. 5. According to the histogram in Fig. 5, as the color turn from blue to red, the error distance increases. As the heat map shows, the accuracy of human figures is highest, as they are covered by blue. Moreover, the error distance of almost all points is lower than 0.02 m, while only a few points reached an error distance greater than 0.04 m.

5.3   Transparent Visualization Results

As the temple is an approximately square building, the full view of these reliefs cannot be viewed at a certain point when using opaque visualization due to the existence of corners. Hence, we reconstructed two old photos of the hidden reliefs representing two panels and applied our transparent visualization method to these reliefs Fig. 6. We simulated the reliefs under the assumption that they cover the two sides of a corner. As a result, the see-through image provides a proper depth feel in a few seconds. We plan to achieve fused visualization using the reconstructed data of the hidden reliefs and scanning data of extant parts of Borobudur, and we will demonstrate that our method will provide a proper depth feel in an interactive time period.

Fig. 6. Transparent visualization result

6   Discussion

In this paper, we applied pre-processing methods to reduce the effects of light condition and noise that our previous work suffered from. A larger data set is also used for proper training of the depth estimation network. The improvement generated by these efforts was confirmed by the accuracy of both the predicted depth map and the reconstructed point clouds. Moreover, by zooming the reconstructed point cloud to the real size of Borobudur reliefs, we found out that our error is 1.5 cm on average, indicating an accuracy of over 90%. Therefore, we demonstrated that the proposed method can be successfully applied to the Borobudur temple reliefs and is efficient and accurate.

In future work, we plan to use a much deeper depth estimation network to improve the details in our depth maps. More training data will also be included for further improvement. The entire temple will be scanned into large-scale point clouds. With the scanning data of extant temple parts and the reconstructed data of the hidden reliefs, we will implement a fused transparent visualization of the entire Borobudur temple.

References

1. Besl, P., McKay, N.D.: A method for registration of 3-D shapes. IEEE Trans. Pattern Anal. Mach. Intell. **14**(2), 239–256 (1992). https://doi.org/10.1109/34. 121791. http://ieeexplore.ieee.org/document/121791/
2. Eigen, D., Puhrsch, C., Fergus, R.: Depth map prediction from a single image using a multi-scale deep network (2014). https://papers.nips.cc/paper/5539-depth-map-prediction-from-a-single-image-using-a-multi-scale-deep-network
3. Gregor, R., Sipiran, I., Papaioannou, G., Schreck, T., Andreadis, A., Mavridis, P.: Towards automated 3D reconstruction of defective cultural heritage objects. In: Eurographics Workshop on Graphics and Cultural Heritage, pp. 135–144 (2014). https://doi.org/10.2312/gch.20141311, http://diglib.eg.org/EG/DL/WS/GCH/GCH2014/135-144.pdf
4. Hermoza, R., Sipiran, I.: 3D Reconstruction of Incomplete Archaeological Objects Using a Generative Adversarial Network (2017). http://arxiv.org/abs/1711.06363
5. Ioannides, M., et al.: Online 4D reconstruction using multi-images available under open access. ISPRS Ann. Photogram. Remote Sens. Spat. Inf. Sci. **2**(5/W1), 169–174 (2013). https://doi.org/10.5194/isprsannals-II-5-W1-169-2013
6. Kersten, T.P., Lindstaedt, M.: Automatic 3D object reconstruction from multiple images for architectural, cultural heritage and archaeological applications using open-source software and web services automatische 3D-objektrekonstruktion aus digitalen Bilddaten für Anwendungen in Archit. Photogrammetrie - Fernerkundung - Geoinformation **2012**(6), 727–740 (2013). https://doi.org/10.1127/1432-8364/2012/0152
7. Kyriakaki, G., et al.: 4D reconstruction of tangible cultural heritage objects from web-retrieved images. Int. J. Heritage Digit. Era **3**(2), 431–451 (2014). https://doi.org/10.1260/2047-4970.3.2.431. http://journals.sagepub.com/doi/10.1260/2047-4970.3.2.431
8. Ladicky, L., Shi, J., Pollefeys, M.: Pulling things out of perspective. In: 2014 IEEE Conference on Computer Vision and Pattern Recognition, pp. 89–96. IEEE (2014). https://doi.org/10.1109/CVPR.2014.19, http://ieeexplore.ieee.org/lpdocs/epic03/wrapper.htm?arnumber=6909413
9. Lu, M., Zheng, B., Takamatsu, J., Nishino, K., Ikeuchi, K.: Preserving the Khmer smile: classifying and restoring the faces of Bayon. In: Proceedings of the 12th International Conference on Virtual Reality, Archaeology and Cultural Heritage, pp. 161–168 (2011). https://doi.org/10.2312/vast/vast11/161-168, https://dl.acm.org/citation.cfm?id=2384521

10. Pan, J., Li, L., Yamaguchi, H., Hasegawa, K., Thufail, F.I., Tanaka, S.: 3D Reconstruction and Transparent Visualization of Indonesian Cultural Heritage from a Single Image, pp. 3–6 (2018). https://doi.org/10.2312/gch.20181363
11. Park, J.H., Muhammad, T., Jae-Hong, A.: The 3D reconstruction and visualization of Seokguram Grotto World Heritage Site. In: Proceedings of the 2014 International Conference on Virtual Systems and Multimedia, VSMM 2014, pp. 180–183 (2014). https://doi.org/10.1109/VSMM.2014.7136646
12. Saxena, A., Chung, S.H., Ng, A.Y.: Learning Depth from Single Monocular Images (2006). https://papers.nips.cc/paper/2921-learning-depth-from-single-monocular-images
13. Tanaka, S., et al.: SEE-through imaging of laser-scanned 3D cultural heritage objects based on stochastic rendering of large-scale point clouds. ISPRS Ann. Photogram. Remote Sens. Spat. Inf. Sci. **3**(July), 73–80 (2016). https://doi.org/10.5194/isprs-annals-III-5-73-2016
14. Tanaka, S., et al.: Application of stochastic point-based rendering to transparent visualization of large-scale laser-scanned data of 3D cultural assets. In: 2014 IEEE Pacific Visualization Symposium, pp. 267–271. IEEE (2014). https://doi.org/10.1109/PacificVis.2014.25, http://ieeexplore.ieee.org/document/6787179/

Simulation Applications

Tolerance Coefficient Based Improvement
of Pedestrian Social Force Model

Ruiping Wang[1], Xiao Song[1(✉)], Junhua Zhou[2], and Xu Li[2]

[1] School of Automation Science and Electrical Engineering,
Beihang University, Beijing, China
Songxiao@buaa.edu.cn
[2] State Key Laboratory of Intelligent Manufacturing System Technology,
Beijing Institute of Electronic System Engineering, Beijing 100854, China

Abstract. In this paper, pedestrian evacuation is investigated by using an extended social force model that considers patience factor which can solve the situation pedestrian in the corner stay where they are until everyone is finished or there is an occasional gap. In the simulation of indoor evacuation, we add the endurance coefficient attribute to pedestrians. When pedestrians are blocked in a corner that is not conducive to passage, there will be temporary waiting. When more and more people behind them are found passing through the narrow gate, pedestrians generate greater "social forces" to enable them to pass through the narrow gate and avoid long waits. Besides, LSTM is used to learn scenario data by normalization of relative positions among pedestrians, transferring velocity vector to scalar and incorporating more path planning information, and thus to make it more adaptive to realistic scenarios. The results shows more realistic speed density curve and generates less trajectory fluctuations compared with social force model.

Keywords: Pedestrian behavior · Long short term memory · Social force

1 Introduction

An effective pedestrian evacuation model can increase effectiveness of evasion for a large number of people when the emergencies occur in limited space. Most people react unconsciously to conditions of panic and scare. They tend to seek the option to leave the danger zone quickly. However, this is not the most effective way to do it.

The reasonable guidance can make pedestrians evacuate orderly, fast and safely. The Current evacuation route are available in general public places, but lacking of reasonable evacuation plan. Most plans ignore their interactions, movements and the different behaviours of people in dangerous situations. Besides, the design of safe routes within room should minimize congestion during the evacuation, preventing high evacuation times and the risk of injuries caused by the crowd dynamics.

Regarding this problem, many researchers analysed evacuation strategies in manifold scenarios such as rooms [1, 2], corridors [3], airports [4], metro stations [4, 5], shopping malls [6], high-rise buildings [7], tour regions [8] and city traffic networks [8, 9] etc. The main issues of these works include how to evacuate people more quickly

© Springer Nature Singapore Pte Ltd. 2019
G. Tan et al. (Eds.): AsiaSim 2019, CCIS 1094, pp. 201–210, 2019.
https://doi.org/10.1007/978-981-15-1078-6_17

under different conditions, such as various disaster locations, different geometry structures, invisibility caused by power failure etc.

Pedestrian modeling is one of the most essential components of evacuation analysis. There are two alternatives for pedestrian modeling: Social force model (SFM) and cellular automata model (CAM). SFM is continuous, CAM is discrete. Considering the CAM is limited in the range of speed and direction changing, we mainly focus on SFM in this paper. There have been numerous studies that tried to improve the original social force model since it was proposed in Helbing [5, 10]. For example, Fernando [11] proposes a spheropolygon shape model to simulate a dense counterflow during a music event. Farina and Fontanelli [12] include heading force and torque to improve the realism of the trajectories. Langston [13] used a three-circle model to simulate the pedestrians' rotation behavior.

Although many efforts have been made to modify the original social force modeling approach, there still exist some interesting problems. For instance, when a group of pedestrians run to an exit door to escape from a room, pedestrians crowded in a corner will stay in place for a long time until an accidental gap appears or pedestrians in the back are evacuated. From our analysis, we think SFM still needs improvement to enable more realistic direction changing ability of pedestrians.

Meantime, many researchers designed evacuation strategies [1, 2, 4, 5, 11–13] to make the pedestrians evacuate more efficiently. However, their study lacks of precise computation of exit capacity (EC). They consider the exit flow is linear to the door width neglecting other important factors such as emergency level and pedestrians' physical strength. In fact, wrong EC computation might lead to wrong instructions and unnecessary exit selection changes, which may incur more accidents during large event. This is a serious problem because each second is precious in emergency scenarios.

The outline of this paper is as follows. Section 2 describes the existing SFM model and how the paper introduced a new property into the existing algorithm. Section 3 discusses how to improve SFM by studying characteristic time of direction changing. Finally, Sect. 4 draws the conclusion.

2 Tolerance Coefficient Based Improvement of Social Force Model

SFM is one the most popular models to simulate pedestrian movement. However, one unrealistic phenomenon observed with SFM is that People running along the wall towards the exit often stay where they are until the occasional gap or the person behind them leaves. This phenomenon is caused by the social forces of the people and walls around it far greater than their own driving forces. The snapshot of our simulation is shown in Fig. 1. The crowd in the red box was all blocked in the queue behind.

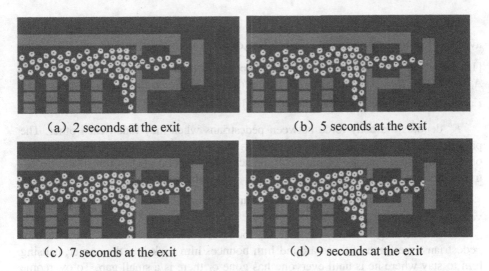

(a) 2 seconds at the exit   (b) 5 seconds at the exit

(c) 7 seconds at the exit   (d) 9 seconds at the exit

Fig. 1. An example of blocked pedestrian at the corner near an exit (Color figure online)

To tackle this problem, we will make improvement in a better characteristic time of direction changing of SFM.

Before this improvement, let us revisit the original social force model, which is the change of velocity at time t given by the acceleration with Eqs. (1)–(4) [14–16].

$$\vec{F_i} = m_i \frac{d\vec{v_i}}{dt} = \vec{F_i^d} + \vec{F_i^r} + \vec{F_i^w} \tag{1}$$

$$\vec{F_i^d} = \frac{m_i}{\tau_i}(v_i^0 \vec{e_i^0} - \vec{v_i}) \tag{2}$$

$$\vec{F_i^r} = \sum_{j(j \neq i)} \vec{F_{ij}} = \vec{F_{ij}^a} = A_i \exp(d_{ij}/B_i) \vec{n_{ij}} \tag{3}$$

$$\vec{F_i^b} = \sum_{b} \vec{F_{ib}} = k_1 g(d_{ij}) \vec{n_{ij}} + k_2 g(d_{ij}) \Delta v_{ji}^t \vec{t_{ij}} \tag{4}$$

In SFM, $\vec{F_i^d}$ represents the self-driven force in Eq. (2). It means each pedestrian moves with a certain desired speed v_i^0 in a certain direction $\vec{e_i^0}$, which can often be simulated with path planning algorithms such as A*, Dijkstra etc. [17]. Meantime, the person can change his actual velocity $\vec{v_i}$ with a certain characteristic time τ_i. For Chinese adult, the shoulder width $2r = 0.36$–0.44 m, $m_i = 40$–70 kg, $\tau_i = 0.5$ s, $v_0 = 1.4$–3 m/s.

The repulsive psychological force is denoted by $\vec{F_i^r}$ and $\vec{F_i^b}$ in Eqs. (3)–(4). To avoid collisions, the psychological force exists among pedestrians and obstacles [18, 19]. $\vec{F_i^r}$ denotes the repulsive force between pedestrians when they are not touched. $A_i = 2000$ N, $B_i = 0.08$ m. d_{ij} is the actual distance between the center of pedestrian i and j. $\vec{n_{ij}}$ is the unit vector in the normal direction.

$\vec{F_i^b}$ denotes the body force between pedestrians when they touch each other. The parameters $k_1 = 1.2 \times 10^5$ kg $\cdot$ s^{-2} and $k_2 = 2.4 \times 10^5$ kg $\cdot$ m^{-1} $\cdot$ s^{-1} determine obstruction effects in case of physical contact. The function g(x) is zero if the pedestrians do not touch each other ($d_{ij} < 0$), and otherwise equal to the argument x. $\vec{t_{ij}} = (-n_{ij}^2, n_{ij}^1)$ is the tangential direction and $\Delta v_{ji}^t = (\vec{v_j} - \vec{v_i}) \cdot \vec{t_{ij}}$ is the tangential velocity difference.

After analyzing SFM with Fig. 1, we found one main issue is that in the rush of pedestrians, the force of those around him bounces him back into the corner, causing him to stay where he is until everyone has gone or there is a small gap. To overcome this shortcoming, We give each pedestrian a property: the endurance coefficient t_{i0}, which indicates how long he can wait in the "corner" mentioned above. The greater the tolerance coefficient, the longer he is willing to wait; The lower the tolerance coefficient, the less time he is willing to wait.

We assume that the tolerance coefficients are normally distributed. Most pedestrians have a tolerance coefficient in the middle, and only a few are particularly tolerant and impatient. Besides, we stipulate that the tolerance coefficient is an integer from 0 to 9, that is to say, the simulated population is divided into 10 categories.

According to the simulated pedestrian evacuation experiment, we set the endurance time corresponding to the endurance coefficient. When the endurance coefficient is 0–2, the endurance time increases rapidly; when the endurance coefficient is 3–6, the endurance time grows slowly; when the endurance coefficient is 7–9, the endurance time increases fastest. The details are shown in the following Table 1.

Table 1 Tolerance level and time

Tolerance level	Tolerant time t_{i0} (s)
0	0
1	1
2	2
3	2.5
4	3
5	3.5
6	4
7	5
8	7
9	10

Finally, we design a functional mapping between endurance time and the generation of additional social forces. The longer the endurance, the greater the value of the function, that is, the greater the social force it exerts on others. So, we chose the exponential function to simulate this situation. The formula is as follows:

$$p_i = \begin{cases} 1 & (t_i < t_{i0}) \\ kt_1 \cdot \exp(kt_2 \cdot (t_i - t_{i0})) & (t_i > t_{i0}) \end{cases} \tag{5}$$

In SFM, the corresponding modification item is $\vec{F}_i^r$:

$$\vec{F}_i^r = \sum_{j(j \neq i)} \vec{F}_{ij} = \vec{F}_{ij}^a = p_j A_i \exp(d_{ij}/B_i) \, \vec{n}_{ij} \tag{6}$$

3   The Effect of Door Size on Evacuation Efficiency

In order to study the effect of gate width on evacuation efficiency, we set the gate width as 1 m and 2 m respectively, as shown in Fig. 2, and calculated the evacuation time when the evacuation population was 10, 20, 30, 40 and 50 respectively by using the social force model.

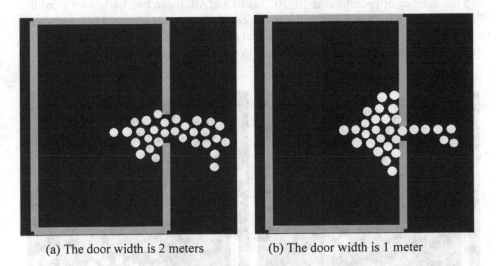

(a) The door width is 2 meters   (b) The door width is 1 meter

Fig. 2. Evacuation with various door width

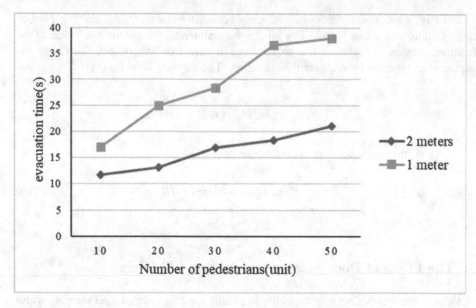

Fig. 3. Evacuation time against the number of pedestrians

Figure 3 shows evacuation time when the door width is 1 m and 2 m respectively, and the number of pedestrian is 10, 20, 30, 40 and 50. It can be clearly seen from the Fig. 3 that when the number of pedestrian is equal, the evacuation speed of a room with a door width of 1 m is much slower than that of a room with a door width of 2 m. The more pedestrians, the greater difference in evacuation speed.

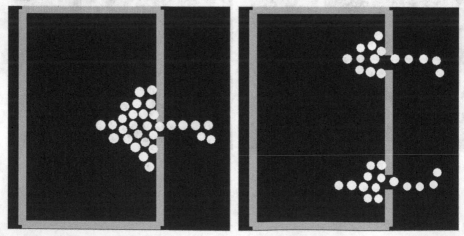

(a) The exit width is 1 meter   (b) The width of two exits is 1 meter respectively

Fig. 4. Comparison of the influence of various exit widths

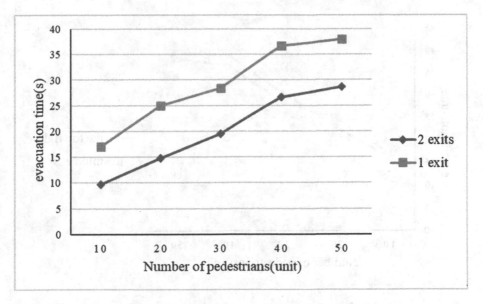

Fig. 5. The impact of door width

In Fig. 4, (a) is the evacuation simulation with exit width of 2 m, and (b) is the evacuation simulation with two exit widths of 1 m. Figure 5 shows the evacuation time required for the two rooms when the number of pedestrians is 10, 20, 30, 40 and 50 respectively. It can be clearly seen from Fig. 5 that when the number of pedestrians is equal, the increase of exits will reduce the evacuation time by approximately equal proportion.

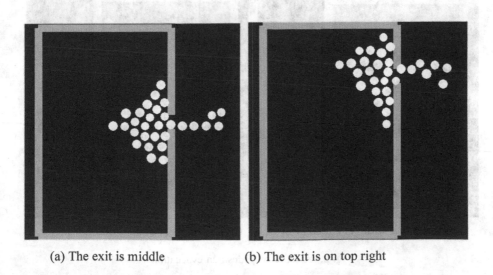

(a) The exit is middle   (b) The exit is on top right

Fig. 6. Different positions of the door

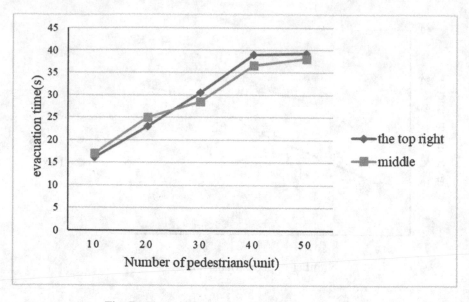

Fig. 7. The evacuation time of pedestrian evacuation

In Fig. 6(a) is the evacuation simulation of the exit in the middle, and (b) is the exit at the upper right with the same width of 1 m. Figure 7 shows the evacuation time required for the two rooms when the number of pedestrians is 10, 20, 30, 40 and 50 respectively. Figure 7 shows that when the indoor space is not large, the exit location has no obvious influence on evacuation speed.

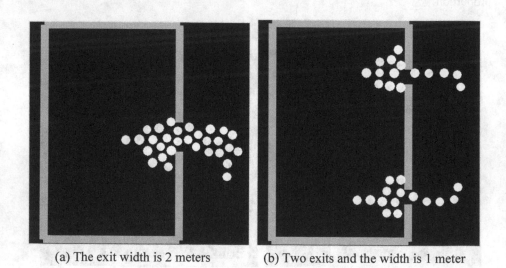

(a) The exit width is 2 meters   (b) Two exits and the width is 1 meter

Fig. 8. A scene of pedestrian evacuation

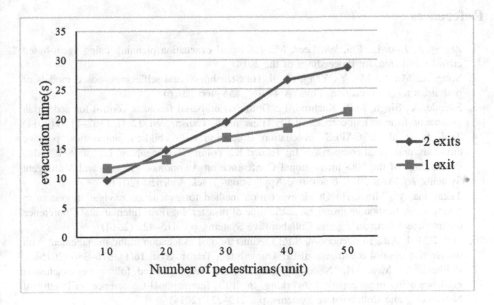

Fig. 9. Comparison of different exit design

In Fig. 8 the exit width of a is 2 m, and (b) is two exits, each 1 m wide. Figure 9 shows the evacuation time required for two rooms when the number of pedestrians is 10, 20, 30, 40 and 50 respectively. Figure 9 shows that when the number of pedestrians is small (no more than 18 pedestrians), the evacuation efficiency of one exit is less than that of two exits, with the total width of exits equal; When more pedestrians are evacuated (more than 20), the efficiency of two exits was lower than that of one exit. From the analysis of evacuation process: there is a small number of people at one exit, congestion will occur, while the two exits will not. So the evacuation efficiency of the two exits is high; When the number of pedestrians is large, congestion will occur at both exits. At this time, evacuation efficiency of one exit is higher.

4   Conclusion

In this paper, we use the traditional social force model to simulate indoor pedestrian evacuation. It is can be seen that when people are crowded at the exit, people near the corner will stagnate for a long time by simulations, which is different from the actual situation. We added a "endurance coefficient" attribute to each pedestrian, and summarized the endurance time corresponding to the endurance coefficient through multiple simulation experiments, so as to improve the traditional social force model. In addition, the influence of exit width on evacuation time is studied by using the improved model.

References

1. Zhong, J., Luo, L., Cai, W., Lees, M.: EA-based evacuation planning using agent-based crowd simulation. In: Proceedings of the 2014

2. Song, X., Ma, L., Ma, Y., Yang, C., Ji, H.: Selfishness- and selflessness-based models of pedestrian room evacuation. Phys. A **447**(6), 455–466 (2016)

3. Shende, A., Singh, M.P., Kachroo, P.: Optimization-based feedback control for pedestrian evacuation from an exit corridor. IEEE Trans. Intell. Transp. Syst. **12**(4), 1167–1176 (2011)

4. Tsai, J., et al.: ESCAPES- evacuation simulation with children, authorities, parents, emotions, and social comparison. In: Tumer, K., Yolum, P., Sonenberg, L., Stone, P. (eds.) Proceedings of the 10th International Conference on Autonomous Agents and Multiagent Systems, AAMAS 2011. Innovative Applications Track, Valencia (2011)

5. Takayama, Y., Miwa, H.: Quick evacuation method for evacuation navigation system in poor communication environment at the time of disaster. In: IEEE International Conference on Intelligent Networking and Collaborative Systems, pp. 415–421 (2014)

6. Hui, F., Pel, A.J., Hoogendoorn, S.P.: Optimization of evacuation traffic management with intersection control constraints. IEEE Trans. Intell. Transp. Syst. **16**(1), 376–386 (2015)

7. Fujihara, A., Miwa, H.: Necessary condition for self-organized follow-me evacuation guidance using opportunistic networking. In: IEEE International Conference on Intelligent Networking and Collaborative Systems, pp. 213–221 (2014)

8. Kinugasa, S., Izumi, T., Nakatani, Y.: Evaluation of a support system for large area tourist evacuation guidance: Kyoto simulation results. In: IEEE SCIS-ISIS 2012, Kobe, Japan, pp. 439–445 (2012)

9. Caggianese, G., Erra, U.: Parallel hierarchical A* for multi agent-based simulation on the GPU. In: an Mey, D., et al. (eds.) Euro-Par 2013. LNCS, vol. 8374, pp. 513–522. Springer, Heidelberg (2014). https://doi.org/10.1007/978-3-642-54420-0_50

10. Schadschneider, A., Klingsch, W., Klupfel, H., Kretz, T., et al.: Evacuation dynamics: empirical results, modeling and applications, pp. 517–551 (2008). https://arxiv.org/abs/08021620

11. Langston, P.A., Masling, R., Asmar, B.N.: Crowd dynamics discrete element multi-circle model. Saf. Sci. **44**, 395–417 (2006)

12. Kang, J., Jeong, I.-J., Kwun, J.-B.: Optimal facility-final exit assignment algorithm for building complex evacuation. Comput. Ind. Eng. **85**(4), 169–176 (2015)

13. Song, X., Sun, J., Xie, H., et al.: Characteristic time based social force model improvement and exit assignment strategy for pedestrian evacuation. Phys. A Stat. Mech. Appl. **505**(9), 530–548 (2018)

14. Song, X., Han, D., Sun, J., Zhang, Z.: A data-driven neural network approach to simulate pedestrian movement. Phys. A Stat. Mech. Appl. **509**(11), 827–844 (2018)

15. Song, X., Xie, H., Sun, J., Han, D., Cui, Y., Chen, B.: Simulation of pedestrian rotation dynamics near crowded exits. IEEE Trans. Intell. Transp. Syst. (2018). https://doi.org/10.1109/TITS.2018.2873118

16. Liu, J., Song, X., Sun, J., Xie, Z.: Global A* for pedestrian room evacuation simulation. In: 2018 IEEE International Conference on Big Data and Smart Computing, vol. 1, Shanghai, China, pp. 573–577 (2008)

17. Luo, L., Zhou, S., et al.: Agent based human behavior modeling for crowd simulation. Comput. Animat. Virtual Worlds **19**, 271–281 (2008)

18. Bruneau, J., Pettré, J.: Energy-efficient mid-term strategies for collision avoidance in crowd simulation. In: ACM SCA (2015)

19. Luo, L., Chai, C., Ma, J., et al.: Proactive crowd: modelling proactive steering behaviours for agent-based crowd simulation. Comput. Graph. Forum **37**(1), 375–388 (2018)

Capturing Human Movements
for Simulation Environment

Chengxin Wang[✉], Muhammad Shalihin Bin Othman[✉], and Gary Tan[✉]

School of Computing, National University of Singapore, Singapore, Singapore
{wangcx,gtan}@comp.nus.edu.sg, mshalihin@u.nus.edu

Abstract. In this paper, we proposed a novel data-driven framework to translate human movements from real-life video feeds into a virtual simulator in Unity 3D. In the proposed framework, YOLOv3 is used for pedestrian detection. Thereafter, a modified offline tracking algorithm with the min-cost flow was built to associate detected pedestrians from frame to frame. Finally, 2D trajectories are produced where a script would translate them into the Unity 3D platform. The proposed framework has the ability to display realistic behavior patterns where we would be able to introduce threats and analyze different strategies for improving evacuation and rescue in disaster situations.

Keywords: Computer vision · Multiple object tracking · Simulation

1 Introduction

Natural disasters, bomb threats and heavy congestion leading to numerous accidents are real issues of today and they can occur at any time, anywhere. It is impossible to derive any form of mathematical or analytical model due to the unprecedented nature of these events. However, such events would also be inappropriate and dangerous to simulate in real life. Therefore, an effective way to model and simulate such situations computationally and yet be as close to real-life is imperative.

Crisis management and planning have drawn increasing attention in recent years. The government, academia, and related industries have been actively pushing this area of research. Resource management and deployment in response to a disaster situation call for effective strategies in evacuation and rescue. However, this problem is non-trivial due to several issues such as how humans react in panic and the numerous variables that could affect an outcome. Disaster-events or crisis situations more often than not come with casualties. Thus, being able to strategize an efficient and effective rescue-evacuation plan in real-time is crucial. High delays could possibly result in higher fatalities due to the failure of timely attention to injured victims or failure to evacuate while the crisis continues to escalate. In order to accommodate human reaction in a computational model, several works have sought to integrate social sciences, such as BDI aspects, into

© Springer Nature Singapore Pte Ltd. 2019
G. Tan et al. (Eds.): AsiaSim 2019, CCIS 1094, pp. 211–221, 2019.
https://doi.org/10.1007/978-981-15-1078-6_18

Multi-Agent Systems, where each agent (people involved in the simulation) has their own unique characteristics and behaviors.

Again, it is still non-trivial to assign each agent a set of unique characteristics where the combinations of attributes are realistic enough to simulate real-life expectations. Therefore, we consider developing a data-driven framework to collect human behavioural data and translate them into a virtual simulator for a more realistic simulation. This is especially crucial in crisis management since an increase of efficiency by a matter of seconds could possibly result in lower casualty rates. Hence, this paper presents the work we have done to integrate computer vision techniques into agent-based simulation for microscopic studies. Through this automated framework, different possible threats can be applied and we present how different strategies can affect evacuation and rescue. In an overview, the aim of this paper is to introduce a conceptual framework for integrating computer vision and agent-based simulation for a 3-dimensional virtual reality simulation. The methods proposed in the framework ensure a quick and efficient technique to achieve this goal.

The organization of this paper will start with an overview of the related works in Sect. 2, followed by the description of methodologies and the proposed framework in Sect. 3. Section 4 will present a case study using the full framework, and finally, Sect. 5 will draw conclusions and discuss possible future directions.

2   Related Work

To achieve high fidelity in behavioral simulation from video feeds, object detection and multiple object tracking are two critical factors, among others. There has been an increasing amount of research in these areas. Hence, in this literature, we take a look at the latest advancements for both and briefly cover some existing platforms for simulation modeling, as well as collision avoidance schemes for agent-based simulations.

A popular method for object detection, Fast R-CNN, takes an image as input to process through several convolutional and max-pooling layers along with a list of object proposals to score, relying on a selective search [1]. Faster R-CNN introduces a Region Proposal Network (RPN) to replace selective search algorithm. It is able to predict object bounds and object scores simultaneously at each position and merge them with Fast R-CNN into a single network [2]. Unlike Fast R-CNN and Faster R-CNN, the You-Only-Look-Once (YOLO) model predicts bounding box coordinates and class probabilities using a single convolutional network which makes it faster and with fewer background errors [3]. Single Shot Multi-Box Detector (SSD) uses a single deep neural network with a small convolutional filter for predicting object categories and offsets the location of the bounding box, which could achieve better accuracy than YOLO [4]. More recently, YOLOv3 was able to achieve three times speedup as compared to SSD, while maintaining the same level of accuracy [5]. Although there may be better detection algorithms through the use of deeper networks such as Mask R-CNN [6], the YOLOv3 model provides faster performance time with a sufficient level of accuracy.

For multiple object tracking, most of the works done focus on online tracking. Many online tracking algorithms such as recurrent auto-regressive networks [7] and Simple Online and Real-time Tracking (SORT) [8] aims to perform data association frame-by-frame. The SORT model uses Kalman filter framework [9] for object inter-frame displacements prediction and associating current detections with existing objects using the Hungarian algorithm [10]. As for offline tracking models, most works use global tracking approach to utilize more information for reducing detection errors. Yu et al. [11] proposed an offline tracker, which improved the existing H^2T [12] algorithm, used to handle a mixture of different scale targets and introduced the affinity matrix for K-Dense Neighbors. Zhang et al. [13] proposed an iterative approach built upon the min-cost flow algorithm to solve long-term occlusions. However, the proposed method was not aimed at addressing missing detection problems.

Several Multi-Agent Simulation (MAS) tools and platforms are available today. Mason [14] is a fast discrete-event multi-agent simulation library core in Java, which provides more than enough functionality for many lightweight simulation needs. D-Mason [15] is a distributed version of Mason, harnessing multiple processing units for increasing performance time. NetLogo [16] is much like Mason but with lesser back-end interference. However, it is not ideal for simulations that require an immense amount of detail. Unity 3D is great for logging data, creating controls and viewers. Although Unity [17] may not be ideal for running simulations that require several formulas, it is still possible to build a shell in Unity that handles the visuals where the outcomes are calculated through a separate program or script outside of the Unity platform.

Agent navigation and collisions avoidance schemes are important factors in crowd simulation models [18] in order to simulate the movements of pedestrians realistically with respect to its surrounding environment. The second version of Reciprocal Collision Avoidance (RVO) model, RVO2 [19], is an algorithm designed for crowded environments where a large number of agents in a two-dimensional space interactively navigate towards their individual goals. Other advanced crowd models based on agent simulation [20,21] where human-like decision-making process that are affected by internal attributes such as the current situation, social states, feelings, and physical conditions, are introduced into the behavioural models, were also explored. However, Hybrid Reciprocal Velocity Obstacle (HRVO) [22] approach and the RVO2 approach are more popular in crowd simulation due to its simplicity and capabilities. Although the HRVO have better local interaction results, the RVO2 model is much faster in terms of performance time. Hence, we chose the RVO2 for our collision avoidance scheme in this paper for a straightforward integration of our methods in simulation.

Thus, based on the knowledge gathered through the literature, we propose a framework that would seamlessly integrate object detection and tracking for replicating human behaviours in a multi-agent simulation. To the best of our knowledge, this is the first work that attempts to provide a modular framework that is flexible and capable of mimicking real world scenario into a virtual scene for simulation of crisis.

3   Methodologies and Framework

The framework proposed in this paper aims to provide a test-bed that can introduce crisis and danger under normal circumstances for crisis management and analysis. Hence, a system to study real-life behavioral movements of pedestrians in an area is developed so as to realistically generate agents in a simulation model for analyzing possible crisis scenarios. Figure 1 shows the overview of our framework.

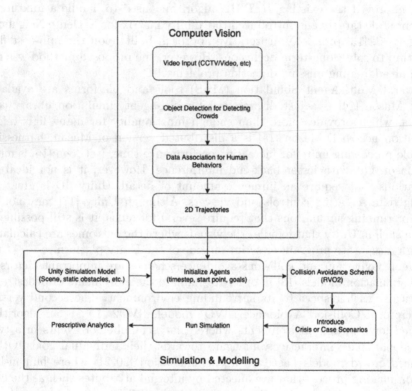

Fig. 1. Framework overview

In the event of a crisis, behaviours and goals may change. Hence, each agent is equipped with an intelligent collision avoidance scheme, RVO2, as discussed in Sect. 2. In the following sub-sections, we will break down the framework into individual systems. Firstly, the detection of pedestrians from video footage, followed by the extraction of trajectories, which is then used for generating agents in the Unity platform for simulation of crisis situations.

3.1   Pedestrian Detection and Tracking

To date, there are several current research on pedestrian or object detection, as discussed in Sect. 2. Each of them has its advantages and disadvantages.

Our proposed framework may adopt any of such detection approaches as long as the approach is able to identify the bounding box of detected objects with labels that specify the type of object it is.

In this work, we use a lightweight algorithm, YOLOv3, for detecting pedestrians in each frame. We then build a cost-flow network for every detection in the current frame and its immediate previous frame based on the paper by Zhang et al. [13]. Finally, after solving for the Minimum Cost Flow, we introduced a simple offline algorithm to handle occlusions and missed detection in-between frames so as to improve the overall tracking accuracy, which the original paper lacks in. Algorithm 1 describes the full procedure, returning a list of trajectories for each unique person in the video.

Algorithm 1. Offline Tracking Algorithm

1: **for each** frame ∈ video **do**
2:     detections[$frame\_count$] = YOLOv3(frame)
3:     **for each** detected object i ∈ detections[$frame\_count$] **do**
4:         **if** i is a person with probability $> \tau$ **then**
5:             Create nodes u_i and v_i with costs $C_{entr,i}, C_{exit,i}, C_i$
6:             **for each** detected object j ∈ detections[$frame\_count - 1$] **do**
7:                 **if** LS$(i,j) > \hat{\tau}$ **then**
8:                     Create arc(v_i, u_j) with cost $C_{i,j}$
9:                 **end if**
10:             **end for**
11:         **end if**
12:     **end for**
13:     increment $frame\_count$
14: **end for**
15: Solve for the min cost flow   ▷ generate initial trajectories
16: **for each** t_i ∈ set of trajectories **do**
17:     **for each** t_j ∈ set of trajectories **do**
18:         **if** t_i is not t_j AND $LBS(t_i[-1], t_j[0]) > \bar{\tau}$ **then**
19:             Combine t_i and t_j
20:         **end if**
21:     **end for**
22: **end for**

Algorithm 1 begins by scanning frame by frame for objects. In each frame, each detected object is added into a cost flow network with its entry cost $C_{entr,i}$, exit cost $C_{exit,i}$ and the cost C_i for the arc between the nodes u and v. The costs are computed based on [13] as follows, where P_{entr}, P_{exit} are constants and β is the probability score given by the YOLOv3 detector (between $0 - 1$):

$$C_{entr,i} = -\log P_{entr}(x_i) \tag{1}$$

$$C_{entr,i} = -\log P_{exit}(x_i) \tag{2}$$

$$C_i = \log \frac{\beta_i}{1 - \beta_i} \tag{3}$$

In order to associate detections between frames, each of the detected objects in the current frame scans through all the detections in the previous frame to compute the location score (LS), $LS_{i,j}$, as follows:

$$HD_{i,j} = \min(BB_i, BB_j) - \max(BT_i, BT_j) \tag{4}$$

$$WD_{i,j} = \min(BR_i, BR_j) - \max(BL_i, BL_j) \tag{5}$$

$$LS_{i,j} = HD_{i,j} * WD_{i,j} / (BH_i * BW_i + BH_j * BW_j - HD_{i,j} * WD_{i,j}) \tag{6}$$

$HD_{i,j}$ is the height difference and $WD_{i,j}$ is the width difference. BB, BT, BR, BL are the bounding box bottom, top, right and left positions respectively. BW and BH are the width and height of the bounding box. Objects that are far away from each other are unlikely to be associated, hence, if the LS is larger than a certain threshold $\hat{\tau}$, we create an arc with cost $c(v_i, u_j) = C_{i,j}$.

$$C_{i,j} = -\log P_{link}(x_j | x_i) \tag{7}$$

In the above equation, P_{link} is the appearance score (AS), which represents the association of the two objects based on their appearance. To calculate AS, the HSV from the two detected objects are used to compute its Bhattacharyya distance [23], as follows, where H is the normalized histograms of its appearance:

$$d(H_i, H_j) = \sqrt{1 - \frac{1}{\sqrt{H_i \overline{H_j} N^2}} \sum_1 \sqrt{H_i(I) \cdot H_j(I)}} \tag{8}$$

$$AS_{i,j} = 1 - d(H_i, H_j) \tag{9}$$

An explicit occlusion model proposed in [13] expands the observation set by adding the occluded objects into the cost-flow network. However, identity switches may occur when two observations are detected by a single bounding box. In order to address this issue, we first measure the distance and scale difference for any two detections from 2 consecutive frames so as to identify possible occlusion case. For every x_i from a previous frame directly occluded by x_j in the current frame, a new node x_i^j is created with the following properties, where p_j and t_j are the position and time step of x_j, and s_i and a_i are the size and appearance of x_i:

$$x_i^j = (p_j, s_i, a_i, t_j) \tag{10}$$

Finally, we solve for the min-cost flow and address fragmentation issues due to missing detections and occlusions. This method of global association is adapted for linking two or more sets of trajectories that may be fragmented due to the aforementioned reasons. In order to effectively achieve this, a link back score (LBS) is derived based on distance and appearance of the last object in a set of trajectories and the first object in another set of trajectories. Firstly, the distance score (DS) $DS_{i,j}$ is computed as follows:

$$DT_{i,j} = FI_{i,j} * FD \tag{11}$$

$$DS_{i,j} = DT - (D(i,j)/TS)/DT \tag{12}$$

DT is the distance threshold given by the frame interval (FI) and frame displacement(FD), learned from training data. $D(i,j)$ is the distance between detected bounding boxes, and TS is the timestep between these two detections. Finally, $LBS_{i,j}$ is defined as:

$$LBS_{i,j} = DS_{i,j} * AS_{i,j} \tag{13}$$

If the LBS score between two sets of trajectories is greater than the threshold $\bar{\tau}$, we combine these two trajectories into one. Finally, we will have a whole new set of complete trajectories for each unique person in the video.

3.2   Translating Trajectories into a Virtual Reality Simulation

With the techniques explained in Sect. 3.1, we would be able to process any surveillance videos and extract actual trajectories at different times of day and week for a particular area under study. The aim is to be able to replicate actual movement behaviours of pedestrians into a virtual reality platform, so as to safely introduce crisis and dangers into the scene for analysis and planning.

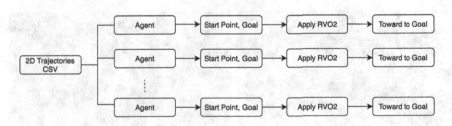

Fig. 2. An illustration of trajectory translation

The Unity 3D platform is utilized to replicate the scene and static obstacles. An illustration of trajectory translation from the tracking result to the Unity3D is showed in Fig. 2. Subsequently, a script was developed to read in trajectories extracted from the videos and generate agents for every unique person. These agents are then spawned at the respective time steps and initialized to follow the trajectories from start to finish. The agents are also equipped with the RVO2 mechanism for avoiding obstacles. During runtime, each agent senses the environment independently and then computes a collision-free motion according to the optimal reciprocal collision avoidance formulation. Thus, it enables agents to regulate their speed in order to avoid danger and potential collisions while the simulation is running. Since the actual trajectories are extracted while no crisis was taking place, the RVO2 implementation will help the agents to change their course and speed only when we have introduced new obstacles, that may include fire hazards, bomb threats, etc.

Thus, with these in place, crisis simulation can be done by introducing threats in the scene and studying evacuation behaviours. Strategies to improve evacuation and rescue can also be implemented. Furthermore, the level of panic can be manipulated in the RVO2 response to collision by increasing speed and allowing collisions that would reflect actual world scenarios during such panic situations.

We will discuss several opportunities for further work in Sect. 5. In this work, we focus our scope on the general framework. Therefore, the next section will discuss an experimental case study we have carried out using the proposed framework and what we can achieve from it.

4   Case Study

The Town Centre Dataset [24] includes video footage of a busy street in a typical town area, recorded on a single camera with an average of sixteen people visible at every frame. The frame size of the dataset is 1920×1080 and the frame rate is 25 frames per second (fps). The dataset also includes the ground truth for verification and validation, hence ideal for use in our experiments. For this case study, we followed the full framework and methods as discussed in Sect. 3. Figure 3 shows an example of pedestrian detection and tracking from the video.

Fig. 3. Example of detected persons from Town Centre Dataset

With the ground truth provided, we were able to verify that the detection and associations are correct. After extracting the 2D trajectories from the video, we treat each set of trajectories for every unique person as an agent in Unity and attached the RVO2 collision avoidance scheme. The agent's entry point will be the first detection location and the destination will be the last detection location. Each of them will move from the source to destination with the speed synchronized based on the video frame number (timestep). Figure 4 presents the example of the agents generated on an empty plane in Unity to replicate the movement behaviours in the video. The result shows our framework can translate the human trajectory successfully. Moving forward, we can now introduce crisis situations and evacuation strategies to analyze and test, as mentioned in Sect. 3.2.

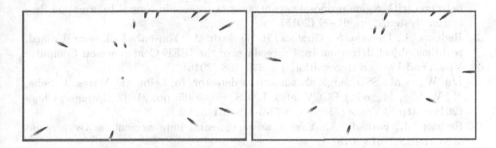

Fig. 4. Example of detected persons generated in Unity3D

Due to the scarcity of data in crisis, no statistical tests can be done to analyze its performance at this point. Since this is a theoretical framework, we have shown how it can be used and what it can achieve.

5   Conclusion and Future Directions

Taking advantage of the recent advancements in computer vision, we are able to drill deeper into understanding crowd behavior by studying individuals rather than the movements of masses in a crowd. With that, we are able to reconstruct the scenes into a virtual simulation environment from video sequences, then simulate case scenarios and events that may be too costly or dangerous to carry out in real-life. Unlike other pedestrian simulation methods [20,21,25] designed to model the behavior of humans, our framework uses a data-driven approach and tries to learn these behavior from real-life video feeds directly. Doing so also improves the level of realism since they are adapted from actual footage of the area under study.

With more advanced human detection, face detection, and behavior prediction technique in computer vision, the results and analysis produced from the framework will certainly improve. In future work, we consider introducing an artificial intelligence (AI) model to learn human movement behaviours effectively and predict possible paths, arrival rates, etc. based on the time and day. Some crisis scenarios will be introduced after we obtain the crisis data, with which the human behavior in crisis could be studied. Furthermore, we will look into developing novel methods to semi-automate/automate data collection for continuously processing surveillance footage. This would enable real-time simulation where prescriptive analytics that makes robust recommendations for rescue and evacuation strategies can be proposed as soon as an incident occurs or perhaps even before it does so as to avoid or make better mitigation plans for any crisis situations.

References

1. Girshick, R.: Fast R-CNN. In: Proceedings of the IEEE International Conference on Computer Vision, pp. 1440–1448 (2015)
2. Ren, S., He, K., Girshick, R., Sun, J.: Faster R-CNN: towards real-time object detection with region proposal networks. In: Advances in Neural Information Processing Systems, pp. 91–99 (2015)
3. Redmon, J., Divvala, S., Girshick, R., Farhadi, A.: You only look once: Unified, real-time object detection. In: Proceedings of the IEEE Conference on Computer Vision and Pattern Recognition, pp. 779–788 (2016)
4. Liu, W., et al.: SSD: single shot multibox detector. In: Leibe, B., Matas, J., Sebe, N., Welling, M. (eds.) ECCV 2016. LNCS, vol. 9905, pp. 21–37. Springer, Cham (2016). https://doi.org/10.1007/978-3-319-46448-0_2
5. Redmon, J., Farhadi, A.: Yolov3: an incremental improvement. arXiv preprint arXiv:1804.02767 (2018)
6. He, K., Gkioxari, G., Dollár, P., Girshick, R.B.: Mask R-CNN. CoRR, vol. abs/1703.06870 (2017). http://arxiv.org/abs/1703.06870
7. Fang, K., Xiang, Y., Li, X., Savarese, S.: Recurrent autoregressive networks for online multi-object tracking. In: 2018 IEEE Winter Conference on Applications of Computer Vision (WACV), pp. 466–475. IEEE (2018)
8. Bewley, A., Ge, Z., Ott, L., Ramos, F., Upcroft, B.: Simple online and realtime tracking. In: 2016 IEEE International Conference on Image Processing (ICIP), pp. 3464–3468. IEEE (2016)
9. Kalman, R.E.: A new approach to linear filtering and prediction problems. J. Basic Eng. **82**(1), 35–45 (1960)
10. Kuhn, H.W.: The hungarian method for the assignment problem. Naval Res. Logistics Q. **2**(1–2), 83–97 (1955)
11. Yu, F., Li, W., Li, Q., Liu, Y., Shi, X., Yan, J.: POI: multiple object tracking with high performance detection and appearance feature. In: Hua, G., Jégou, H. (eds.) ECCV 2016. LNCS, vol. 9914, pp. 36–42. Springer, Cham (2016). https://doi.org/10.1007/978-3-319-48881-3_3
12. Wen, L., Li, W., Yan, J., Lei, Z., Yi, D., Li, S.Z.: Multiple target tracking based on undirected hierarchical relation hypergraph. In: Proceedings of the IEEE Conference on Computer Vision and Pattern Recognition, pp. 1282–1289 (2014)
13. Zhang, L., Li, Y., Nevatia, R.: Global data association for multi-object tracking using network flows. In: 2008 IEEE Conference on Computer Vision and Pattern Recognition, pp. 1–8. IEEE (2008)
14. Luke, S., Cioffi-Revilla, C., Panait, L., Sullivan, K., Balan, G.: Mason: a multiagent simulation environment. Simulation **81**(7), 517–527 (2005)
15. Cordasco, G., De Chiara, R., Mancuso, A., Mazzeo, D., Scarano, V., Spagnuolo, C.: A framework for distributing agent-based simulations. In: Alexander, M., et al. (eds.) Euro-Par 2011. LNCS, vol. 7155, pp. 460–470. Springer, Heidelberg (2012). https://doi.org/10.1007/978-3-642-29737-3_51
16. Sklar, E.: Netlogo, a multi-agent simulation environment (2007)
17. Unity. The world's leading real-time creation platform (2019). https://unity3d.com/unity
18. Zhong, J., Cai, W., Luo, L., Zhao, M.: Learning behavior patterns from video for agent-based crowd modeling and simulation. Auton. Agent. Multi-Agent Syst. **30**(5), 990–1019 (2016)

19. van den Berg, J., Guy, S.J., Snape, J., Lin, M.C., Manocha, D.: Rvo2 library: Reciprocal collision avoidance for real-time multi-agent simulation (2011)
20. Luo, L., Chai, C., Ma, J., Zhou, S., Cai, W.: Proactivecrowd: modelling proactive steering behaviours for agent-based crowd simulation. In: Computer Graphics Forum, vol. 37, no. 1, pp. 375–388. Wiley Online Library (2018)
21. Luo, L., et al.: Agent-based human behavior modeling for crowd simulation. Comput. Animation Virtual Worlds 19(3–4), 271–281 (2008)
22. Snape, J., Guy, S.J., Vembar, D., Lake, A., Lin, M.C., Manocha, D.: Reciprocal collision avoidance and navigation for video games. In: Game Developers Conference, San Francisco (2012)
23. OpenCV. Histogram comparison, January 2019. https://docs.opencv.org/2.4/doc/tutorials/imgproc/histograms/histogram_comparison/histogram_comparison.html
24. Benfold, B., Reid, I.: Stable multi-target tracking in real-time surveillance video. In: CVPR, pp. 3457–3464, June 2011
25. Moussaïd, M., Perozo, N., Garnier, S., Helbing, D., Theraulaz, G.: The walking behaviour of pedestrian social groups and its impact on crowd dynamics. PLoS ONE 5(4), e10047 (2010)

Simulation Model Selection Method Based on Semantic Search in Cloud Environment

Siqi Xiong, Feng Zhu[✉], Yiping Yao, and Wenjie Tang

College of Systems Engineering, National University of Defense Technology,
Changsha 410073, China
siqi@mail.ustc.edu.cn, zhufeng@nudt.edu.cn

Abstract. Search and selection of simulation model is an important process of building simulation application of complex system based on model composition in cloud architecture environment. This paper aims to solve the problem of lacking model correlation search and quality of service (QoS) weighted selection. The knowledge graph is used to describe the simulation models and their correlations. According to the model attributes (such as model name, domain, type, time scale, model granularity, etc.) and the model correlation (such as equipment model carrying relationship, etc.) set by users, the initial set of simulation models satisfying the requirements is found based on semantic search. Then, an optimization selection mechanism based on QoS is proposed to support users in customizing the weights of the QoS indices. The optimally ordered model candidate set is provided for selecting according to the weighting comparison of QoS indices. The experimental results show that the proposed method based on semantic search can support the effective selection of simulation models in cloud environment and the composite modeling of complex systems.

Keywords: Cloud computing environment · Knowledge graph · Semantic search · QoS-based model selection method

1 Introduction

Cloud simulation which technologically driven by cloud computing has become an important trend in the development area of complex system simulation [1, 2]. In the combined process of constructing complex system simulation applications, if a part of simulation models are stored in the cloud architecture as the form of shared simulation services, users can heterogeneously invoke them to run cooperatively in the corresponding simulation task. Then simulation users could effectively use the computing resources provided by cloud computing technology and the utilization of simulation model resources can be raised. That finally could raise the flexibility and efficiency, and reduces the cost of the construction of complex system simulation applications.

In order to construct complex system simulation applications in cloud environment, it is necessary to search the initial set of simulation models which meet user's requirements in the cloud and select the optimal simulation models in the set, so as to quickly and efficiently construct the required application [3]. Therefore, the search and

© Springer Nature Singapore Pte Ltd. 2019
G. Tan et al. (Eds.): AsiaSim 2019, CCIS 1094, pp. 222–233, 2019.
https://doi.org/10.1007/978-981-15-1078-6_19

selection of simulation model is the important process of constructing complex system simulation applications in the cloud environment [4]. Traditional simulation model search methods based on web service description language (WSDL) [5, 6] mainly search for simulation models through keywords matching. In this way, the accuracy is low and the simulation models are limited in the result of search. Complex system simulation applications are composed of a large number of simulation model entities, and there are intricate interactions and correlations between model entities [7]. Ontology web language [8] (OWL)-based simulation model search method lacks the mechanism that could search simulation models through models' correlations efficiently, which is insufficient to support user in searching related models conveniently. The simulation models for building simulation applications are usually stored in the cloud environment as services. These models are developed independently by different institutions which may have similar functions and attributes, but differ in QoS. QoS is the key factor for model selection to build complex system simulation application with high quality [9]. Current QoS-based optimization selection algorithms for simulation models lack the induction of QoS attributes for simulation models in the cloud environment and lack a mechanism to select models based on users' QoS preferences.

The concept of knowledge graph [10] was proposed by Google in 2012 which was developed from semantic network. Knowledge graph is usually stored by graph database and mainly used to describe various entities existing in the real world and their relationships. Knowledge graph has powerful semantic descriptive ability and correlation search capability [11]. Since each simulation model is also an entity in the real word, this paper uses a simulation model description method based on knowledge graph to describe simulation models; establishes a model semantic search framework (MSSF) in the constructed model description knowledge graph under which users can set attributes and correlation of models to find the required models through semantic search. A QoS weighted-based model selection mechanism (QWSM) is proposed, which can select the simulation models according to the customized QoS weight set by user. MSSF and QWSM can provide effective search and selection of simulation models in cloud environment, and support for composite modelling of cloud computing-based complex system simulation.

The organizational structure of this paper is as follows: Sect. 2 is related works, introducing the research status of related fields in recent years, and describing the shortcomings of current study and the problems that this paper wants to solve. Section 3 introduces the simulation model selection method based on semantic search in cloud environment. Section 4 is the experimental part, which proves the feasibility and effectiveness of the method proposed in this paper. Section 5 is the summary and the outlook for future work.

2 Related Works

2.1 WSDL-Based Simulation Model Search Method

Early web services were primarily described using the WSDL, similarly, the early simulation model was also described by the WSDL basic description framework.

WSDL lacks the semantic description of simulation models, and when building a complex system simulation application, users' search requirements for simulation models are often based on semantics. WSDL-based search method searches models by keyword matching, so this method not only has low accuracy but also can't make full use of a large number of simulation models that meet the requirements semantically with the same function but do not match the keywords, which is limited in model searching [12]. Therefore, the search method of simulation model based on keywords matching can't meet the demand for model searching of users in the process of building complex system simulation applications.

2.2 OWL-Based Simulation Model Search Method

Ontologies in the Semantic Web can describe simulation models at the semantic level. Web service ontology description language (OWL-S) was designed to make the Web service an entity that computers can understand based on the description of ontology. OWL-S describes Web services in three aspects: (1) service profile (2) service model, and (3) service grounding [12, 13]. Ontology can improve the accuracy of simulation model search by describing simulation models based on semantics [14, 15]. In order to support the combinatorial modeling of complex system simulation applications, some experts have carried out research on simulation service description methods based on semantics and have proposed description ontologies of simulation model resources (such as OWL-SS [16] and OWL-SM [17]). At present, OWL-based simulation model description methods generally lack descriptions of the characteristics of simulation models in the cloud environment [18], and lack expression of the correlations between simulation models, which are not effective enough to support users in searching and selecting relevant models conveniently through the correlations between models in the cloud environment.

2.3 QoS-Based Simulation Model Selection Method

Similar to Web services, QoS is a key factor in choosing simulation models stored in the cloud environment as a service [19]. At present, many researchers have defined suitable QoS indices for simulation services and have proposed model selection mechanisms based on QoS [20]. However, current descriptions of simulation models lack the induction of QoS attributes of simulation models in the cloud environment [21], and current selection algorithms lack a selection mechanism that could select models in the cloud environment according to users' preferences for QoS indices, which cannot meet users' specific requirements in QoS when constructing complex system simulation applications.

In summary, in order to improve the semantic correlation search ability of simulation models in cloud environment and support users in selecting models through the weight allocation of QoS indices, so as to provide better support for composite modelling of complex systems, this paper carries out the research on simulation model selection method based on semantic search in cloud environment.

3 Simulation Model Selection Method Based on Semantic Search in Cloud Environment

3.1 MSSF

The traditional WSDL-based simulation model search mechanism uses keyword matching to find simulation model description texts with the same keywords. Knowledge graph uses a more expressive way to describe simulation models by semantic description, and the search method based on knowledge graph can find simulation models at the semantic level through the link relations between data and things. Compared with ontology description language, knowledge graph stores RDF [22] triples in the graph database directly, which means the correlations between simulation models can be described in a simple and intuitive way by knowledge graph.

This paper uses the description method of cloud simulation model resources based on knowledge graph [23] to describe simulation models, which describes the characteristics of cloud simulation models and their QoS indices, and then designs a MSSF based on the simulation model description knowledge graph. MSSF provides two patterns for simulation model search: (1) users can associate the required simulation model by attribute information such as the name, domain, type, time scale, and granularity of the simulation model; or (2) users can search for the required simulation model by the correlations between models. According to the search conditions input by the user, simulation models that meet the search conditions can be found in the knowledge graph that stored in the graph database (see Fig. 1).

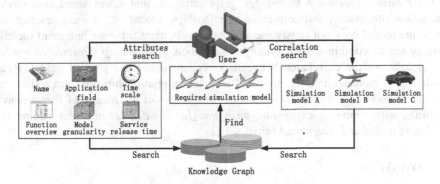

Fig. 1. Simulation model semantic search framework

Under MSSF, users input model attribute requirements as semantic search conditions stored in an array *Attributes_conditions [M]*. Each item of the array corresponds to 1 to M attribute requirements of the simulation model. The user can input one or more attribute requirements (such as model name, domain, category, time scale, model granularity, etc.) as semantic search conditions to search for simulation models that meet the requirements of these attributes. The user can also input the required association model and specific association relationships (such as command relationship, equipment-carrying relationship, etc.) as semantic search conditions stored in the variables *Correlated model* and *Relationship* respectively, to search for simulation models that have a certain relationship with the correlated model. The input of correlated models is necessary in this search pattern. Algorithm 1 shows the semantic search process.

Algorithm 1: Semantic_search

Input: Attributes _conditions[M], the vector for storing model attributes requirements;
      Correlated model; Relationship, the relationship with correlated model;

Output: Ω, simulation model initial set;

1 Boolean flag1 ← true, flag2 ← true;
2 **if** (*Attributes_conditions* ≠ *null*)||(*Relationship_search_conditions* ≠ *null*) **then**
3   **for each** *model* ∈ *Data_Base* **do** // Loop traversal of the simulation model
4   **for** i ← 0 **to** M **do**   // Loop traversal of model attribute requirements condition
5   **if** *model* ≮ *Attributes_search_conditions*[i] **then** flag1 ← false;
6   **end for**
7   **if** *relationship*(*Correlation model, model*) ≠ *NULL*
8   **if** *Relationship* ≰ *relationship*(*Correlation model, model*)
              then flag2 ← false;
9   **else** flag2 ← false;
10   **if** (*flag1 & flag2*) **then** *push_into_list(model, Ω)*;
11   **end for**
12 **end if**
13 **return** Ω

Data_Base represents a knowledge graph database that stores simulation model description information and correlation relationships. *model* ≮ α indicates that the simulation model does not satisfy the attribute requirement α by the judgment method of fuzzy search combined with synonym expansion. *relationship (Correlated model, model)* indicates the correlation between correlated model and present model. Relationship ≰ β indicates that the specified association relationship does not satisfy the correlation between correlated model and present model by means of fuzzy search combined with synonym expansion. *push_into_list (model, Ω)* indicates adding the simulation model into the model initial set Ω.

3.2 QWSM

The simulation model that the user needs to use has to not only meet the requirements of its function but also have high QoS to reach the quality requirements of building complex system simulation applications. The simulation models obtained under the MSSF proposed in Sect. 3.1 are not unique, and they have similar functions and attributes, but differ in QoS. In order to build higher-quality complex system simulation applications, after the initial set that meets the search conditions under the MSSF is acquired, it is necessary to order that set through a QoS-based selection mechanism to select the optimal simulation models from the ordered candidate set (see Fig. 2).

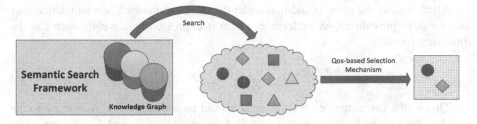

Fig. 2. Search and selection process of simulation model

The QWSM proposed in this paper can support users in customizing QoS index weights and selecting the optimal simulation model from the initial set according to the weighted comparison of QoS indices. The specific method is as follows:

Definition of QoS indices: Referring to the QoS indices of Web services, and considering the uniqueness of the simulation model as a kind of special Web service [20, 24], the QoS indices of the simulation model in the cloud environment can be summarized as follows:

1. Model performance (Q_M) is determined by the computation of the model. A simulation model with more computation has lower model performance.
2. Communication capability (Q_C) reflects the communication capability of the link between the user's terminal node and the cloud server.
3. Availability (Q_A) indicates the probability that the simulation model can be called and used, which reflects the reusability of a simulation model. It is defined by the mean time between failures and the mean time to repair.
4. Reliability (Q_R) is defined by the execution success rate of the service, which reflects the robustness of a simulation model and refers to the probability of obtaining the correct response to the user's requirements within the maximum expected time range.
5. Security (Q_S) measures data management capability, which mainly depends on the user's experience after using the service. Security can be defined as the average score on data management capability given to the simulation model by terminal users.

QoS weighted-based selection algorithm: The above five attributes (Q_M, Q_C, Q_A, Q_R, and Q_S) are all positive metrics, that is, the higher the value, the higher the quality. In order to eliminate the gap between the different QoS indices, this paper use the following formula [21] to limit their values to the range of [0, 1]:

$$V(Q_i^k) = \frac{maxQ_i^k - Q_i^k}{maxQ_i^k - minQ_i^k}. \tag{1}$$

These five QoS indices are assigned numbers 1–5. Q_i^k indicating the value of the ith QoS index of the kth model in the candidate set; $maxQ_i^k$ and $minQ_i^k$ indicate the maximum and minimum values, respectively, that the QoS index may reach; and $V(Q_i^k)$ indicates the value after standardization of this QoS index.

After entering the search condition under the search framework, the simulation user also needs to provide a QoS preference, which is expressed by a weight vector as the following formula:

$$W = (w_i, \ 1 \leq i \leq 5, \ \sum w_i = 1). \tag{2}$$

That is, the percentage each QoS index should be accounted for. According to the weight vector given by the user, the total QoS index of the kth model in the candidate set is

$$Q^k = \sum_{i=1}^{5} w_i \cdot V(Q_i^k). \tag{3}$$

The model that meets the user's search conditions under the MSSF will be added to the initial set. According to the weight vector representing the QoS preference provided by the user, the target QoS index Q of each model in the initial set is obtained by the above formulas. Finally, the candidate set of simulation models ordered by Q will be provided to the user for selection. Algorithm 2 shows the QoS weighted-based selection process.

Algorithm 2: QoS weighted-based_selection

Input: W, Simulation model QoS index weight vector;
        Ω, Simulation model initial set (from Algorithm 1);

Output: Φ, Ordered model candidate set;

1 **if** $\Omega \neq$ null **then**
2   **for each** $model \in \Omega$ **do**   // Loop traversal of model initial set
3   **for each** $i \leftarrow$ 0 to 5 **do**   // Loop through 5 QoS indices
4        $V(Q_i) \leftarrow \frac{maxQ_i - Q_i}{maxQ_i - minQ_i}$ // Calculate the standard value of the QoS index
5        $Q \leftarrow \sum_{i=1}^{5} w_i \cdot V(Q_i)$ // Calculate the target QoS value of the simulation model
6        $push\_into\_list$(<model,Q>, Φ)   // Insert the binary <model, Q> into the set Φ
7   **end for**
8   **end for**
9    $rank\_list\_by$ (Φ, Q)   // Sort the elements in Φ by Q
10 **end if**
11 **return** Φ

---

4   Case Study

4.1   Building an Instance of Simulation Model Description Knowledge Graph

In order to prove the feasibility and effectiveness of simulation model selection method based on semantic search proposed in Sect. 3, taking military weapon equipment simulation as an example, this paper constructs some simulation models with different QoS indices as a supplement. According to the description method of cloud simulation model based on knowledge graph proposed in paper [23], the description information of these simulation models are added to the database that stores the model description knowledge graph.

Figure 3 takes a single simulation model (*fighter plane A* simulation model) as an example, displaying the description information of the simulation model in the knowledge graph, including the static information, dynamic function, and interface information of the model. The blue nodes and the purple nodes together describe the static information of the simulation model. The purple nodes represent the simulation model entities and the correlations between these three simulation model entities, which could be used for model correlation search. The blue node describes various attributes of the *fighter plane A* model which could be used for attributes search (some attributes can also be stored directly in the model entity node) and the QoS information that could be used for model optimization selection. The gray nodes describe the interface information of *fighter plane A* model. The red nodes indicate the statuses of its subject node, and there are certain conversion conditions between them which describe the dynamic function of the simulation model.

After the construction of simulation model description knowledge graph, this paper realizes the simulation model selection method based on semantic search by the connection and operation of graph database in an inquiring statement called Cypher.

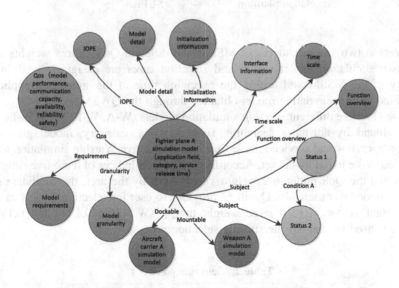

Fig. 3. Model description knowledge graph

4.2 Analysis of Simulation Model Selection Method Based on Semantic Search

The experiment uses military weapon equipment simulation models to build a simulation application called Sea Battle. The simulation platform is SUPE, and all experiments were run on two compute nodes with a Linux (centos7) operating system.

Each node was equipped with a 3.40 GHz Intel(R) Core(TM) i7-6700 quad core CPU processor. In this experiment, all the simulation objects instantiated by the selected simulation model are distributed to one node, and the remaining simulation objects are in another node. A simulation time was set up corresponding to the physical time of 10 min to study the actual system of 5 days, so each simulation promotes the logical simulation time of 720. Each piece of experimental data in the analysis chart is the average value after 10 test runs. The specific experimental parameters are shown in Table 1.

Table 1. Simulation scenario parameters

Experimental parameters	Description/Value
Number of fighter planes	50
Number of reconnaissance planes	10
Number of warships	50
Number of submarines	50
Number of aircraft carriers	2
Simulation run time	720
Degree of parallelism	2
Simulation platform	SUPE

Direct at two search patterns of MSSM and different QoS indices weights set by user, two simulation model search and selection cases are designed, verifying the veracity of the MSSM and testing the execution time of the simulation application assembled by the simulation model obtained through the QWSM.

Case (1): Five different *warship* simulation models (W-A, W-B, W-C, W-D, W-F) can be found by attributes searching such as name, category, model granularity, function overview and service release time, etc. These five Warship simulation models are added in the initial model set. According to the QoS indices of these five simulation models and the QoS preference weight vector input by the user, the candidate set of simulation models ordered by Q will be provided to user for selecting. In this case, the QoS weight vector gives a large weight to Q_M (W = $(0.6, 0.1, 0.1, 0.1, 0.1)$) and Table 2 is used to analysis the specific selection process.

Table 2. Selection process 1

	QoS1[0, 100]	QoS2[0, 10]	QoS3[0, 1]	QoS4[0, 1]	QoS5[0, 10]	Q
W-A	46(0.46)	7(0.7)	0.93	0.95	9(0.9)	0.624
W-B	60(0.6)	6(0.6)	0.92	0.95	9(0.9)	0.697
W-C	85(0.85)	6(0.6)	0.94	0.96	10(1)	0.86
W-D	73(0.73)	7(0.7)	0.91	0.96	10(1)	0.795
W-E	52(0.52)	6(0.6)	0.92	0.94	9(0.9)	0.648
W = $(0.6, 0.1, 0.1, 0.1, 0.1)$						
Ordered candidate set: {W-C, W-D, W-B, W-E, W-A}						

The QoS indices of simulation models are firstly standardized by the Formula (1), and then the target QoS index value Q is calculated according to the given QoS weight vector and Formula (3). Finally, the ordered candidate set will be output. The optimized candidate model set {W-C, W-D, W-B, W-E, W-A} can be obtained through that calculation process. The five *warship* models are added to the simulation application and the execution times of the five simulation applications are shown in Fig. 4(a).

These applications can run effectively and it can be seen that the simulation application assembled by the model W-C, which is ranked first in the candidate set, has the shortest running time (2115 s). Because the simulation model with higher computational performance spends less time for calculating.

Case (2): Under the MSSF, the required models can also be found by the correlations between models, for example: Four *fighter plane* simulation models (FP-A, FP-B, FP-C, FP-D) can be found through the search of fighter plane which is dockable on the *aircraft carrier* simulation model. The selection process is the same as Case (1), and the ordered candidate set will be output. In this case, the QoS weight vector gives a large weight to Q_C ($W = (0.1, 0.6, 0.1, 0.1, 0.1)$) and Table 3 is used to analysis the specific selection process.

Table 3. Selection process 2

	QoS1[0, 100]	QoS2[0, 10]	QoS3[0, 1]	QoS4[0, 1]	QoS5[0, 10]	Q
FP-A	70(0.7)	8(0.8)	0.94	0.96	10(1)	0.84
FP-B	68(0.68)	4(0.4)	0.93	0.95	9(0.9)	0.586
FP-C	80(0.8)	7(0.7)	0.94	0.96	10(1)	0.79
FP-D	75(0.75)	4(0.4)	0.92	0.95	9(0.9)	0.592
$W = (0.1, 0.6, 0.1, 0.1, 0.1)$						
Ordered candidate set: {FP-A, FP-C, FP-D, FP-B}						

The calculation process of Q is the same as Case (1). The optimized candidate model set is {FP-A, FP-C, FP-D, FP-B}. The four *fighter plane* models are added to the simulation application and the execution times of the four simulation applications are shown in Fig. 4(b).

These applications can run effectively and it can be seen that the order of the fighter plane models corresponding to the execution efficiency of the five simulation applications is not completely consistent with the optimization order in the model candidate set, because when selecting the model to construct a simulation application without detailed analysis, it is unable to accurately quantify the extent to which the model performance and communication capability affect the execution efficiency of the entire simulation application.

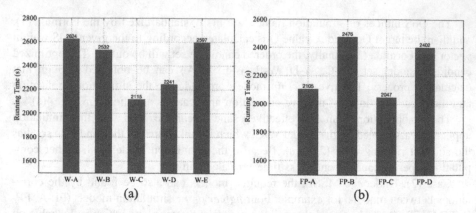

Fig. 4. Execution times of simulation applications

4.3 Discussion

The experiment verifies the MSSF proposed in this paper. It can search and find the correct simulation model that meets the requirements through the attributes search and correlation search and the model could work together with other models. And the QWSM can support the effective selection of simulation model according to customized requirements of users, but it cannot always give the optimum solution that could optimize the overall performance of the simulation system.

5 Summary and Future Work

The simulation model selection method based on semantic search proposed in this paper can support users in searching simulation models accurately by attributes and correlations of models and provide effective selection of simulation model that satisfies users' QoS preferences in cloud environment. The method could support the composite modelling of complex system simulation applications.

The follow-up work will further improve the QWSM, confirm the metric of model QoS indices, and study how to assign the corresponding QoS index weights directing at specific simulation applications, which could help users to select simulation models that can optimize the comprehensive performance of the entire simulation system.

Acknowledgment. This work was supported in part by the National Natural Science Foundation of China (no. 61903368).

References

1. Calheiros, R.N., Ranjan, R., Beloglazov, A., Rose, C.A.F.D., Buyya, R.: CloudSim: a toolkit for modelling and simulation of cloud computing environments and evaluation of resource provisioning algorithms. Softw. Pract. Exp. **41**(1), 23–50 (2011)

2. Sotiriadis, S., Bessis, N., Antonopoulos, N., et al.: SimIC: designing a new inter-cloud simulation platform for integrating large-scale resource management. In: IEEE International Conference on Advanced Information Networking and Applications (2013)
3. Taylor, S.J.E., et al.: Grand challenges for modelling and simulation: simulation everywhere —from cyber infrastructure to clouds to citizens. Simulation **91**(7), 648–665 (2015)
4. Moghaddam, M., Davis, J.G.: Service Selection in Web service Composition: A Comparative Review of Existing Approaches. Springer, New York (2014). 10.1007/978-1-4614-7518-7_13
5. Christensen, E., et al.: Web services description language (WSDL). In: Encyclopedia of Social Network Analysis and Mining (2003
6. Moreau (Canon), J.: Web services Description Language (WSDL) Version 1.2: Bindings (2003)
7. Yao, Y., Liu, G.: High-performance simulation computer for large-scale system-of-systems simulation. J. Syst. Simul. **23**(8), 1617–1623 (2011)
8. Bechhofer, S.: OWL: web ontology language. In: Encyclopedia of Information Science and Technology, vol. 63(45), 2nd edn., pp. 990–996 (2004)
9. Zeng, L., et al.: QoS-aware middleware for Web services composition. IEEE Trans. Softw. Eng. **3**(4), 449–470 (2004)
10. Pujara, J., Miao, H., Getoor, L., Cohen, W.: Knowledge graph identification. In: Alani, H., et al. (eds.) ISWC 2013. LNCS, vol. 8218, pp. 542–557. Springer, Heidelberg (2013). https://doi.org/10.1007/978-3-642-41335-3_34
11. Xu, Z.-L., Sheng, Y.P., He, L.-R., Wang, Y.F.: Review on knowledge graph techniques. J. Univ. Electron. Sci. Technol. China **45**, 589–606 (2016)
12. Xin, W.: Realizing Semantic Web services Description with OWL -S Ontology. New Technology of Library & Information Service (2005)
13. Sheng, B., Zhang, C., Yin, X., et al.: Common intelligent semantic matching engines of cloud manufacturing service based on OWL-S. Int. J. Adv. Manuf. Technol. **84**(1–4), 103–118 (2016)
14. Kanthavel, R., Maheswari, K., Padmanabhan, N.: Information retrieval based on semantic matching approach in web service discovery. Int. J. Comput. Appl. **64**(16), 54–56 (2013)
15. Purohit, L., Kumar, S.: Web service selection using semantic matching. In: International Conference on Advances in Information Communication Technology and Computing (2016)
16. Zhang, T., Liu, Y.S.: Semantic Web-based approach to simulation services dynamic discovery. Comput. Eng. Appl. **43**(32), 15–19 (2007)
17. Song, L.L., Qun, L.I.: Research on simulation model description ontology and its matching model. Comput. Eng. Appl. **44**(30), 6–12 (2008)
18. Li, T., Li, B.H., Chai, X.D.: Layered simulation service description framework oriented to cloud simulation. Comput. Integr. Manuf. Syst. **18**(9), 2091–2098 (2012)
19. Cheng, C., Chen, A.Q.: Study on cloud service evaluation index system based on QoS. Appl. Mech. Mater. **742**, 683–687 (2015)
20. Zhang, T., Liu, Y., Zha, Y.: Optimal approach to QoS-driven simulation services composition. J. Syst. Simul. **21**(16), 4990–4994 (2009)
21. Liu, J., Sun, J., Jiang, L.: A QoS evaluation model for cloud computing. Comput. Knowl. Technol. **6**(31), 8801–8803, 8806 (2010)
22. T. M. Organization: Resource Description Framework (RDF). Encyclopedia of GIS, pp. 6–19 (2004)
23. Xiong, S., Zhu, F., Yao, Y.P., Tang, W.J.: A description method of cloud simulation model resources based on knowledge graph. In 4th International Conference on Cloud Computing and Big Data Analytics, Chengdu, pp. 655–663. IEEE (2019)
24. Huang, Y.: The Research on Evaluation Model of Cloud Service Based on QoS and Application. Zhejiang Gongshang University (2013)

Short Papers

Short Papers

Research on New Generation of Multi-domain Unified Modeling Language for Complex Products

Lin Zhang[1,2(✉)], Li-Yuanjun Lai[1,2], and Fei Ye[1,2]

[1] School of Automation Science and Electrical Engineering, Beihang University, Xueyuan Rd. No. 37, Haidian District, Beijing, China
zhanglin@buaa.edu.cn
[2] Engineering Research Center of Complex Product Advanced Manufacturing Systems, Ministry of Education, Xueyuan Rd. No. 37, Haidian District, Beijing, China

Abstract. Modeling and simulation has become an important method to support designing and developing complex products. It's an urgent issue to combine design and simulation together in order to support the efficient development of multi-disciplinary and full-process collaborative design work of complex products. For this problem, a new generation of multi-domain unified modeling language framework for complex products is proposed, which supports multi-disciplinary and full-process collaborative design and cross-domain collaborative simulation optimization for complex products, and realizes the full process standardization and collaborative modeling of complex products. Finally, the goal of precision modeling, global simulation, and optimal synergy is achieved.

Keywords: Complex product · Modeling language · Collaborative design · Simulation optimization

1 Introduction

Complex products refer to a class of products with complex customer requirements, system components, product technology, manufacturing processes, test and maintenance, project management, and complex working environment [1]. It has the characteristics of high design difficulty, high cost of test operation and maintenance, strict quality requirements, and large demand for intelligence. At the same time, it faces major challenges such as one-time success, on-time delivery, cycle and cost compression. To solve the above problems, it's essential to rely on modeling and simulation. In recent years, Model-based Systems Engineering (MBSE) has become the main solution for complex system modeling and design [2]. MBSE transforms traditional document and physical model driven research method into model-driven research and development (R&D) method. The formal description makes MBSE reusable, unambiguous, easy to understand, easy to spread, etc., and has received extensive attention in academic and business circles.

MBSE uses System Modeling Language (SysML) to model the whole process of the system to achieve unified model-based management and optimization of the whole process of product development [3]. Since SysML does not have the description capability of physical model, it cannot be used for simulate directly. Therefore, other multi-domain modeling and simulation methods are required to verify the correctness and completeness of the model.

At present, there are three main methods for multi-domain modeling and simulation: methods based on commercial simulation software interfaces in various fields [4], methods based on high-level architecture [5] and methods based on unified modeling language. Among them, the method based on unified modeling language is a unified description of system components in different fields, thus achieving seamless integration and data exchange of multi-domain models [6], making it the most popular method of multi-domain modeling and simulation methods.

For the complex products of the integrated types including machine, electricity, liquid and control, the current practice is to perform requirements modeling and architecture design based on system modeling language (such as SysML, IDEF, etc.). Based on unified modeling physical modeling Language (such as Modelica, etc.) and the integration of standard specifications (FMI, HLA, etc.), the development and integration of physical models is achieved. Through the mapping between the system model and the physical model for system-wide modeling and simulation, unified product management is achieved during different development stages.

2 Related Works

In the research of system layer design and simulation integration, Schamai et al. [8] proposed a mapping method ModelicaML based on the UML extension method for Modelica transformation. It uses state machine diagram as the carrier of discrete and continuous behavior hybrid modeling. Adding comments to state transitions to express continuous behavior, it provides a more complete solution for design behavior and simulation behavior integration. However, this method lacks formal model expression. The description based on plain text can not effectively express and manage the model, and the parameter correspondence between state machine diagram and structure model is not solved, which makes ModelicaML unable to fully support all grammar standards of Modelica.

Cao et al. [7] proposed a unified behavior model extension method based on SysML. This method is combined with Matlab/Simulink to realize the automatic conversion of design model and simulation model by establishing simulation supplementary model. However, this method is more focused on the simulation of the control system field, and the support for the multi-domain modeling and simulation of the physical system is weak, so it is not suitable for the simulation of complex system engineering.

Gauthier et al. [9] used the ATL (ATL Transformation Language, ATL) to map the SysML model to the Modelica model based on the SysML4Modelica extension package proposed by the Object Management Group (OMG) to verify the accuracy and completeness of the design model. Compared with the QVT (Query/View/Transformation) mapping method applied by OMG, Gauthier et al. have some innovations in the mapping method. However, due to the incomplete definition of the SysML4Modelica extension package, the description of the Modelica syntax is not perfect.

Li et al. [10] proposed a visual model transformation method based on SysML from the meta-model transformation level. The SysML source model and the Modelica target model were determined by the instantiation hierarchical modeling of transformation rules and transformation activity meta-models. The conversion relationship performs a dynamic conversion activity to achieve the conversion. However, this method establishes a mapping relationship with Modelica based on the existing model-elements of SysML, and does not extend SysML. Therefore, the specific description of complex products is insufficient, which makes the conversion between the two languages incomplete.

Zhou et al. [11] constructed the SysML extension package M-Design for Modelica based on the Modelica meta-model, and then defined the mapping rules between the two according to the extended SysML and Modelic metamodels, thus implementing the automatic conversion from SysML design model to Modelica simulation model. However, the extension package only defines the basic meta-model of Modelica, and some advanced features cannot be described. Moreover, the ATL-based mapping method only implements the one-way model conversion from SysML to Modelica, and fails to implement bidirectional model conversion.

In summary, the current research on complex product modeling and simulation integration still has the following problems: ① The system modeling language is out of touch with the physical domain modeling language, and the connection needs to be realized through conversion, and the versatility is not strong; ② It is difficult to support the modeling and simulation of truly complex products, such as spacecraft, ships, large aircraft, etc., where continuous and discrete, qualitative and quantitative, linear and nonlinear models of different characteristics coexist. The above scheme is difficult to be applicable; ③ Insufficient support for smart products and intelligent design. Especially in China, there is a lack of unified standards in different fields. In a system, there are often a large number of legacy models with different language systems and different modeling tools. The lack of a unified language system to achieve common, accurate, and complete cognition and association has made it difficult to utilize these heterogeneous models in the development of new products. Therefore, in order to solve the above problems, it is necessary to concentrate on the research of multi-disciplinary and full-process collaborative design and simulation requirements of complex products, and a new generation of multi-domain unified modeling language for complex products, which will realize the standardized and collaborative modeling of complex products to achieve the goal of precise modeling, global simulation and optimal synergy.

3   A New Generation of Multi-domain Unified Modeling Language Research Framework

In order to realize a new generation of multi-domain unified modeling language for complex products, it is necessary to research the association and collaborative description of complex product cross-domain models, the intelligent semantic design of unified modeling language, and the analytic method of cross-domain modeling of grammar/semantic perception, as shown in Fig. 1.

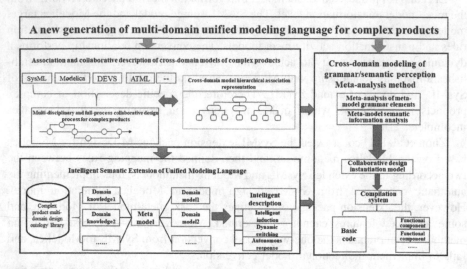

Fig. 1. Modeling language research framework

3.1   Association and Collaborative Description of Cross-Domain Models

For the problem of cross-domain difficulty and interaction of various modeling languages, the existing mainstream modeling languages such as DEVS, Modelica, SysML and other model representation structures are extracted, and the common mechanism and interaction mechanism of multi-domain models are mined. Research on the top-down division of the model and the model connection mechanism forms the top-level representation of the model synergy association. At the system level, SysML is used to describe the system construction requirements, and based on this, the system process description logic, process model interface and driven mechanism are designed. At the model simulation level, since SysML does not have the ability to simulate the designed model, it is necessary to convert the SysML design model into a Modelica simulation model for verification based on the metamodel mapping method. At the model architecture level, considering the ability of DEVS to support discrete event simulation, the middleware is transformed based on this design model to better support the simulation capabilities of various models.

3.2   Intelligent Semantic Design of Unified Modeling Language

Aiming at the multi-domain knowledge complex problem in complex product collaborative design, firstly, the semantic tree of multi-domain modeling for complex products is extended based on the existing subject ontology, and the domain ontology, feature map and functional map are established to improve the construction of semantic tree. Secondly, the extended description semantic rules such as product, collaborative design process and system model design are designed, including semantic similarity analysis and quantification of various models, semantic rules and models, and their operation mode mapping derivation. Finally, the description of the new import model is semantically labeled and functional component association, and the new description is deduced by using the time series neural network, which not only achieves the association model matching, but also realizes the dynamic update of the semantic tree.

3.3 Syntactic/Semantic Perception Cross-Domain Modeling Meta-Analysis Method

The top-down factor decomposition method is used to construct the element analysis rules of meta-language. Through analyzing the grammar and semantics contained in the language, and adding the design pattern dynamic adaptation and collaborative process auto-interaction mechanism, unified language-based model intelligence combination and code quick link in complex product multi-domain collaborative design process can be realized. Firstly, the three-layer grammar structure of system-subsystem-model is parsed and mapped, and the semantic tree search and link method is designed for the name, characteristics and function of the model. Then, the object code generation logic is designed in combination with the code generation mechanism of the existing mainstream language, and the model description is parsed into a high-level programming language for compilation processing. For the reuse of existing models, the FMI standard-based connection calling mechanism is designed for different domain object models. Finally, based on the grammar library and semantic tree of modeling primitives, the automatic editing rules of modeling language code and the visual editing and analysis interface of modeling primitives are written to construct the analytical system.

In summary, modeling semantics (Sect. 3.2) is based on the extended description of modeling grammar (Sect. 3.1), which together form a unified modeling semantics, and dynamic analysis (Sect. 3.3) provides prototype system support for model instantiation and engineering application of modeling languages.

4 Conclusion

MBSE has promoted the transformation of complex product development from document-based models to model-based, improving the ability to model complex product designs, but it still lacks simulation capabilities. In order to solve the problem that the current complex product design modeling language is out of sync with the simulation language, this paper proposes a new generation multi-domain unified modeling language method for complex products. On this basis, it studies multi-disciplinary full-process collaborative design modeling and simulation optimization of complex products. The framework realizes the whole process, multi-disciplinary and inter-stage collaborative design modeling and simulation optimization through requirements, design, experiment, operation and maintenance. The next step will be based on existing theories and frameworks, focusing on the design and implementation of a multi-domain unified modeling language.

Acknowledgements. The authors would like to gratefully acknowledge the financial support of the National Key Technologies R&D Program of China (Project No. 2018YFB1701600).

References

1. Lin, Z., Lei, R., Fei, T.: Complex product manufacturing digital integration platform technology. Def. Manuf. Technol. **4**, 4–10 (2010)
2. Ana Luisa, R., Jose, F., Jaume, B.: Model-based systems engineering: an emerging approach for modern systems. IEEE Trans. Syst. Man Cybern. Part C **42**(1), 101–111 (2011)
3. Sanford, F., Alan, M., Rick, S.: OMG systems modeling language (OMG SysML™) tutorial. In: INCOSE International Symposium (2006)
4. Yu, T.: Study on Objected-oriented Bond Graph Modeling and Simulation of Multi-domain Complex Mechatronic System. Institute of Mechanical Science (2006)
5. Xiaobo, C., Guangleng, X., Bin, G., et al.: Research on multi-disciplinary modeling based on HLA. J. Syst. Simul. **15**(11), 1537–1542 (2003)
6. Jianjun, Z., Jianwan, D., Fanli, Z., et al.: Modelica and its mechanism of multi-domain unified modeling and simulation. J. Syst. Simul. **18**, 570–573 (2006)
7. Schamai, W.: Modelica Modeling Language (ModelicaML): A UML Profile for Modelica. Institute of Technology (2009)
8. Yue, C., Yusheng, L., Hongri, F., et al.: SysML-based uniform behavior modeling and automated mapping of design and simulation model for complex mechatronics. Comput. Aided Des. **45**(3), 764–776 (2013)
9. Gauthier, J.-M., Bouquet, F., Hammad, A., Peureux, F.: Tooled process for early validation of SysML models using modelica simulation. In: Dastani, M., Sirjani, M. (eds.) FSEN 2015. LNCS, vol. 9392, pp. 230–237. Springer, Cham (2015). https://doi.org/10.1007/978-3-319-24644-4_16
10. Xinguang, L., Jihong, L.: A method of SysML-based visual transformation of system design-simulation models. J. Comput. Aided Des. Comput. Graph. **28**(11), 1973–1981 (2016)
11. Shuhua, Z., Yue, C., Zheng, Z., et al.: System design and simulation integration for complex mechatronic products based on SysML and modelica. J. Comput. Aided Des. Comput. Graph. **30**(4), 728–738 (2018)

Improved Grey Relational Analysis for Model Validation

Ke Fang[✉], Yuchen Zhou, and Ju Huo

Harbin Institute of Technology, Harbin 150001, China
hitsim@163.com, zhouyuchen-01@163.com

Abstract. GRA (Grey Relational Analysis) is a typical time series similarity analysis method. However in model validation, it cannot satisfy the feature of monotonicity, and the result is lack of precision. Based on several similarity measurement criteria of time series data, traditional GRA method is developed and modified to satisfy normalization, symmetry and monotonicity. Case study shows that, improved GRA can produce a better similarity analysis result, which is in accordance with the result of TIC (Theil's Inequality Coefficient).

Keywords: Improved grey relational analysis · Model validation · Similarity analysis · Monotonicity · TIC

1 Introduction

Model is the key component of a simulation, which has to be carefully validated to guarantee acceptable credibility. Typical model validation methods can be categorized into three types: statistics methods for randomized variants (Mullins [1] and Ling [2]), time domain and frequency domain methods for time series variants (Jiang [3] and Liu [4]), and expert methods for subjective judgments (Min [5] and Ahn [6]). Regarding as the models of continuous system and continuous-discrete combined system, they have outputs in form of non-periodic time series.

The main solution of similarity analysis on non-periodic time series, is to conduct error/distance calculation between each pair of time point data. Crochemore [7] and Hauduc [8] summarized the model validation methods based on error/distance measurements. Consonni [9] discussed the application of MAE (Mean Absolute Error) in model validation. Kheir [10] and Dorobantu [11] used TIC (Theil's Inequality Coefficient) to validate simulation model of air vehicle. Zhou [12] combined several time series measurements and used ensemble learning method to realize rapid analysis of massive data sets. Wei [13] used GRA (Grey Relational Analysis) to validate missile system simulation model. Ning [14] discussed a modified GRA method.

Different similarity analysis methods for time series have different concerned characteristics of comparison. Similarly, different data sets have different requirements to the analysis methods. However, in general time domain analysis methods have to satisfy the features of normalization, symmetry and monotonicity. GRA cannot satisfy monotonicity with single set of simulation data, which limits the application of the method. It is necessary to improve the formula and make the result more reasonable.

G. Tan et al. (Eds.): AsiaSim 2019, CCIS 1094, pp. 243–250, 2019.
https://doi.org/10.1007/978-981-15-1078-6_21

2 Traditional Grey Relational Analysis

2.1 The Principle of the Method

GRA is a classical similarity analysis method to compare two data sets in time series. The main principle is as the following:

Set $X_0 = (x_0(1), x_0(2), \cdots, x_0(n))$ as observed data set from real world system, and $X_i = (x_i(1), x_i(2), \cdots, x_i(n))$ as simulation data set from simulation model output. The grey relational degree between X_0 and X_i can be calculated as:

$$\gamma(X_0, X_i) = \frac{1}{n} \sum_{k=1}^{n} \gamma(x_0(k), x_i(k)) \tag{1}$$

$$\gamma(x_0(k), x_i(k)) = \frac{\min\limits_{i \in [1,m]} \min\limits_{k \in [1,n]} |x_0(k) - x_i(k)| + \rho \max\limits_{i \in [1,m]} \max\limits_{k \in [1,n]} |x_0(k) - x_i(k)|}{|x_0(k) - x_i(k)| + \rho \max\limits_{i \in [1,m]} \max\limits_{k \in [1,n]} |x_0(k) - x_i(k)|} \tag{2}$$

where $|x_0(k) - x_i(k)|$ denotes the absolute error between observed data and simulation data at time point k, $\min\limits_{i \in [1,m]} \min\limits_{k \in [1,n]} |x_0(k) - x_i(k)|$ denotes the minimum value of absolute error, $\max\limits_{i \in [1,m]} \max\limits_{k \in [1,n]} |x_1(k) - x_2(k)|$ denotes the maximum value of absolute error, and $\rho \in (0, 1)$ denotes the resolution coefficient which is often set as 0.5.

2.2 The Features of Time Domain Similarity Analysis

In general, time domain similarity analysis has to satisfy the following features:

Normalization. The normalization feature can be described as: $\Psi(X, Y) \in [0, 1]$, $\Psi(X, Y) = 1 \Leftrightarrow X = Y$, where Ψ denotes the analysis method of time domain, X denotes the observed data set, and Y denotes the simulation data set.

Symmetry. The symmetry feature can be described as: $\Psi(X, Y) = \Psi(Y, X)$.

Monotonicity. The monotonicity feature can be described as: $\forall a > b \geq 1$, $\Psi(X, bX) > \Psi(X, aX)$; $\Psi(X, bX) = \Psi(X, aX) \Leftrightarrow \Psi(X, X) = 1$ or $\Psi(X, X) = 0$.

2.3 The Features of Traditional GRA

Normalization. Let $X_0 = X_i$ and substitute into Formula (2), it can be deduced as:

$$\gamma(x_0(k), x_i(k)) = \frac{0 + \rho \max\limits_{i \in [1,m]} \max\limits_{k \in [1,n]} |x_0(k) - x_i(k)|}{0 + \rho \max\limits_{i \in [1,m]} \max\limits_{k \in [1,n]} |x_0(k) - x_i(k)|} = 1 \tag{3}$$

So $\gamma(X_0, X_i) = 1$. Because $\min\limits_{i \in [1,m]} \min\limits_{k \in [1,n]} |x_0(k) - x_i(k)| \leq |x_0(k) - x_i(k)|$, $0 \leq \gamma(x_0(k), x_i(k)) \leq 1$, then $0 \leq \gamma(X_0, X_i) \leq 1$, GRA satisfies normalization.

Symmetry. Switch $x_0(k)$ and $x_i(k)$ in Formula (1) and (2). Because of the absolute symbols in Formula (2), the result is unchanged. GRA satisfies symmetry.

Monotonicity. Let $X_0 = X, X_1 = aX, a \geq 1$. Substitute them into Formula (2) with $i = 1$.

$$\gamma(x_0(k), ax_0(k)) = \frac{\min_{k \in [1,n]} |x_0(k) - ax_0(k)| + \rho \max_{k \in [1,n]} |x_0(k) - ax_0(k)|}{|x_0(k) - ax_0(k)| + \rho \max_{k \in [1,n]} |x_0(k) - ax_0(k)|}$$

$$\Rightarrow \gamma(x_0(k), ax_0(k)) = \frac{(a-1) \min_{k \in [1,n]} |x_0(k)| + (a-1)\rho \max_{k \in [1,n]} |x_0(k)|}{(a-1)|x_0(k)| + (a-1)\rho \max_{k \in [1,n]} |x_0(k)|} \tag{4}$$

$X_0 = X, X_1 = bX, b \geq 1$ has the similar result of Formula (4). Then obviously $\forall a > b \geq 1$, $\Psi(X, bX) = \Psi(X, aX)$. GRA cannot satisfy monotonicity at $i = 1$. It is easy to prove when $i > 1$, GRA satisfies monotonicity.

2.4   The Dead Zone of Traditional GRA

In Formula (2), because the error $|x_0(k) - x_i(k)|$ only appears as denominator, the grey relational degree at the maximum error point is still not prominent enough when $\rho = 0.5$. See the formula:

$$\gamma(x_0(k^*), x_i(k^*)) \geq \frac{0 + 0.5 \max_k |x_0(k) - x_i(k)|}{1.5 \max_k |x_0(k) - x_i(k)|} = \frac{1}{3} \tag{5}$$

So at the maximum error point the grey relational degree is $1/3$, which creates a "dead zone" of $[0, 1/3)$ for the result when $\rho = 0.5$. Decrease the value of ρ can alleviate the problem but may reduce the influence of maximum error at other points.

3   Improved Grey Relational Analysis

3.1   The Principle of the Method

Here propose an improved GRA method to satisfy the monotonicity feature and eliminate dead zone effect. The formula is:

$$\gamma_\alpha(X_0, X_i) = \gamma_M(X_0, X_i) - [\alpha R_{mean}(X_0, X_i) + (1 - \alpha)R_{int}(X_0, X_i)] \tag{6}$$

where R_{mean} denotes the mean relative error, R_{int} denotes the relative error in the focused area/points. $\alpha \in [0, 1]$ denotes the balance factor. Expand the formula as:

$$\gamma_M(\boldsymbol{X}_0, \boldsymbol{X}_i) = \frac{1}{n} \sum_{k=1}^{n} \frac{\rho \sup_{\forall X_i \in X} \max_{k \in [1,n]} |x_0(k) - x_i(k)|}{|x_0(k) - x_i(k)| + \rho \sup_{\forall X_i \in X} \max_{k \in [1,n]} |x_0(k) - x_i(k)|} \tag{7}$$

$$R_{mean}(\boldsymbol{X}_0, \boldsymbol{X}_i) = \frac{1}{n} \sum_{k=1}^{n} \frac{2|x_0(k) - x_i(k)|}{|x_0(k)| + |x_i(k)| + \varepsilon} \tag{8}$$

$$R_{int}(\boldsymbol{X}_0, \boldsymbol{X}_i) = \frac{1}{card(\boldsymbol{K}_{int})} \sum_{k \in K_{int}} \frac{2|x_0(k) - x_i(k)|}{|x_0(k)| + |x_i(k)| + \varepsilon} \tag{9}$$

where $\sup_{\forall X_i \in X} \max_{k \in [1,n]} |x_0(k) - x_i(k)|$ denotes the estimated value from analyzer's domain knowledge, which can be substituted as $U \max_{k \in [1,n]} |x_0(k) - x_1(k)|, U > 10$. If the maximum error from other simulation data sets does not exceed it, continue to use the value. K_{int} denotes the focused area of points. ε denotes a small constant.

3.2   The Features of Improved GRA

Normalization. Obviously, $\forall k, x_i(k) = x_0(k) \Rightarrow \gamma_M(x_0(k), x_i(k)) = 1 \Rightarrow \gamma_M(\boldsymbol{X}_0, \boldsymbol{X}_i) = 1$; and $\lim_{x_0(k) - x_i(k) \to \infty} \gamma_M(x_0(k), x_i(k)) = 0 \Rightarrow \lim_{\forall k, x_0(k) - x_i(k) \to \infty} \gamma_M(\boldsymbol{X}_0, \boldsymbol{X}_i) = 0$. So $\gamma_M(\boldsymbol{X}_0, \boldsymbol{X}_i) \in [0,1]$ and $\gamma_M(\boldsymbol{X}_0, \boldsymbol{X}_i) = 1 \Leftrightarrow \boldsymbol{X}_i = \boldsymbol{X}_0$. By setting coefficient ε, we can make $R_{mean} + R_{int} \leq \gamma_\alpha(\boldsymbol{X}_0, \boldsymbol{X}_i)$, and $R_{mean}, R_{int} \geq 0$. So $\gamma_\alpha(\boldsymbol{X}_0, \boldsymbol{X}_i) \in [0,1]$ and $\gamma_\alpha(\boldsymbol{X}_0, \boldsymbol{X}_i) = 1 \Leftrightarrow \boldsymbol{X}_i = \boldsymbol{X}_0$. Improved GRA satisfies normalization.

Symmetry. Because of the absolute symbols in Formula (7)–(9), $\gamma_\alpha(\boldsymbol{X}_0, \boldsymbol{X}_i) = \gamma_\alpha(\boldsymbol{X}_i, \boldsymbol{X}_0)$. Improved GRA satisfies symmetry.

Monotonicity. We can select U (Sect. 3.1) big enough to make the estimated maximum error a constant S. So to prove monotonicity we only need to prove:

$$\frac{\rho S}{|x_0(k) - bx_0(k)| + \rho S} > \frac{\rho S}{|x_0(k) - ax_0(k)| + \rho S} \tag{10}$$

$$\frac{|x_0(k) - bx_0(k)|}{|x_0(k)| + |bx_0(k)| + \varepsilon} < \frac{|x_0(k) - ax_0(k)|}{|x_0(k)| + |ax_0(k)| + \varepsilon} \tag{11}$$

Because $(b-1)|x_0(k)| < (a-1)|x_0(k)|$, Formula (10) is true. Use reduction to absurdity to prove Formula (11). Suppose the opposite inequality is true, which is:

$$\frac{b-1}{b+1+\varepsilon/|x_0(k)|} \geq \frac{a-1}{a+1+\varepsilon/|x_0(k)|} \tag{12}$$

Let $\eta = \varepsilon/|x_0(k)| \geq 0$, then $(b-1)(a+1+\eta) \geq (a-1)(b+1+\eta)$, which can be further derived as $(a-b)(2+\eta) \leq 0$. Because $a > b$ and $\eta \geq 0$, this is false. So Formula (11) is true, and improved GRA satisfies monotonicity.

4   Case Study

4.1   Numerical Case Analysis

Use test functions in Table 1 to explain the effectiveness of improved GRA. The functions are selected to emphasize monotonicity and "dead zone" problem. For each function, select 100 random points to analyze.

Table 1. The functions used to generate observed data and simulation data.

No.	Data	Group A function	Group B function
1	Observed data X_0	$x_0(t) = 2t + 1, t \in [6, 12]$	$x_0(t) = -t^2 + 50t + 100, t \in [0, 50]$
2	Simulation data X_1	$x_1(t) = 2t + 1 + U(0, 0.2)$	$x_1(t) = -t^2 + 50t + 100 + U(0, 5)$
3	Simulation data X_2	$x_2(t) = 1.05x_0(t)$	$x_2(t) = 1.05x_0(t)$
4	Simulation data X_3	$x_3(t) = 1.25x_0(t)$	$x_3(t) = 1.25x_0(t)$
5	Simulation data X_4	$x_4(t) = 2x_0(t)$	$x_4(t) = 2x_0(t)$

In Experiment 0, use all 4 sets of simulation data to compare with observed data, we can get 4 grey relation degrees. In Experiment 1, only use simulation data X_1 to compare with the observed data. and X_2 for Experiment 2, X_3 for Experiment 3, X_4 for Experiment 4. Perform the analysis above for Group A and Group B data. Here select $\rho = 0.5$ in Formula (2). The results of traditional GRA are shown in Table 2. The value before "/" symbol is for Group A, and after "/" symbol is for Group B.

Table 2. The results of traditional GRA for Group A data.

Experiment	$\gamma(X_0, X_1)$	$\gamma(X_0, X_2)$	$\gamma(X_0, X_3)$	$\gamma(X_0, X_4)$
Exp. 0	0.9923/0.9930	0.9295/0.9342	0.7265/0.8773	0.4018/0.4369
Exp. 1	0.5590/0.5559	–	–	–
Exp. 2	–	0.8197/0.5575	–	–
Exp. 3	–	–	0.8197/0.5575	–
Exp. 4	–	–	–	0.8197/0.5575

In Table 2, the results of $\gamma(X_0, X_2)$, $\gamma(X_0, X_3)$ and $\gamma(X_0, X_4)$ are the same in Experiment 2–4, which reveals the non-monotonicity problem of traditional GRA. The minimum grey relational degree is around 0.4, which reveals a "dead zone" of $[0, 1/3)$.

Use improved GRA to perform experiments with the same data generated by the functions in Table 1. Here select K_{int} as the 5% points with the most difference, which is $t \in [11.72, 12]$ in Group A, and $t \in [23.50, 26.00]$ in Group B. Select $\alpha = 0.2$ for both two groups. The results are shown in Table 3.

Table 3. The results of improved GRA for Group A and Group B data.

Group	$\gamma_\alpha(X_0, X_1)$	$\gamma_\alpha(X_0, X_2)$	$\gamma_\alpha(X_0, X_3)$	$\gamma_\alpha(X_0, X_4)$
A	0.9922	0.9390	0.7300	0.2385
B	0.9840	0.9427	0.7456	0.2764

Table 3 shows that when data is different significantly, the grey relational degree is lower than traditional GRA, which means improved GRA can obtain better discrimination between observed data and simulation data. Meanwhile, with maintaining the influence of maximum error, improved GRA has no "dead zone" effect, which can covers the interval of credibility $[0, 1]$ better.

4.2 Simulation Model Analysis

Take a flying vehicle model as an example (Ma [15] and Hundertmark [16]) to perform simulation model analysis. Two outputs are taken into account, the vehicle's height H and velocity V. Figure 1 shows the curves of the data, where V_0 and H_0 are observed data, V_i and H_i are simulation data, $i = 1, 2, 3$.

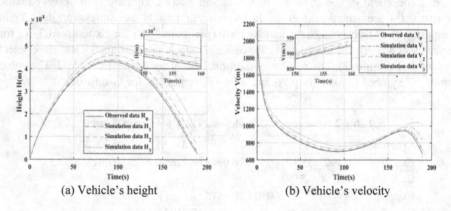

(a) Vehicle's height   (b) Vehicle's velocity

Fig. 1. Curves of the observed data and simulation data for vehicle's height and velocity

Use TIC and improved GRA method to analyze the similarity. Use $1 - \rho$ to convert the result of TIC. Select K_{int} as the 5% points with the most difference for improved GRA, which is $t \in [162.5, 171.5]$ for the vehicle's height, and $t \in [180.5, 189.5]$ for the vehicle's velocity. Select $\alpha = 0.5$ for both two outputs. The results are shown in Table 4. The value before "/" symbol is for the vehicle's height, and after "/" symbol is for the vehicle's velocity.

Table 4. The results of TIC and improved GRA method.

Method	$(H_0/V_0, H_1/V_1)$	$(H_0/V_0, H_2/V_2)$	$(H_0/V_0, H_3/V_3)$
TIC	0.9874/0.9922	0.9532/0.9726	0.8988/0.9474
Improved GRA	0.9124/0.9616	0.7504/0.8680	0.6027/0.7502

Table 4 shows that H_0 and H_1, V_0 and V_1 have the highest similarity, which means the simulation model with H_1 and V_1 output has the highest credibility. The sequence of TIC and improved GRA results is the same, which indicates improved GRA result is coincident to TIC. Meanwhile, when observed data and simulation data differ more, improved GRA results drop lower than TIC, which means improved GRA can discriminate data set difference better.

5 Conclusion

GRA is a typical time domain analysis method widely used in model validation. It satisfies the normalization, symmetry, and monotonicity features when multiple simulation data sets are available. However, if there is only one simulation data set, GRA fails to satisfy monotonicity. Meanwhile, GRA uses the whole time span of observed data and simulation data to measure the similarity, but without a preferred area.

Improved GRA is able to satisfy all features of time domain analysis, no matter there has one simulation data set or multiple of them, and it can focus on a preferred area to emphasize interested part of the data to avoid "dead zone" effect. Case study shows that, improved GRA has better ability to discriminate the difference between observed data and simulation data. However, there are no strict criteria or formal methods to determine the balance factor α in Formula (6) and the small constant ε in Formula (8) and (9), which makes the method ad-hoc by some mean. Future study may focus on this issue and regulate the result more convincing and reasonable.

References

1. Mullins, J., Ling, Y., Mahadevan, S., et al.: Separation of aleatory and epistemic uncertainty in probabilistic model validation. Reliab. Eng. Syst. Saf. **147**, 49–59 (2016)
2. Ling, Y., Mahadevan, S.: Quantitative model validation techniques: new insights. Reliab. Eng. Syst. Saf. **111**, 217–231 (2013)
3. Jiang, X., Mahadevan, S.: Wavelet spectrum analysis approach to model validation of dynamic systems. Mech. Syst. Signal Process. **25**(2), 575–590 (2011)
4. Liu, W., Hong, L., Qi, Z.: Model validation method of radar signal model based on spectrum estimation. Microcomput. Inf. **28**(5), 161–163 (2012)
5. Min, F., Yang, M., Wang, Z.: Knowledge-based method for the validation of complex simulation models. Simul. Model. Pract. Theory **18**(5), 500–515 (2010)
6. Ahn, J., Weck, O., Steele, M.: Credibility assessment of models and simulations based on NASA's models and simulation standard using the Delphi method. Syst. Eng. **17**(2), 237–248 (2014)
7. Crochemore, L., Perrin, C., Andreassian, V., et al.: Comparing expert judgement and numerical criteria for hydrograph evaluation. Hydrol. Sci. J. **60**(3), 402–423 (2015)
8. Hauduc, H., Neumann, M.B., Muschalla, D., et al.: Efficiency criteria for environmental model quality assessment: a review and its application to wastewater treatment. Environ. Model. Softw. **68**, 196–204 (2015)
9. Consonni, V., Ballabio, D., Todeschini, R.: Evaluation of model predictive ability by external validation techniques. J. Chemom. **24**, 194–201 (2010)

10. Kheir, N.A., Holmes, W.M.: On validating simulation models of missile systems. Simulation **30**(4), 117–128 (1978)
11. Dorobantu, A., Balas, G.J., Georgiou, T.T.: Validating aircraft models in the gap metric. J. Aircr. **51**(6), 1665–1672 (2014)
12. Zhou, Y., Fang, K., Ma, P., Yang, M.: Complex simulation model validation method based on ensemble learning. Syst. Eng. Electron. **40**(9), 2124–2130 (2018)
13. Wei, H., Li, Z.: Grey relational analysis and its application to the validation of computet simulation models for missile systems. Syst. Eng. Electron. **2**, 55–61 (1997)
14. Ning, X.L., Wu, Y.X., Yu, T.P., et al.: Research on comprehensive validation of simulation models based on improved grey relational analysis. Acta Armamentarii **37**(3), 338–347 (2016)
15. Ma, P., Zhou, Y., Shang, X., Yang, M.: Firing accuracy evaluation of electromagnetic railgun based on multicriteria optimal Latin Hypercube design. IEEE Trans. Plasma Sci. **45**(7), 1503–1511 (2017)
16. Hundertmark, S., Lancelle, D.: A scenario for a future European shipboard railgun. IEEE Trans. Plasma Sci. **43**(5), 1194–1197 (2015)

Resources Optimisation in New Hospital Central Kitchen Design – A Discrete Event Simulation Approach

Kian Ann Chan[1(✉)], Mack Jia Jia Pan[2], Beng Tee Chua[2],
Xiu Ming Hu[2], and Malcolm Yoke Hean Low[1]

[1] Singapore Institute of Technology, Singapore, Singapore
1602506@SIT.singaporetech.edu.sg
[2] Woodlands Health Campus, Singapore, Singapore

Abstract. This paper describes a simulation study to design the workflow and improve the process efficiency of a hospital central kitchen. The scope of the study includes reducing unnecessary activities and operators' movement, minimize traffic crossing in kitchen, increase employee productivity, and halal & non-halal food segmentation. Simulation models developed in the commercial simulation software Flexism are used in this study to verify the current design by logistics consultants and end-users to ensure that the central kitchen workflow meets the design guidelines and service levels recommended by the Ministry of Health Singapore. Experimental results from the simulation models are analyzed and recommendations are made to the hospital management for resource optimization planning.

Keywords: Simulation modelling · Hospital central kitchen · Process efficiency improvement · Resources optimization

1 Introduction

Woodlands Health Campus (WHC) [1] is a new public health campus which will be developed in the northern region of Singapore and is slated for completion by 2022. The campus will span 1800 beds in size and offer integrated health services including an acute and community hospital, specialist clinics as well as a nursing home where patients can be seamlessly cared for from acute to step-down care. Process improvement, resources optimization, technology innovation & care re-design are key strategies deeply embedded in WHC's DNA to direct its target towards achieving the corporate mission and vision. WHC's Analytics department focuses on generating insights from data and analysis to facilitate and inform decision making for the teams devising the campus functional planning units. The hospital central kitchen is one of the key facilities identified for process improvement in WHC's hospital planning.

The central kitchen handles patients' food preparation and dishwashing which cover three meals a day – breakfast, lunch and dinner. These processes are performed concurrently so that meals can be delivered promptly before each meal's scheduled slot at the ward levels. Food preparation is required for food variation based on food texture

© Springer Nature Singapore Pte Ltd. 2019
G. Tan et al. (Eds.): AsiaSim 2019, CCIS 1094, pp. 251–259, 2019.
https://doi.org/10.1007/978-981-15-1078-6_22

as well as patient ethnicity and religion requirements. Hence, the food preparation area is further segmented into the non-Halal zone and Halal zone in order to comply with Halal certification requirements [2]. With these requirements in mind, it is essential for hospital planners to allocate adequate resources such as kitchen operators and food preparation machines in an accurate and timely manner so that utilization can be optimized leading to an improvement in the overall central kitchen processes.

Simulation is an effective tool to study and improve complex process flows such as the central kitchen in a hospital [3, 4]. By incorporating simulation model analysis into the planning stage, it allows hospital planners to map and visualized process flows, generate scenarios, and lastly, recommendations can be derived from the study results. For this study, the simulation model is developed in Flexism Enterprise 2017.

Flexsim offers 3D visuals, easy-to-use drop-down list, and customization for modelling, simulating and predicting. On top of that, it also provides 3D Charts & graphs and identifying potentials of their systems and optimize through experimentation straight in the model itself.

2   Central Kitchen Workflow

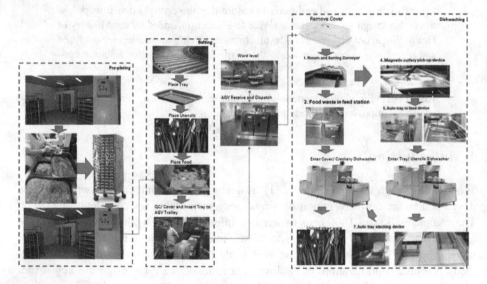

Fig. 1. Kitchen process workflow

Figure 1 shows an overview of the central kitchen process workflow. The food preparation process consists of pre-plating and belting. In the pre-plating step, Gastronorm (GN) trolleys are pushed from the bulk pre-plating area to the pre-plating area. The kitchen operators will then prepare food portioning through scooping food onto the plate. With each filled plate, the operator will insert them into the GN trolleys. Once a GN trolley capacity is full, an operator will push the GN trolley to the pre-plated area for holding. This process is repeated for four food portions.

In the belting area, seven components are placed along the conveyor. They are the food tray, utensils, four portioned-food, and food cover. Operators will perform a visual quality check before putting on the food covers. At the end of the conveyor line, the prepared food trays are inserted into Automated Guided Vehicle (AGV) trolleys. Kitchen operators are required to transfer the portioned food from the pre-plating to the belting area whenever the food supply from the GN trolley runs low.

Once an AGV trolley capacity is full, an operator will push it to the AGV dispatch and return area. Thereafter, the AGV trolley will be transported to the ward level for meal distribution via an AGV. Upon meal completion, the AGV trolleys will be returned to the AGV dispatch and return area and be directed to the dishwashing area.

In the dishwashing area, kitchen operators first remove the food cover from the tray before placing the tray on the conveyor. The conveyor is split into two lines where the first line is meant for crockery and cover, and the second line is meant for utensils and tray. In the first line, kitchen operators will remove the crockery and clear the food waste before placing the crockery on conveyor to go through the dishwasher. In the second line, utensils will be separated from the tray via a magnetic cutlery device before the trays go through the auto tray in-feed device and enter the dishwasher. In both lines, clean wares will be collected at the dishwasher output area.

3 Shift Overview

The central kitchen processes are in progress concurrently and hence there are large human and equipment movements from area to area. Areas that handle fewer processes would require a shorter completion duration and operators may have more idle time. On the other hand, areas that manage complex processes would require more time for task completion. The Halal and non-Halal segmentation would also require a dedicated manpower allocation among operators in these areas.

Figure 2 shows an overview of the central kitchen shift. For breakfast: Pre-plating and tray assembly tasks are completed the day before. The distribution task is carried out the next morning and thereafter followed by dishwashing. For lunch: Pre-plating task is carried out the day before. The tray assembly and distribution task is carried out in the morning on the day itself. Thereafter, the lunch dishwashing task is carried out in the afternoon. For dinner: Pre-plating, tray assembly, and dishwashing task are carried out on the day itself.

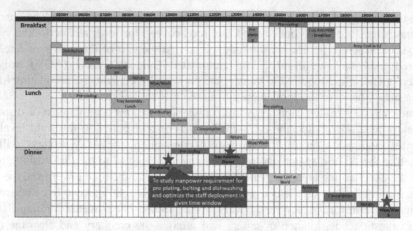

Fig. 2. Overview of Central Kitchen shift

4 Area of Study Assumptions

This section describes the parameters and assumptions used in this study. The test coverage includes 1400 beds from acute and community bed. The number of components and trays is based on a scenario of baseline 50:50 ratio between Halal and non-Halal meals. Thus there will be 700 Halal trays and 700 non-Halal trays.

4.1 Modelling Assumptions

Table 1 shows the modelling assumptions used in the pre-plating area. The number of food components per plate varies from 2 for breakfast to 4 for lunch and dinner. Table 2 shows the modelling assumptions used in the belting and dishwashing area. Different operators are allocated to different tasks in this area.

Table 1. Kitchen pre-plating assumptions

Meal Type	Factors	Value
All	Number of manpower	6
	Manpower allocation	All staff manned at their own plating table. Any available staff is able to push the GN Trolley from bulk holding to pre-plating and pre-plating to pre-plated area
	Number of plating table	6
	Food plating process time per person	Triangular (5,6,5)
	GN trolley capacity	100
Breakfast	Number of food components	2
Lunch		4
Dinner		4

Table 2. Kitchen belting and dishwashing assumptions

Meal type	Area	Factors	Value
All	Belting	Number of manpower	6
		Number of GN trolley	4
		Manpower task allocation	Operator #1: Tray and cutlery Operator #2 to 5: Food placing Operator #6: Cover, QC and insert to AGV Trolley
		Process time	Per tray: Triangular (2,3,2) Per cutlery: Triangular (2,3,2) Per hot food component: Triangular (5,6,5) Per cover and QC: Triangular (5,6,5)
	Dishwashing	Number of manpower	6
		Manpower task allocation	Operator #1: Pick-up Tray, uncovered Tray Operator #2 to 3: Pick, load Ware, and clear food waste Operator #4 to 5: Unload clean ware and cover Operator #6: Organize clean ware
		Process time	Dishwasher: Triangular (170,180,180) Others: Triangular (2,3,2)

To obtain data for the different processing times used in the simulation, we visited other hospital's kitchen to perform time motion study. For instance, to obtain the processing time required for food plating time, we gathered multiple timings to complete one plate to obtain the minimum, maximum and average processing times. The timing obtained is then modelled in the simulation using the triangular distribution, defined as Triangular (min, max, mode).

5 Model Building

As there are four parts of the kitchen to be modelled, the simulation model is divided into four phases as per described in Table 3. During each phase, objects are placed within the model, linked up and configured with the respective process time according to the assumptions. Lastly, network nodes are added to the reachable area within the model to ensure that operators move correctly. Throughout the model building and results evaluation phases, regular meet ups with stakeholders were carried out so that their involvement in a simulation study from the very start will have a greater chance of success [5].

Table 3. Kitchen zone in Flexsim modelling

Pre-plating zone:	Belting zone:
AGV dispatch & receive zone:	Dishwashing zone:

6 Evaluations

We carried out a set of experiments to determine the manpower required to achieve acceptable timings for pre-plating (120 min), belting (90 min) and dishwashing (60 min) respectively in a day setting with no warm-up. The experiments are repeated for non-Halal to Halal ratio of 60:40 and 70:30 for each area. From the model, the start time is obtained from the start of the process and end time is obtained upon completing the entire process. Thereafter, the time difference is computed and compared with the acceptable timing to determine a pass or fail experiment. As the demand for Non-Halal and Halal fluctuates from day to day, the hospital decided to adopt 60:40 and 70:30 ratio requirement as shown in Tables 4, 5 and 6.

From Table 4, in order to meet the 120 min requirement for pre-plating when the ratio is 60:40, we need at least four operators in the non-Halal zone and three operators in the Halal zone. Therefore, to meet the 60:40 requirement for pre-plating, we need a total of seven operators. In order to meet the 70:30 ratio for pre-plating, we need four operators at the non-Halal zone and two operators in the Halal zone. This means a total of six operators is needed to complete pre-plating within 120 min if the ratio is 70:30.

From Table 5, with a 60:40 ratio for belting, we will need a total of twelve operators to complete belting within 90 min. A 70:30 ratio for belting, we will need a total of twelve operators to complete belting in 90 min. From Table 6, with a 60:40 ratio for dishwashing, we will need a total of eleven operators to complete dishwashing in 60 min. Finally, a 70:30 ratio, we need a total of twelve operators for dishwashing to be completed in 60 min.

Table 4. Non-Halal and Halal pre-plating workload based on 60:40 and 70:30 requirement

Non-Halal	Pre-plating (mins)	Manpower	Halal	Pre-plating (mins)	Manpower
3360	73	6	2240	48	6
(840 Tray * 4	87	5	(560 Tray * 4	58	5
Component) – 60%	**100**	**4**	Component) – 40%	72	4
	130	3		**94**	**3**
	197	2		122	2
3920	86	6	1680	39	6
(980 Tray * 4	99	5	(420 Tray * 4	41	5
Component) – 70%	**118**	**4**	Component) – 30%	59	4
	151	3		77	3
	257	2		**120**	**2**

Table 5. Non-Halal and Halal belting workload based on 60:40 and 70:30 requirement

Non-Halal	Belting (mins)	Manpower	Halal	Belting (mins)	Manpower
840 Tray – 60%	78	8	560 Tray – 40%	**57**	**6**
	80	7		102	5
	82	**6**		108	4
	153	5		215	3
980 Tray – 70%	88	8	420 Tray – 30%	38	6
	90	**7**		**90**	**5**
	93	6		92	4
	172	5		179	3

Table 6. Non-Halal and Halal dishwashing workload based on 60:40 and 70:30 requirement

Non-Halal	Dishwashing (mins)	Manpower	Halal	Dishwashing (mins)	Manpower
840 Tray – 60%	**59**	**6**	560 Tray – 40%	40	6
	50	7		**41**	**5**
	49	8		80	4
980 Tray – 70%	66	6	420 Tray – 30%	35	6
	57	**7**		**39**	**5**
	56	8		72	4

With the operators' count derived from the experiments, WHC planners are able to pre-plan the workflow before the actual production starts. For instance, as shown in Table 4, seven operators will be required for pre-plating to complete within 120 mins. If there is a shortage of manpower due to some unforeseen circumstances (e.g. staff taking medical leave), the shortage in manpower in the pre-plating area will cause a delay in the belting phase. Due to the delay, patients will not be able to receive their dinner on time. On the other hand, WHC also does not want to allocate more operators than the required to be on duty as this will incur more staff salary expenses. Therefore, it is essential to allocate the right number of operators to be at each station at any time.

The numbers above also help WHC to better allocate operators based on the needs for a specific day. For example, WHC can also do a check on the percentage of patients that need Halal food and plan the manpower accordingly. Thus, the simulation model that has been developed will allow WHC planners to pre-plan the schedule and improve the overall hospital workflow.

7   Conclusion and Future Work

This paper studied the WHC current workflow within the central kitchen setting. Through our study, we can conclude that for WHC to reach to the maximum efficiency, they will require between five to twelve manpower at their respective kitchen areas depending on the non-Halal to Halal ratio. Each of the central kitchen areas is equally important and they are interlinked. If the operations in any of the areas are delayed, it will affect both the upstream and downstream areas. In summary, the simulation model developed will be very useful to study the manpower requirements to minimize any negative impact on hospital operations.

When WHC turns operational, the planning parameters may be updated accordingly to operational needs. This model could be used to facilitate short term and midterm decision making in central kitchen resources planning and daily operations. This model could also be extended to cover raw food material inflow and AGV prepared food transportation flow to form the whole food supply chain study.

Acknowledgement. This project is a collaboration between the Woodlands Health Campus and the Singapore Institute of Technology. The team would wish to express deep appreciation to the Analytics department, Campus planning department of WHC for their valuable support and assistance in this project.

References

1. Khalik, S.: Woodlands health campus will add 1,800 beds and use technology for better patient care, The Straits Time. https://www.straitstimes.com/singapore/health/woodlands-health-campus-will-add-1800-beds-and-use-technology-for-better-patient. Last accessed 18 Apr 2017
2. MUIS: Halal Certification Conditions: Food Preparation Area Scheme. Majlis Ugama Islam Singapura (MUIS) (2016). https://www.muis.gov.sg/-/media/Files/Halal/Documents/Revised-HCC-FPA-Scheme-Final.pdf
3. Swisher, J.R.: Evaluation of the design of a family practice healthcare clinic using discrete-event simulation (1999). https://vtechworks.lib.vt.edu/bitstream/handle/10919/42176/jrsetd.pdf

4. Fujii, N., Kaihara, T., Uemura, M., Nonaka, T., Shimmura, T.: Facility layout planning of central kitchen in food service industry: application to the real-scale problem. In: IFIP International Conference on Advances in Production Management Systems, APMS 2013, pp. 33–40 (2013)
5. Jahangirian, M., Taylor, S., Young, T., et al.: J. Oper. Res. Soc. **68**, 747 (2017). https://doi.org/10.1057/jors.2016.1

Prototype Development of the Real-Time Quadrotor UAV Simulation in Litmus-RT

Muhammad Faris Fathoni, Yong-Il Jo, and Kyong Hoon Kim[✉]

Gyeongsang National University, Jinju, Republic of Korea
mfarisfathoni@gmail.com, {crues,khkim}@gnu.ac.kr

Abstract. Simulation is a system to imitate the operation of various kinds of real–world facilities or processes for behavior study, training or entertainment purposes. As example, a quadrotor UAV simulator can be used as tool for research on real-time system performance, quadrotor system behavior study and control design (inner loop, outer loop). On the other hand, the benefit of Litmus-RT as a UNIX-like kernel should be used for real-time system. This paper discusses the prototype development of the real-time quadrotor simulation in Litmus-RT. The non-linear quadrotor models are developed, consisting of the stability controllability augmentation system (SCAS) and equation of motion (EOM). Program modules (software) of simulation are implemented in Litmus-RT with earliest deadline first (EDF) scheduling, and run on Ubuntu 16.04 operating system with iteration rate 50 Hz.

Keywords: Real-time simulation · Non-linear simulation · Quadrotor UAV model · Litmus-RT

1 Introduction

Simulation is a process of building mathematical or logical models to represent/imitate existing real–world or hypothetical future systems. By using these models, computer–based experiments may needed to explain or predict the behavior of system, improve the system performance, or design new systems with desirable performances. For example, a quadrotor UAV system simulator can be used as a tool for research on real-time system performance, study of quadrotor system behavior and control design (inner loop: stability controllability augmentation system (SCAS), outer loop: autonomous mission formation flight). Figure 1 shows the quadrotor unmanned aerial vehicle (QR UAV) system configuration. The QR UAV system is consists of motor control SCAS and quadrotor equation of motion (EOM).

On the other hand, a Litmus-RT (Linux Testbed for Multiprocessor Scheduling in Real-Time Systems) is an extension of Linux, which is a widely used open-source UNIX-like kernel for real-time system. There are three benefits of using Litmus-RT: (1) it extends Linux's scheduling infrastructure with an implementation of the sporadic task model, (2) it provides a plugin interface that allows the active scheduling policy to be changed during runtime, and (3) it provides additional system calls for real-time tasks [2].

© Springer Nature Singapore Pte Ltd. 2019
G. Tan et al. (Eds.): AsiaSim 2019, CCIS 1094, pp. 260–266, 2019.
https://doi.org/10.1007/978-981-15-1078-6_23

At the present quadrotor simulation environment, such as Gazebo with ROS (Robot Operating System) and MATLAB Simulink, it provides a platform that only focused on control design (inner-loop and outer-loop). These quadrotor simulation environment does not focused on real-time scheduling performance and virtualization [1]. The Litmus-RT can be used for research on the real-time simulation of heterogeneous large-scale quadrotor UAV with hierarchical hypervisor structure.

This paper discusses the design and implementation of real-time nonlinear dynamic simulation of quadrotor in Litmus-RT.

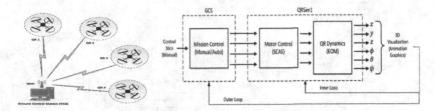

Fig. 1. Quadrotor UAV system configuration.

2 Non-linear Dynamic Model of Quadrotor

A Modeling is activities for developing the model. A Model is representation or formalization in certain language to describe the real world (real system). This section describes the development process of non-linear system dynamic of quadrotor model. Figure 2 shows the variables and parameters of quadrotor model [3].

By using Newton law (translational acceleration = force/mass, rotational acceleration = moment/moment of inertia), the motion equation of quadrotor can be written as a nonlinear first order differential equation as follow.

$$\dot{\mathbf{x}}(t) \dot{=} \frac{d\mathbf{x}(t)}{dt} = f(\mathbf{x}(t), \mathbf{u}(t); t), \ \mathbf{x}(t) = \begin{bmatrix} x & y & z & \phi & \theta & \psi \end{bmatrix}, \ \mathbf{u}(t) = \begin{bmatrix} \delta_l & \delta_r & \delta_p & \delta_y \end{bmatrix}$$

Where: $\mathbf{x}(t)$ is a state variable vector of quadrotor, $\mathbf{u}(t)$ is a control input vector, and t is a continuous time varable (sec); x, y, z are forward, side and vertical positions (m) of quadrotor respectively; u, v, w are forward, side and vertical velocities (m/s) of quadrotor respectively; ϕ is roll angle (deg), θ is pitch angle (deg) and ψ is yaw angle (deg); p, q, r are pitch, roll and yaw velocities (deg/sec) of quad-rotor respectively; δ_l (lift_cmd) is lift command deflection (deg), δ_r (roll_cmd) is roll command deflection for lateral control input (deg), δ_p (pitch_cmd) is pitch command deflection for longitudinal control input (deg), and δ_y (yaw_cmd) is yaw command deflection for directional control input (deg). To calculate all of these variables, numerical integration computation is needed [7].

SCAS in Fig. 1 above is a feedback control system designed to increase the relative damping of a particular mode of the quadrotor motions. The damping is achieved by augmenting the coefficients of the EOM by imposing on the appropriate forces or moments of quadrotor as a result of actuating the control surfaces in response to the feedback signals derived from appropriate motion variables [4–6].

Figure 2(a) shows the data flow diagram (DFD) of quadrotor UAV system model. The quadrotor UAV system consists of four quadrotors, with qr1 as leader. The quadrotor qr1 will receive the command input from ground control station (GCS). The quadrotor qr2, qr3 and qr4 receive the command input from qr1. The state variables of all quadrotor will be sent to GCS.

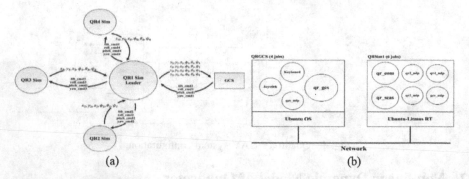

(a)   (b)

Fig. 2. (a) DFD of QR UAV system model and (b) QR simulation structure in Litmus-RT.

3 Structure of Quadrotor Simulation in Litmus-RT

Litmus-RT (Linux Testbed for Multiprocessor Scheduling in Real-Time Systems) is an extension of Linux [2]. Litmus-RT has a number of additional system calls. One of functionality of this system calls is job control for real-time processes (e.g., inquiring the current job sequence number, waiting for job releases, and signaling job completions). A real-time task (thread) set consists of a number of tasks that are subject to real-time constraints. Tasks (threads) are invoked, or released, repeatedly during their lifetimes; each such invocation is known as a job. The real-time scheduling policies are provided for executing real-time task (thread). This scheduling policy is an algorithm used by a scheduler at runtime to determine how to allocate available processor to jobs. Under the global earliest-deadline-first (G-EDF) policy, contending jobs are prioritized in order of nondecreasing deadlines.

The structure of quadrotor simulation in Litmus-RT is shown in Fig. 2(b) above. The qrsim1 consists of six job threads : qr_eom, qr_scas, gcs_udp, qr2_udp, qr3_udp and qr4_udp. The qr_eom job thread computes the quadrotor equation of motion. The qr_scas job thread computes the quadrotor stability controlability augmentation system. The qrgcs is consist of four threads: qr_gcs, gcs_udp, joystick, and keyboard.

4   Implementation of Quadrotor Simulation

The real-time non-linear dynamic simulation of quadrotor is implemented in Litmus-RT with earliest deadline first (EDF) scheduling, written in C language with Open Graphic Library (OpenGL). Simulation softwares are run on Intel based computers with Ubuntu 18.04 operating system platform.

Simulation is a repetition (looping) process with iteration rate in Hz. The quadrotor simulation uses 50 Hz iteration rate, which is 50 times of computation per second. Each iteration will compute force (F), moment (M), numeric integration, displays of the result of simulation to time history plot, and animation graphic.

The implementation of quadrotor dynamic simulation uses two computers connected with peer-to-peer LAN and joystick input. Figure 3 shows the GUI of 3D visualization of the GCS, and the numerical GUI of quadrotor simulation in Litmus-RT.

The simulation computer software configuration item (CSCI) consists of two computer software component (CSC) modules. There are quadrotor equation of motion (EOM) and stability controllability augmentation system (SCAS) module software. The real-time executive software schedules the job thread with iteration rate in Hz. In order to fulfill real-time constraint, iteration rate used in this real-time executives software is 50 Hz. The application software implements quadrotor simulation. The variables of quadrotor are monitored, which are: x position (m), y position (m), z altitude above ground level (m), indicated airspeed (m/s), heading (deg), pitch angle (deg), roll angle (deg), yaw angle (deg), and command deflection (deg).

Fig. 3. GUI of ground control station and GUI of QRSim in Litmus-RT.

Figure 4 shows pseudo code f the implementation of quadrotor simulation in Litmus-RT framework.

```
#include "../include/global.h"          // Invoke job.
#include "litmus.h"                      //     do_exit = job_ecm(); ...
...                                      // } while (!do_exit);
int main(int argc, char** argv)          // 4) Transition to background mode.
{                                        //    return NULL;
// 1) Command line paramter parsing would be done here.   }
// 2) Work environment (e.g., global data structures)
   init_litmus();                        void* rt_thread_scas(void *tcontext) { ... }
// 3) Initialize LITMUS-RT.              void* rt_thread_gcs_udp(void *tcontext) { ... }
                                         void* rt_thread_qr2_udp(void *tcontext) { ... }
// 4) Launch threads.                    void* rt_thread_qr3_udp(void *tcontext) { ... }
pthread_create(task+1,NULL,rt_thread_ecm,(void *)(ctx+1));  void* rt_thread_qr4_udp(void *tcontext) { ... }
pthread_create(task+0,NULL,rt_thread_scas,(void *)(ctx+0));
pthread_create(task+2,NULL,rt_thread_gcs_udp,(void *)(ctx+2));  int job_ecm(void){
pthread_create(task+3,NULL,rt_thread_qr2_udp,(void *)(ctx+3));  {
pthread_create(task+4,NULL,rt_thread_qr3_udp,(void *)(ctx+4));  // Do real-time calculation.
pthread_create(task+5,NULL,rt_thread_qr4_udp,(void *)(ctx+5));  ...   before_ecm = wcgettimeofday(); ...
// 5) Wait for RT threads to terminate.  // update simulation time
   for (i=0; i<NUM_THREADS; i++) pthread_join(task[i],NULL);  ...  qr_nextstate(&qrstate, DT); ...
// 6) Clean up, maybe print results and stats, and exit. ...  after_ecm = wcgettimeofday();
   return 0;                             ctime_ecm = after_ecm - before_ecm;  ...
}                                        // * Don't exit.
void* rt_thread_ecm(void *tcontext)      return 0;
{                                        }
// 1) Initialize real-time settings.     int job_scas(void){ ... }
// 2) Transition to real-time mode.      int job_gcs_udp(void){ ... }
// 3) Invoke real-time jobs.             int job_qr2_udp(void){ ... }
   do {                                  int job_qr3_udp(void){ ... }
// Wait until the next job is released.  int job_qr4_udp(void){ ... }
   sleep_next_period(); ...
```

Fig. 4. Pseudo code of the implementation of quadrotor simulation in Litmus-RT framework

5 Experimental Results

The Experiments have been conducted with quadrotor generic model. Time interval of computation (delta time) is 0.02 s. The value of state variables are measured and recorded for every process. Then the analysis is also conducted on the computing time of this quadrotor dynamics simulations. The experiment simulates quadrotor with mass 1 kg, cg 0.30, trim value 0.0 deg pitch_cmd and 0.0 deg roll_cmd at altitude 2.5 m and velocity 0.0 m/sec. The results with 0.1 deg step input for pitch, roll and yaw input relative to trim position, short period responses are shown in Fig. 5.

Figure 5 shows the step input responses with lift_cmd, roll_cmd, pitch_cmd, and yaw_cmd step input, respectively.

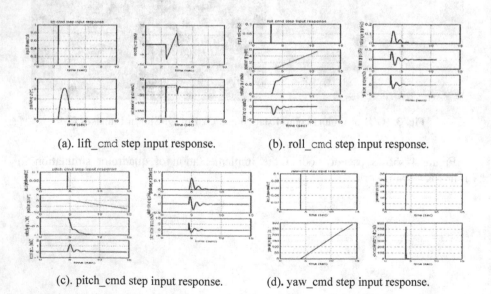

(a). lift_cmd step input response.   (b). roll_cmd step input response.

(c). pitch_cmd step input response.   (d). yaw_cmd step input response.

Fig. 5. Step input response of quadrotor simulation.

The computation time is a simulation time of one cycle simulation process. Time measurement of quadrotor simulation is performed on each step input. The computation time of simulation consists of computation time of EOM (ctime_eom) and computation time of SCAS (ctime_scas). The measurement of the computation time performed on Intel based computers. Figure 6 shows the real-time measurement results of ctime_eom for step deflection input and ctime_scas for step deflection input. The average of computation time ctime_eom is 68.1083 μs and ctime_scas is 0.4903 μs, which is less than 50 Hz real-time requirement constraint (0.02 s = 20000 μs).

Step input	Average ctime_eom (μsec)	Maximum ctime_eom (μsec)	Step input	Average ctime_scas (μsec)	Maximum ctime_scas (μsec)
Lift command	66.956	88	Lift command	0.4504	1
Roll command	68.874	86	Roll command	0.46202	1
Pitch command	69.419	95	Pitch command	0.496	1
Yaw command	67.184	233	Yaw command	0.55298	1

Fig. 6. The real-time measurements of ctime_eom and ctime_scas

6 Conclusions

Based on the experimental results, the quadrotor simulation can be implemented in Litmus-RT. The simulation results shows that the average of computation time ctime_eom is 68.1083 μs and ctime_scas is 0.4903 μs, which is less than 50 Hz real-time requirement constraint (0.02 s = 20000 μs).

Further research, we will study the real-time hypervisor structures for large–scale quad-rotor simulation with implementation on multi-core processor.

Acknowledgements. This work was supported by the Human Resources Development of the Korea Institute of Energy Technology Evaluation and Planning (KETEP) grant funded by the Ministry of Trade, Industry and Energy (No. 20194030202430).

References

1. Akcakoca, M., Atici, B.M., Gever, B.: A simulation-based development and verification architecture for micro uav teams and swarms. In: AIAA Scitech 2019 Forum. AIAA, San Diego (2019)
2. Brandenburg, B.: LITMUS[RT]: a testbed for empirically comparing real-time multiprocessor schedulers. In: Proceedings of the 27th IEEE Real-Time Systems Symposium, pp. 111–123 (2006)
3. Bouabdallah, S.: Design and Control of Quad Rotor with Application to Autonomous Flying, Ph.D. Thesis, Ecole Polytechnique Federal de Lausanne (2007)
4. Das, A., Subbarao, K., Lewis, F.: Dynamic inversion with zero-dynamics stabilization for quad rotor control. IET Control Theory Appl. 3(3), 303–314 (2009)
5. Fax, J.A., Murray, R.M.: Information flow and cooperative control of vehicle formations. IEEE Trans. Autom. Control 49, 1465–1476 (2004)

6. Kushleyev, A., Mellinger, D., Powers, C., Kumar, V.: Towards a swarm of agile micro quad rotors. Auton. Robot **35**, 287–300 (2013)
7. Stevens, B.L., Lewis, F.L.: Aircraft Control and Simulation, 3rd edn. Wiley, New York (2016)

Research on the Secondary Development Method of Finite Element Analysis Module of SIEMENS NX

Lin Wang[✉], Zhiqiang Li, Chenli Deng, and Jialiang Sun

Beihang University, Beijing 100191, China
wanglin1714@buaa.edu.cn

Abstract. In order to improve the efficiency of reliability simulation test, the extraction of finite element simulation results was studied in this paper. Using SIEMENS NX software as the application platform, the finite element simulation module was used to perform thermal analysis, structural static analysis and random response analysis on the reliability simulation model. The result of the calculation of the specified point was taken as the target to extract. In this paper, the requirements analysis and overall design of the application were firstly carried out, and then the functional modules were designed in detail. Finally, under the secondary development framework provided by NX Open, with the help of the secondary development tools, the user interaction interface and the module functions of the application were realized by writing source program files. After the actual test, the application could complete the task of automatically extracting the results of the simulation calculation correctly to meet the design requirements.

Keywords: Secondary development · SIEMENS NX · Reliability simulation · Finite element calculation

1 Introduction

With the widely using of the electronic devices, it is of great significance to study the reliability of them [1]. Among the varied methods, reliability simulation test is getting more attention. An important part of the test is passing the results of calculation of finite element simulation performed by Computer Aided Engineering (CAE) software to the reliability assessment module. The data needs to be transferred is large. If the secondary development can be carried on to the finite element simulation software, this process will be automated, and the work efficiency of reliability assessment can be improved [2].

NX is a new generation digital product development system of SIEMENS PLM Software. The finite element simulation module of SIEMENS NX is based on NAS-TRAN technology. NX provides users with a variety of secondary development tools named NX Open [3, 4]. It supports many programming languages, such as C, C ++, Java, VB.NET, C# and Python. This tool set mainly includes Common API, Journaling, Classic APIs, Knowledge Driven Automation, Other NX Toolkits [5, 6].

© Springer Nature Singapore Pte Ltd. 2019
G. Tan et al. (Eds.): AsiaSim 2019, CCIS 1094, pp. 267–273, 2019.
https://doi.org/10.1007/978-981-15-1078-6_24

2 Basic Principles of Reliability Simulation

The reliability simulation test is mainly based on the physics of failure of solder joints and leads in thermal cycling and vibration environment. It calculate the fatigue life and evaluate the reliability of electronic products.

Material fatigue characteristics can be represented by the S-N fatigue curve, the S-N curve equation is:

$$N_1 S_1^b = N_2 S_2^b \tag{1}$$

In the formula, S is the failure-related stress, N is the number of fatigue cycles corresponding to S, and b is the slope of a fatigue curve drawn on a log-log fatigue curve. In a linear system, the stress is proportional to the displacement Z.

The most famous empirical model for vibration fatigue life prediction of electronic products is the model proposed by Steinberg [7]. For a component mounted on a printed circuit board (PCB), the allowable limit of its dynamic displacement Z is:

$$Z_{limit} = \frac{0.00022B}{Chr\sqrt{L}} \tag{2}$$

Where B is the length of the board, L is the length of the component, h is the thickness of the board, C is the constant of the different types of components, r is the relative position factor of the component, and can be substituted by the relative curvature.

In a given vibration environment, N_{limit} is a constant, the board's maximum response displacement Z_{max} can be calculated by the vibration response acceleration and the natural frequency of the board. Then, the fatigue cycles N_{max} can be got.

A widely used thermal fatigue model is the strain-based Engelmaier model. The specific expression is as follows:

$$N_f = \frac{1}{2} \left(\frac{\Delta\gamma}{2\varepsilon_f} \right)^{\frac{1}{c}} \tag{3}$$

Where N_f is the fatigue life, ε_f is the fatigue ductility coefficient, $\Delta\gamma$ is the total shear strain range, and C is the parameter of temperature stress profile [8, 9].

In conclusion, the data needs to be extracted from the simulation results includes: natural frequency of PCB, vibration response acceleration, x and y positive strain which used for calculating relative curvature, and the temperature at each component.

3 Overall Framework of Software Design

Usually there are thousands of components on a PCB, the simulation model should be simplified. The simulation results of the simplified components can be replaced by the results of the nodes at the same locations on the surface of the board.

The data extracting process is designed as follow [10]. Before the model is meshed, mesh points should be set according to the information provided by the electronic design automation (EDA) file. Then, meshing and material assignment are carried out. After setting simulation environment, calculation can be executed, and the results of the specified nodes can be extracted. The data flow diagram is shown in Fig. 1.

Since the data flow has no obvious transaction center, it can be considered to have general characteristics of the transformed stream, the structure of the application is shown in Fig. 2. The input stream includes project path, mesh point and simulation calculation file. The output stream is the extracted data. The transformation center is the process of data extraction.

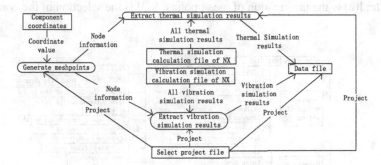

Fig. 1. Data flow diagram of application

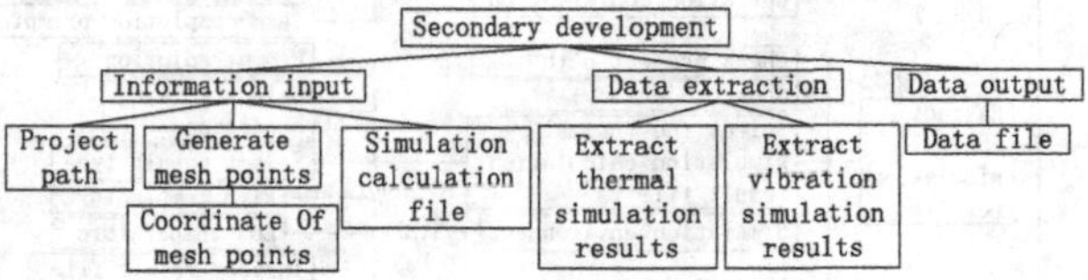

Fig. 2. Application structure diagram

4   Key Functional Implementation

4.1   Detailed Design of the Application

Through accurate description, the system can be designed in detail, so that it can be written in programming language without considering the structure during the coding phase. The following issues are mainly discussed in the detailed design.

(1) Data Transfer. The program calls different dialogs to execute different functions. Since the source files of each dialog are relatively independent, the parameters cannot be passed between files. To ensure the parameters can be delivered reliably and correctly, the application uses the method of passing parameters in configuration file.

(2) Corresponding Problem Between Project and Path. When the user carries out multiple projects in the same period, it is necessary to ensure the data files are stored in the correct path. Since the project folder and the model folder are not consistent, it is better to clearly display the project and the path in the dialog box.

(3) Data Uniqueness. When the user repeats the operation on the same item, the application should ensure the correctness and uniqueness of the data. If the data is already existed, actions like rewriting the data or showing a message box to tell the user what to do should be taken.

(4) User Interaction. User experience is another important aspect of software design. Functions like data extraction have no change on the NX interface, users are not sure if the operation was successful. Therefore, it is better to pop up a message box, indicating the result of the task.

After the above discussion, a detailed design structure of the application can be obtained, part of them is shown in Fig. 3. In the figure, I(1) is the information of coordinate; I(2) is the information of mesh points; S(3) is the selection of the condition.

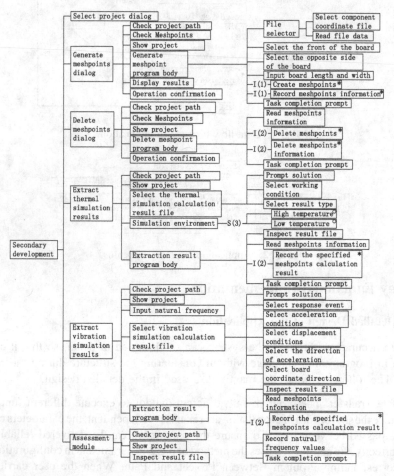

Fig. 3. Part of the detailed structure of application

4.2   Implementation of the Application

Code Design for each Module. The source program of each module is mainly divided into several parts: getting the current working part, creating instances such as parameters and generators, performing the operation, and destroying the instances [11].

The application needs to obtain the current working part first, and then it can perform various operations on the specified part. The current part is a workFemPart class object, and it has many kinds of properties and methods. The mesh points are built mainly based on the CreateMeshpointOnFaceBuilder method.

The result of calculation is stored in a iterator, the Result class provides the interface to query the results. It needs to be created by NXOpen.CAE.ResultManager. This result manager provides a variety of results-related methods. The Create-ResultAccess method can obtain a resulting interface, using the CreateResultParameters and AskNodalResult method, the result of the calculation of the specified node can be extracted.

Interface Design for each Module. Good interface design is very important. Using the method of combining menus and dialogs, the overall structure will be simple and modular, it is also convenient for debugging.

The menu file is written in the MenuScript language, the menu structure is shown in Fig. 4(a). NX Open provides users with the NX-style dialog editing tool Block UI Styler. It has various defined blocks to form the dialog [12].

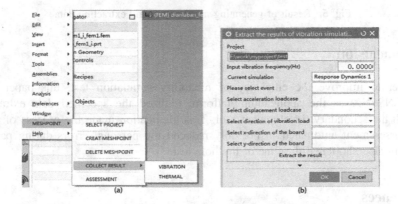

Fig. 4. Menu structure and dialog of extracting vibration simulation results

The main code in source program includes creating a dialog class and an instance of this class. The method of this class includes a variety of system callback functions and user callback functions. The coding is concentrated on several functions. Among them, the initialize_cb is a menu initialization function for setting the initial contents of the menu, update_cb is a response function to the button operation. When the user changes the value of any block, this function will be called. Figure 4(b) shows an example of a dialog box generated by applying the above method:

4.3   Application Testing

The application was tested by a simulation model, partial results are shown in Fig. 5. Figure a shows the dialog of generating mesh points. In this module, the EDA information was passed to the program and mesh points were generated on the surface of the board. Figure b is the dialog box for extracting thermal simulation results respectively. The dialog box could identify the currently active solution, by selecting the corresponding result type, simulation environment, and other parameters, the program can correctly extract the required data into the data file.

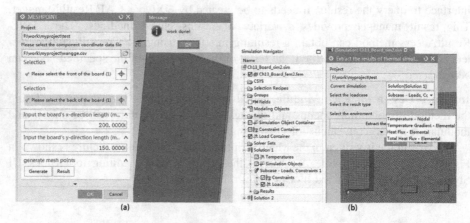

(a)   (b)

Fig. 5. Result of generating mesh points and extracting data

5   Conclusion

In order to improve the efficiency of reliability simulation test, this paper used SIEMENS NX as the application platform, realized the specified data extraction through the secondary development tool. This application made the process of reliability assessment automated. It not only reduced the personal errors during passing data, but also shortened the time of the hole test.

References

1. Rui Zhang, F., Kaiwei Wang, S., Zhengrong Shen, T.: Application research of high reliability electronic equipment reliability simulation test technology. Electron. Prod. Reliab. Environ. Test **30**(6), 13–19 (2012)
2. Weishan Zhang, F., Shoumei Xiong, S., Baicheng Liu, T.: Study on a CAD/CAE system of die casting. J. Mat. Process. Technol. **63**(1–3), 707–711 (2017)
3. Yuanxun Fan, F., Yahong Zhuang, S., Huakun Wang, T.: Application of UG secondary development tool. Mach. Manuf. Autom. **6**, 70–72 (2002)

4. Xinhua, L.F., Qi, L., Youhui, L.S., et al.: Development of a rapid design system for aerial work truck subframe with UG secondary development framework. Procedia Eng. **15**, 2961–2965 (2011)
5. Linzhen Zhou, F., Qingzhu Li, S., Ke Qin, T.: Secondary Development Based on UG NX System. Jiangsu University Press, Zhenjiang (2012)
6. Rong Mo, F., Zhiyong Chang, S., Hongjun Liu, T., et al.: Illustration of UG NX Secondary Development. Electronic Industry Press, Beijing (2008)
7. Dave, S., Steinberg, F.: Vibration Analysis for Electronic Equipment, 3rd edn. John Wiley and Sons, New York (2000)
8. Steinberg, F.: Thermal Circulation and Vibration Fault Prevention of Electronic Equipment. Aeronautical Industry Press, Beijing (2012)
9. Xiaoyan Li, F.: Research on Integrated Assessment Technology of Temperature Fatigue Life of Electronic Products Based on CAE. Beihang University, Beijing (2015)
10. Haifan Zhang, F.: Introduction to Software Engineering, 3rd edn. Tsinghua University Press, Beijing (1998)
11. SIEMENS Product Lifecycle Management Software Inc.: Getting Started with NX Open. 12th edn (2017)
12. SIEMENS NXOpen Python Reference Guide. https://docs.plm.automation.siemens.com/data_services/resources/nx/12/nx_api/custom/en_US/nxopen_python_ref/index.html. Last accessed 25 June 2016

Author Index

Printed in the United States
By Bookmasters